The HR Answer Book

Second Edition

The HR Answer Book

An Indispensable Guide for Managers and Human Resources Professionals

Second Edition

**Shawn Smith, J.D.,
Rebecca Mazin**

AMACOM

American Management Association

New York · Atlanta · Brussels · Chicago · Mexico City · San Francisco
Shanghai · Tokyo · Toronto · Washington, D.C.

Bulk discounts available. For details visit:
www.amacombooks.org/go/specialsales
Or contact special sales:
Phone: 800-250-5308
E-mail: specialsls@amanet.org
View all the AMACOM titles at: www.amacombooks.org

This publication is designed to provide accurate and authoritative information in regard to the subject matter covered. It is sold with the understanding that the publisher is not engaged in rendering legal, accounting, or other professional service. If legal advice or other expert assistance is required, the services of a competent professional person should be sought.

Library of Congress Cataloging-in-Publication Data
Smith, Shawn A., 1958–
    The HR answer book : an indispensable guide for managers and human resources professionals / Shawn Smith and Rebecca Mazin. —2nd ed.
        p. cm.
    Includes index.
    ISBN-13: 978-0-8144-1717-1 (hbk.)
    ISBN-10: 0-8144-1717-5 (hbk.)
    1. Personnel management—Handbooks, manuals, etc. I. Mazin, Rebecca A. II. Title.
    HF5549.17.S62 2011
    658.3—dc22   2011003898

About AMA
American Management Association (www.amanet.org) is a world leader in talent development, advancing the skills of individuals to drive business success. Our mission is to support the goals of individuals and organizations through a complete range of products and services, including classroom and virtual seminars, webcasts, webinars, podcasts, conferences, corporate and government solutions, business books, and research. AMA's approach to improving performance combines experiential learning—learning through doing—with opportunities for ongoing professional growth at every step of one's career journey.

Printing number
10 9 8 7 6 5 4 3 2 1

Contents

Preface

SINCE THE PUBLICATION of the first edition of *The HR Answer Book* in 2004, it has been most gratifying for us to see the book on so many office and library bookshelves. It has been even more satisfying to meet and hear from our readers, telling us how the book made their lives as HR professionals and managers easier, or how they read our examples of HR practices that are "worth repeating" or "better forgotten" and smiled (or winced!) in recognition. We know from both firsthand experience and the feedback we receive that the combined voices of an attorney and human resources professional provide a unique and helpful perspective.

Because the fields of human resources and employment law are constantly changing, we knew even as the first edition of *The HR Answer Book* went to press that a second edition would be inevitable. It has been only seven years, but times have changed, and this new edition keeps you abreast of the latest changes in workforce laws and best practices. We tell you about the new laws and regulations that affect the employment environment, and we give you practical advice to minimize your legal liability. We bring you up to date on the changes in health care legislation. We have added or enhanced hot topics such as Web-based recruiting, wage and hour classifications, and the challenges that arise from the emergence of social networking sites such as Facebook and Twitter. And because many companies have had the unfortunate need to downsize over the past several years—either due to the challenging economic climate or to redundancies created by mergers and acquisitions—we have included a new chapter on effective reductions in force that will guide you through the process. This new edition reflects the realities of the ever-evolving workplace while retaining the timeless, commonsense advice on sound management and communications practices that made the first edition so successful.

New readers will appreciate the organization by topical area in an easy-to-use question and answer format that allows you to quickly zero in on the subject of interest. From reference checks to severance packages to discussions of complex legal issues, you will find clear explanations in plain language that you don't need to be a lawyer or a human resources expert to understand. Checklists, charts, and specific illustrations clarify the contents of each chapter, and our "worth repeating" and "better forgotten" sections provide real-life examples of the best and worst practices in human resources management. You will also find helpful sample forms and other documents in our Tools and Templates section, ready to be adapted for use by your organization.

This edition of *The HR Answer Book* has been written and revised to:

- Help business owners and executives interpret and understand ever-increasing amounts of information to make better-informed decisions and enable more effective business administration

- Be used as a timely, relevant guide for managers about everyday workplace issues

- Continue to be a trusted resource for human resources professionals, managers, and business owners in establishing, revising, and maintaining employee policies and procedures

- Provide a comprehensive, up-to-date overview of the human resources field, suitable for the growing number of management instructors who choose this volume as their course textbook

We are confident that this book will be a valuable tool to help you to solve problems, set direction, maintain legal compliance, and enable your organization to focus its energy on reaching business goals.

Shawn Smith
Rebecca Mazin

The HR Answer Book

Second Edition

Employee Selection

How Do I Find, Attract, and Select the Best?

HIRING IS A BASIC NEED for any employer that has at least one employee who is not a partner or family member. This is where the employment relationship begins. Policies and procedures for employee selection will set the tone for the interactions that follow throughout an individual's time with the organization.

Hiring someone is easy. Hiring the best candidate isn't always as simple, and it will require planning and a logical process. Whether you have one job opening or one hundred, the process and procedures you use for employee selection will be directly reflected in the results you achieve.

FINDING YOUR CANDIDATES

"Isn't it as easy as posting the job on the Web?"
Web-based job postings are an important part of an effective recruitment strategy, but not the first step. Technology and the exponential rise in the use of online social networking have dramatically expanded the sources and methods for identifying candidates, but jumping right in without planning and preparation can bog down the process.

Some Preliminary Steps

Before identifying the best recruiting sources, you must clearly identify the parameters of the job. While a complete job description is helpful, it may not be available and does not always include all the information you need. Answering the following questions will help you define the job parameters. If you are the hiring manager, you will probably have the answers to these questions already or you know where to get them. If you are not the hiring manager, then the hiring manager is a good starting point.

* *What is the job title and who does the job report to?* In your company, a particular job title or level may have certain benefits or perks attached to it. Does your company allow flexibility or creativity with job titles? One candidate may only accept a job with a "director" title, while another may be satisfied with a lesser title if you add the word "senior." Employers often add words like "senior" or "junior" with the intention of upgrading an individual or adding an entry-level spot in a department. Use care in creating these new titles. While the title of "senior sales associate" will add status, a title such as "junior sales associate" can be a detriment. Think of the customers or other employees who will interact with this person. Does dealing with a "junior" inspire confidence? Creative titles are terrific as long as they are appropriate for your culture both internally and externally. "Brand Champion" might have a nice ring, but may not translate into an understandable role in every business-to-business situation.

    Speak to the person to whom the job reports to determine this individual's needs and expectations. In a larger department, the position may report to a level below the hiring manager. In this situation, you should speak with both persons.

* *When does the position have to be filled, and how much does it pay?* A manager may demand a quick hire. Before you rush to offer the job to the first available candidate, remember that the cost of hiring the wrong person is potentially higher than leaving the position vacant. The wrong person can make expensive mistakes or cause dissatisfaction and turnover among other employees. Set realistic hiring timelines that also take into account the availability of necessary resources such as space, equipment, training, and supervision.

If you are filling an existing position, find out what the pay range has been in the past. If it is a new position, ensure that the pay rate is appropriate. If your company paid sign-on bonuses, relocation expenses, or other incentives or special benefits in the past, determine if they are available for this position and, if so, how much money is available. Extra perks are far less common when candidates are plentiful but may be necessary in industries or environments where skills shortages exist.

- *Who needs to meet or interview this person, and who will make the job offer?* Identify everyone who needs to be part of the hiring decision and determine their general availability to conduct interviews. Also, think about people who will be helpful in attracting candidates. These people may include employees from a promising candidate's hometown or alma mater, as well as those with exceptional personalities who might be effective salespeople for the organization.

It is often helpful to obtain many different perspectives on an applicant, from both prospective superiors and peers. Consider having an employee who is at the same job level as the open position either conduct an interview, give a tour of the facility, or take a coffee break with candidates. Not only is employee involvement in the selection process good for morale, it will provide valuable feedback—and a peer can help to "sell" the company.

The job offer should be made by the person with the authority to make decisions and respond to demands. This can be the hiring manager, a senior manager or executive, a member of the HR staff, or a search firm, if one is used.

Worth Repeating: Tour Guide Obtains References
For a mid-management position in a service industry, a strong performer met the candidate as part of a tour. The manager identified all they had in common, including people they both knew and had worked for. These names became the first references to be called.

- *What are the skills/education needed for this position? What is the work experience required for this position?* Create a list of the core skills, education, and experience needed to get the job done. You can add additional skills and experience that would be helpful and designate these elements as optional for successful performance of the job.

- *Was someone promoted or fired? Where did the last person come from?* If the vacancy was created by a promotion, gather information about the position from the person who last held the job. Check with the hiring manager to ensure that the job content is not changing. If the vacancy was created because someone was fired, find out if the termination was due to poor job performance or a lack of specific knowledge or skills.

  If the last person in the job had been hired within the past year, check for a file of resumes of other candidates who applied for the position. Find out whether the person came from a search firm, Internet posting, networking, or other source, then make it a priority to return to this source if it had previously generated strong candidates. Maintaining applicant flow logs in a spreadsheet or database will facilitate the process, particularly when resumes are filed electronically. A sample format can be found in the Tools and Templates section of this book.

Better Forgotten: Great Post, Wrong E-Mail Address

A start-up in a major city placed a job posting on a site focused on the town and industry. The posting included an e-mail address to send resumes and responses to. The e-mail address was incorrect and responses went into cyberspace. Candidates were lost and frustrated. Double-check any information included in an employment posting.

Internet Recruiting

"How do I make the most out of the Internet for recruiting?"

With more than ten thousand Web sites focused on recruitment and the prevalence of online social networking, the Internet has become a significant source for candidates for many employers. However, before you jump in to make your presence known on the Web, plan ahead. Internet resources can be a valuable part of your recruitment strategy, or they could take too much time without generating strong results.

The first step in Web-based recruitment is a review of your own company Web site. Online job seekers should find a site that is representative of the culture and environment of your workplace, provides good information about the organization, and is easy to navigate. Embedded videos of employees sharing career experiences can help create a picture of the company. Have a designated location, button, or tab where job openings are posted. Make sure it's visible on and accessible from your home page with a click on a button such as "Careers at XYZ Company."

To maximize the effectiveness of your employment Web page, include information about career paths, expectations of experience and education, and how to apply for open positions. If you consistently solicit resumes whether or not there are any immediate openings, put this information on your Web site. Be sure to keep the information up to date. Provide a direct link that allows candidates to apply online. Do not force potential applicants to take the extra step of printing an application or mailing or faxing a resume.

"Shouldn't I just post the opening on a large recruitment Web site?"

Posting your job on Monster or Careerbuilder may seem like a logical step, but sometimes the jumbo sites may be your least productive source of qualified job candidates.

If you are seeking a candidate in a highly competitive field where the number of job openings is far greater than the number of people in the workforce with the necessary skills, then many employers with similar needs will probably be posting jobs as well. The people who are successfully employed in a high-demand field are usually not spending time scrolling through job boards. In these circumstances, your posting is likely to generate either very few responses or responses from individuals who lack the necessary qualifications.

If the job opening is for a position with few requirements, or in a field that is overpopulated, you are likely to receive a very large response. A flood of resumes does not ensure the highest-quality candidates, and the larger the response, the more work you may need to do.

If you feel it is important to generate a large candidate pool, make certain you are able to handle the applicants properly. A large candidate pool is useless if you cannot screen and respond to the resumes.

Effective use of recruitment sites requires research before you begin, preferably before a need occurs. An easy way to start your inquiry is to navigate one of the large popular sites. Recruitment sites feature separate sections for employers and job seekers. Gain an understanding of what types of jobs are posted—and how candidates get to view the postings—by searching for openings similar to yours in the job seekers' section. The employer section of the site will include information about costs for both posting and viewing resumes and may also provide facts about the candidate database or typical visitor.

Once you are familiar with the basic components of recruitment sites, begin researching sites that will best fit your needs. The annually updated *Weddle's Guide to Employment Sites on the Internet* includes a top 100 list with a full page of information on each and a listing of more than ten thousand sites identified as "The Best & the Rest" divided into helpful categories. Using this and other resources, you can identify sites that cater to your geographic location or industry specialty. Industry-specific sites can be as all-encompassing as www.dice.com, with more than seventy thousand technology jobs posted, or very specific, such as www.idealist.org, for nonprofits. Using a targeted site, whether it is local or industry/skill-specific, is likely to increase the number of quality responses. You can also find niche employment Web sites through a community search, area business groups such as the chamber of commerce, or local newspapers. Online versions of newspapers typically post all jobs that appear in their print editions and partner with the big job boards.

Worth Repeating: Find the Niche Site

A nonprofit in an urban area launched a search for an IT manager. In a candidate-saturated market the organization targeted associations and sites that expressly served nonprofits. These postings were more effective because they generated candidates who were more likely to understand the different work environment in an organization that serves a public interest. Recruitment sites targeted to nonprofits were also cheaper.

Internet posts typically cost approximately $200 to $400 per job listed. In this crowded industry, first-time user discounts and packages that include multiple postings will provide savings. A little checking can uncover less expensive options, including free and low-cost job boards managed by employer or industry associations and nearby schools. Craigslist, a popular free site with classifieds of all types, has grown to become a host for job opportunities throughout the world, with available openings listed by job category functions and geography. Craigslist jobs are predominantly entry-level, hourly, semiskilled, and skilled up to middle management.

"How do I write an online job posting?"

Follow these guidelines when you find the right site for your job posting:

✓ Write a creative job posting that reflects not only the position, but also the culture of your company.

✓ Job postings are more effective if they avoid repetition and use abbreviations and language that all readers can understand. Even though there is generally plenty of space, and you are not paying by the word, you still want to attract and hold the candidate's attention.

✓ Select the proper category that includes job or industry type. Research these factors by checking existing job postings. Don't combine two or more openings into one posting. This can make it impossible to categorize or find effectively.

If you fill the job or a posted position becomes inactive, remove the posting immediately. Don't frustrate potential applicants by posting jobs that are not available. Most sites have a feature allowing employers to view resumes in their databases, usually for an additional fee. Before paying to view resumes, determine the exact criteria used by the database so you'll know whether the resumes are current and contain the background, skills, geographic location, and salary requirements that match your search.

Larger companies that receive numerous resumes use computer software programs to receive, organize, and track submissions. The biggest general recruitment sites also offer services or programs that perform these functions. Check out offerings that allow small to mid-size companies the ability to take advantage of this technology at more attractive rates, available through a variety of vendors from software to payroll providers. One step to help sort a flood of resumes is to use a dedicated e-mail address, or multiple addresses by type of position, such as jobs@abcaudio.com or techjobs@abcaudio.com.

Consider using an advertising agency that specializes in recruitment advertising. These companies have transitioned from ad writers who earned their fees from newspapers to partners who can facilitate online postings and manage much of the process. These companies' services range from screening to providing virtual resume storage, employment branding, and candidate database management.

"How do I search social media sites to find potential employees?"

Job boards are not the only venues for online recruiting. The Internet has become a hotbed of virtual networking for job seekers and employers. With hundreds of millions of users interacting and sharing information online, employers now use social media to actively search for and connect with potential employees—sometimes as a first step before even turning to job sites. Social networking can take two forms: announcing your opening through different channels and seeking and identifying individual candidates.

Worth Repeating: Spread the Word on the Web
Sodexho, the global service company, has eighteen links on its Web site for career information. Job seekers can check out company information and employee input on blogs, Facebook, Twitter, and a range of career networks.

"Isn't Facebook for party and vacation photos?"

The majority of Facebook users are not the teenagers and college students who initially flocked to the site. Facebook is still the home for hundreds of millions of photos of vacations, families, and friends, but increasingly it is an important venue for employers seeking to broaden their Web presence.

Employers enhance their branding by creating Facebook pages that:

* Spread news about products and people

* Share information about innovations and successes

* Announce job openings or link to postings

* Provide a glimpse of the organizational culture and work environment through tone, images, video links, and comments by employees

The very presence of a Facebook page can give candidates the impression that an employer is progressive and modern, and the page provides a forum and format for research about a prospective employer that can be attractive to potential hires. Investor information does not belong on Facebook, but a description of a new marketing campaign, including links to sample commercials, fits perfectly into the format. Check fan pages of competitors or employers in your geographic area for examples. A consultant or internal staff member with expertise in social media can guide this process.

Social networking sites offer limitless potential to connect with people, but they should be used with care. If you have lost track of an engineer who left the company five years ago who could be a great rehire or referral source, you might reconnect with him simply by searching his name on Facebook. However, as with any recruiting search method, do not target some candidates and exclude others based on race, gender, religion, or other protected category. For example, a search that targets only candidates who openly espouse a particular religious affiliation could create problems.

"How do I find a director to produce a video?"

Videos that highlight and focus on stories of actual employees can be a powerful tool to create an impression of life at the workplace. While some companies upload professional quality videos to YouTube, you do not need a director and production team to achieve impact. Consider creating an in-house video with employees describing "why we like working at . . ." Some basic editing will often suffice, or you can add captions or voiceover. Add a title that will attract the viewers you seek, and link to the videos from your company Web site and Facebook fan pages rather than waiting for employees or potential employees to find you on YouTube.

"Can anyone describe a job opening in 140 characters?"
Twitter, the idea-sharing site that allows users to post short messages, or "tweets," has rapidly become a global bulletin board for sharing information, ideas, and opinions. Like Facebook, employers can best use Twitter as part of a recruitment strategy to communicate quickly and maintain an image. You can announce job openings in tweets, or post a job, preferably with a link to apply, on free spots within the community. Search "using Twitter to post jobs" to find sites and get additional suggestions.

"Why should I spend time on LinkedIn?"
With a membership count approaching one hundred million users around the world, LinkedIn has become the premier online professional networking site. Members post individual profiles with the ability to invite contacts they know to connect and interact in affinity groups, categorized by industry, job type, alma mater, and location. LinkedIn offers employers the opportunity to post jobs at reasonable rates and to spread the word about a position by posting an "activity update," starting a "discussion," or sending out information to connections and groups. For example, employers in the alternative energy business can join the Wind Energy Professionals Group on LinkedIn and communicate a job opening to the more than 19,000 members.

You can also use LinkedIn to search for profiles of individuals employed by target companies or alumni. As with Facebook, since most people include a photo in their profiles, take care in the search to avoid making employment decisions based on appearance.

Worth Repeating: Does the LinkedIn Profile Match the Resume?
A recruiter conducted a preliminary telephone interview with a candidate who responded to a LinkedIn posting for an executive position. After the conversation, the recruiter had some questions about the individual's experience. She checked his LinkedIn profile and found that it did not match the information contained in his resume. The candidate's explanation for the discrepancy was not sufficient to put him back into consideration for the position.

*"Do I need to hire an eighteen-year-old
to keep track of our social media presence?"*

It doesn't take a member of Generation Y to manage social media, but it is important to monitor and update your presence on the various outlets to make sure your content is consistent across sites and that it effectively conveys the company's message and culture. Appoint an individual on the recruiting team, or someone close to the hiring process, to be responsible for recruiting through social media. This person should also monitor questions and comments posted about the company on these sites and respond with messages that reinforce the company's message or clarify misinformation. A robust, positive, online conversation adds buzz about products and employment opportunities.

"Does anyone still run help wanted ads in newspapers?"

Hard copy help wanted ads are only a tiny minority of twenty-first century employment advertising, but they can be a creative option. These ads can still be found in alternative publications, such as college, trade, or industry journals or community newspapers. Check the free publications to see if they include a help wanted section that could be relevant for your needs.

Other Referral Sources

*"How can my business contacts help
me to find qualified candidates?"*

Networking is possibly the single most effective way to generate candidates. Begin your networking with the hiring manager. The hiring manager may have resumes from a previous search or know the names of people in similar positions at other companies. Contact these potential candidates to ask if they know of anyone else who might be interested in the opening or if it is a position they would like more information about for themselves. Ask all managers for referrals. Besides referring specific individuals, managers can help identify other companies employing individuals in similar positions that would be good sources of candidates. Compile a list of all likely sources and call them to ask if they know of anyone who might be interested in the opening. Other networking sources include industry or trade associations and business organizations such as chambers of commerce. Newspapers and industry magazines often highlight people and awards programs, which will generate additional names.

Networking can also be as simple as calling a counterpart at another company. Other organizations may not have the same need, but they will have resumes or know of potential candidates elsewhere. Former employees are also an outstanding source of referrals for the same reasons. Many companies have established informal or formal alumni programs as an effective form of networking for candidates. You can begin these programs with simple lists, phone calls, e-mail blasts, invitations to new product launches and tours, mailings of employee news updates and job openings, and invitations to alumni events. Not only is networking a cost-effective way to identify candidates, but because it is a direct method you will also save time.

Worth Repeating: Host an Event

A mid-size company did not have to send its managers far to attend an industry conference in a nearby city. It maximized company visibility and collected business cards and names of potential future hires, or referral sources, by hosting one of the industry events at its own site. This was a great chance to take advantage of professionals visiting in the company's backyard.

"How can I develop an effective employee referral program?"

An employee referral program is another form of networking under which a company rewards current employees for identifying new employees. You do not have to offer a huge—or even monetary—reward in order to attract interest. Rewards as small as $100, as well as gift certificates or noncash prizes, will be sufficient to generate considerable enthusiasm if your program is well-run. Most employees are motivated to participate as a way of contributing value to and receiving recognition from their organizations.

The most critical elements of a successful employee referral program are clear communication and follow-through. If your employees don't know about the program, the existing job openings, or how to participate, you can have a very attractive program and still not generate a single referral.

Create a forum in which to communicate current job openings. This can be an employee bulletin board, newsletter, e-mail blasts, or the company's intranet site. Publicize the guidelines of the program along with the job openings. Promptly and accurately follow up with referring employees. You want to let them know the status of candidates referred and thank them for their participation. Distribute awards promptly and make these distributions visible. When employees see their coworkers receiving rewards and/or recognition, they will become more excited about participating themselves.

You do not have to apply your referral program to all positions. You can limit eligibility to specified, hard-to-fill positions. Again, communicate eligibility requirements clearly and accurately. Misunderstanding as to what positions are covered and the nature of the reward will only generate hard feelings, not future referrals.

"Should I put up a 'Help Wanted' sign?"

Putting up a sign announcing job openings can be a terrific way to generate candidates if you have a high-traffic workplace frequented by potential employees. Your sign should say much more than "Help Wanted, Apply Within." Like all good advertisements, effective signs are creative and target the customer or client with the greatest potential for becoming an employee. In a retail setting, you might post a sign asking, "Do you tell your friends about our products?"

Your sign should contain specific instructions for how to apply for a job, including a telephone number, hours to apply, or a Web address. When individuals inquire about your sign, instead of merely leaving a stack of blank applications on a table or handing them out, provide an instruction card or flyer describing both the position(s) and the application process. Consider the audience when determining the requirements. It does not make sense, for example, to require a resume for lower-skilled positions.

Consider carefully the location where the candidate will complete the application. It can be distracting and potentially disruptive for customers or your workers to have groups of candidates filling out applications in the middle of an establishment. Distributing a job application for completion "at home" does not guarantee that the candidate will be the person who fills it out. The instructions should direct candidates to an appropriate location, or you might have them return at specified times when business is slower. Whenever you use a Web-based employment application, either at your location or generally available online, make certain that the process is checked by an individual who is not IT-savvy to ensure that it is user-friendly.

"Where are the recent college graduates, and how can I attract them?"

Successful college recruiting is not limited to large companies with high visibility. Recruiting from colleges, universities, and graduate schools can be just as effective for filling one position as for filling a dozen. Large companies often receive special treatment for the funding and goods they provide, but educational institutions recognize smaller employers as strong sources of information, assistance, and potential jobs.

Worth Repeating: College Kids Love Temporary Work
A retailer staffed a "pop-up" short-term site using college students. It wasn't hard to find them after representatives of the retailer handed out flyers at the student union that prominently displayed popular products.

While college recruiting can certainly pay off when a company has a specific opening, the most effective programs flow from ongoing relationships that can provide part-time employees, paid and unpaid interns, and contacts for more experienced workers as well as recent graduates. If you are not aware of the college and university resources in your community or for your industry or specialty, begin by locating the applicable schools. Start your research with a basic college guide such as *Barron's Profiles of American Colleges*. These are indexed by location and by major. The guides are written for prospective students, not employers, so you will need to do some additional research to make the best contacts. After choosing the programs or schools that would provide students who best fit your requirements, contact the school's career or internship office.

To develop relationships before openings occur, speak to the career center director, internship coordinator, or head of the department whose students or graduates are of interest to you. Introduce yourself and your company and obtain the following information:

- Details about the curriculum, to determine whether the students and/or graduates fit your hiring needs.

- Calendar of on-campus recruiting events, the process for scheduling interviews, and a list of companies that recruit on campus for similar positions.

- Availability of ongoing job postings for current students and alumni, including how the information is accessed and any costs charged for alumni postings. Don't be surprised if you are directed to an online resource that allows you to post at multiple schools from one site.

- Guidelines for any paid and unpaid internship programs, including the application process (e.g., do you meet and approve the intern before the program, or are they assigned?), calendar of internships, hours, and supervision/evaluation required.

- A list of classes at which someone from your company can guest lecture, or a list of student clubs or preprofessional groups that use outside speakers. Offer tours of your work site if it might be beneficial for any classes.

- Calendar of any career fairs, including costs and logistics.

- Calendar of classes, availability of students for internships, and graduation dates.

Identify any alumni of the school within your company and enlist them to help nurture this relationship. Alumni can establish instant rapport with students as employer representatives at a career fair.

"How do I find a recent college graduate in February?"
Don't assume that you can hire recent college graduates only in May or June. Many students graduate at different times of the year. Others graduate without a position or take time off and maintain contact with a career services office.

If you have an immediate job opening, ask your contact at the school for referrals. Career services professionals generally know their students and have contact with alumni. Colleges often have a job posting system that includes alumni as well. Ask to review any available resumes of students or graduates who are interested in your industry or geographic area.

Developing ongoing paid or unpaid internship programs will provide valuable resources for recruiting. Internships provide opportunities for an employer to get to know prospective employees and gain motivated representatives who return to campus and spread positive information about the company. Certain colleges have programs with work-study components, through which students work full-time for three to nine months. Consider scheduling work-study students or interns in advance to cover leaves of absence or peak business periods. Encourage interns and college students who are employed in summer jobs to become ambassadors for your company on campus. Keep in touch with them even if you know they are heading to graduate school or another employer. An enthusiastic student can spread the word about a wonderful work environment faster than any career center.

"What happens at a job or career fair?"

Job or career fairs come in many forms. They range from on-campus career days sponsored by colleges to large programs at convention centers run by recruitment businesses, with events catering to specific needs in between. Participation in a career fair can generate candidates and increase the visibility of a company as an employer.

The cost of participating in a career fair can range from a few hundred dollars for a college or local job fair to thousands of dollars for a convention center program that promises to attract thousands of candidates. Before making a commitment, speak with other employers that have attended the fair in the past to evaluate their experiences. Obtain a list of participating companies to determine whether the event is appropriate for your company. A small employer with a small booth will be lost in a sea of very large employers with large booths. Being a "little fish in a big pond" will probably not generate strong candidate traffic flow and will certainly not improve visibility.

Plan ahead for effectiveness. The following steps will improve results:

- See that your booth is adequately staffed. It may give many attendees their first impression of your company. If you are setting up at an on-campus career fair, have alumni at the table.

- Prepare a few key questions for each candidate who presents a resume. Asking the same questions will make it easier for you to remember and rank candidates.

- Treat everyone who approaches the booth with respect. Don't forget rules about appropriate and inappropriate interview questions simply because you are standing up or are in a less formal setting.

- Be prepared to inform promising candidates then and there about the "next step." This can range from setting up an appointment to discuss an immediate opening to keeping in touch by following up with notes and/or phone calls. Plan to follow up on all resumes using the same process you use for other resumes you receive.

- Have something at the booth that will catch people's eye, such as a pen, keychain, or other take-away gift, as well as marketing materials about your organization. Food, even small snack items, is usually a draw. You do not need slick recruitment information to display a positive image.

- Walk around and meet the representatives of other companies. These people can become part of your network for finding job candidates.

Search Firms

"What can headhunters do for me, and what should I look for?"

Recruitment firms can be called many things, from staffing agencies to executive search firms. The most important thing to remember in choosing, and using, a firm is that *you*, the employer, direct the search.

When deciding whether to use a search firm, consider your recruitment budget, available time, and in-house resources. The most costly searches are retained searches. Retained searches are exclusive searches where a specific recruiter is hired to fill a position, usually for a fee of up to one-third of the position's annual compensation. Generally, there is an up-front "deposit" and charges for expenses, with the balance payable after a hire is made. Before you agree to a retained search, clarify the types of expenses that will be reimbursable and the methods the recruiter will use in conducting the search. Remember that once you sign an exclusive agreement, you must pay a fee even if you hire a person you located through another source.

Contingent search firms charge a fee equal to a percentage of a candidate's annual compensation, but you have to pay this fee only if you hire a candidate introduced to you by the firm. Therefore, you can use several contingent search firms simultaneously to fill one position. But be aware that having many recruiters chasing the same people can lead to arguments about who first made contact with a candidate.

Many search firms will negotiate the amount of the fee they charge. Searches for a 20 percent fee are common in some areas and industries, and it is possible to obtain even lower rates. When negotiating a fee, be clear about what will be included in the calculation of compensation. If the position includes an incentive or bonus, the fee is typically based on the maximum that can be earned. Most search firms will offer some type of guarantee or reduction in a subsequent fee if a candidate does not remain employed for a specific period. If the search firm does not offer you a guarantee or reduction, ask for one. Get all terms in writing prior to accepting resumes from any recruiter.

While a nonretained search may offer a cost advantage, be aware that the quality of contingent search firms varies widely. An inferior firm will often produce an abundance of candidates who have not been well-screened. Be firm and clear with the person conducting the search. State your requirements, the steps you have already taken to locate candidates, and your preferred means of communication and scheduling. Do not let a search firm talk you into a candidate. If the consultant assigned to your search does not meet your needs, request a different one.

When it comes time to make an offer, do not let the search firm handle the salary negotiations or complete the reference checks. Chances are it will not be as diligent as you. If the firm informs you that it has already conducted reference checks, request copies of notes or records of conversations and follow up to verify or add to the information.

"I heard there are tax breaks for hiring certain people.
What are they and how can I get them?"

One valuable and often overlooked source is the group of programs designed to employ people with disabilities or move individuals from welfare to work. There are many reasons for hiring people with disabilities and utilizing welfare-to-work programs to fill entry-level positions. Often these programs can be a good source for candidates in low unemployment locations where employment ads do not produce results. Financial incentives are often available to employers to hire from these sources, and they provide a satisfying and visible way to give back to the community.

Under disability and welfare-to-work programs, participants complete preemployment training before they are referred to employers. At minimum, this training includes job readiness classes where students learn resume and interview skills, plus lessons about responsibility, accepting supervision, and the importance of good attendance. During the training and in the interview and placement process, job coaches or counselors guide participants. These counselors help determine if there is a match between the candidate and the job opening, and they resolve issues that occur on the job. They also can coordinate supplemental benefits (such as government-provided transportation, child care, and clothing allowances) potentially available to the individual and financial incentives for the employer. This training and counseling is not available to you when you hire someone "off the street."

To find disability and welfare-to-work programs, you can start with local business alliances, such as chambers of commerce. Qualified applicants with disabilities can be located through vocational rehabilitation or education departments in each state. These groups will be listed in the telephone book under state government agencies. Other links can be found through the Department of Labor and the Social Security Administration. Each state also operates offices to help people with disabilities and One Stop employment centers for employers and job seekers.

National or local stimulus programs often provide tax breaks for other types of hiring. An accountant or payroll provider should be able to provide details of any available hiring incentives, including the necessary documentation and reporting you will need to qualify.

CONDUCTING THE INTERVIEW

"How do I make the most of the interview process?"

Just as candidates should prepare for interviews, an employer needs to prepare as well. The first step is to conduct a brief prescreening with the applicant to determine whether the candidate meets the basic requirements of the position and is appropriate for an interview. This is generally done by telephone but may be handled in person, at a career fair, for example. The prescreening can be conducted by an employee with a minimum amount of training and should seek to determine the following information:

Does the Candidate Meet the Skill or Knowledge Requirements of the Position? This can be determined with a few basic, structured questions that are used for all candidates.

What Is the Candidate's Salary Requirement? Many people believe that an employer should not discuss salary early in the interview process. However, you do not want to waste time interviewing someone for a $60,000-a-year job when that person is looking for $120,000 a year. If the candidate does not want to answer this question directly, ask for a range. Avoid disclosing the salary range for the position until you have learned more about the candidate, because the individual may be more qualified for a different position with a different rate of pay. If the salary or wage is fixed and nonnegotiable, just ask the candidate if it is an acceptable rate.

Does the Position Meet the Candidate's Criteria? People have different interpretations of job titles. Provide a brief description of the position, including any details about hours or requirements.

Are There Logistical Considerations That Would Affect the Candidate's Ability to Perform the Job? Obtain information such as days, hours, and locations at which the applicant can work, and the individual's availability for an interview.

"How do I develop incisive interview questions?"

Outline your interview questions in advance and you will be more likely to obtain all the information you need during the interview. Review the resume and the prescreening documentation as a starting point for questions that should verify, clarify, and elaborate on any information provided. If there is any gap in employment or unusual positions or accomplishments, you will want to develop questions to gather additional details. Do not limit yourself to questions based on specifics already detailed in the resume or application. While it is important and useful to ask questions that verify information, well-prepared questions will provide a wealth of insight beyond what the candidate has chosen to tell you on paper.

Ask behaviorally based questions rather than questions that will merely elicit feelings or opinions. Behaviorally based questions focus on what the individual actually did in a given situation. For example, asking, "Are you a good team player?" is likely to bring forth a response such as, "Yes, I love to work with people." However, asking the candidate to describe a time when he or she was successful at getting buy-in from others will give you an actual example rather than a potentially biased self-assessment.

Behaviorally based questions can be used to determine a candidate's actual job experience and to assess skills that are less structured and less easily defined. If the job requires the management of multiple tasks, ask, "Can you describe a time when you managed multiple tasks? What strategies did you use and how successful were you?" These types of questions are also good predictors in interviews with candidates who may have the talent but not the direct experience. For example, if an individual without previous supervisory experience applies for a position that supervises others, ask this candidate to tell you about situations in which he or she led a team, committee, or group or demonstrated leadership.

Ask open-ended questions, not closed-ended ones that can be answered with a yes or no. Closed-ended questions do not create a conversation and will not provide the information needed to make a decision about a candidate. They are only appropriate for eliciting specific facts. Here's a closed-ended question about business growth: "Have you been involved in a business that went through an expansion?" The open-ended version asks, "Describe a time when you worked in a company where there was an expansion, including your role, and describe the results of the actions you took." Which is more likely to give you better insight into whether the candidate could help your company in a period of rapid growth?

Interviewers often select very common, overused questions, such as asking the candidate to describe his or her strengths and weaknesses. Here you are practically guaranteed to receive an answer that has been rehearsed. A more effective way of asking this, and making it more relevant to the conversation, would be: "Describe the strengths you would bring to this position."

An oft-repeated query of an interviewer who did not prepare specifically for the interview is, "Tell me about yourself." The candidate is sure to have a rehearsed response ready, and when the interview is over, the interviewer will have learned little. You and your own interviewing experience are an excellent source for interview questions. So are other managers who conduct interviews. Ask them to provide examples of questions they have found to be effective.

Better Forgotten: *"I scooped ice cream too!"*
A recruiter for a major pharmaceutical company spent 90 percent of an interview reminiscing with a candidate about their shared experiences working at an ice cream shop during high school. It was a pleasant and enjoyable conversation with virtually no information shared about the candidate's more relevant work experience for the job opening.

"What is an illegal interview question?"

If a question does not relate to the candidate's qualifications and ability to do the job, there is no reason to ask it during an interview. Questions that have the effect of discriminating against a candidate by screening for age, sex, marital status, race, ethnicity, religion, disability, genetic information, and, in many locations, sexual orientation are illegal. Many questions that appear innocuous can actually be considered discriminatory. The following guidelines include questions that can and cannot be asked in some of the most common categories:

Marital Status. Questions about marital status including, "Do you plan to have children?" and "How much money does your husband make?" do not relate to the applicant's ability to do the job and can be viewed as discriminating against women. To determine availability for work or long hours, it is more appropriate to ask, "What hours can you work?" or "Are you available for overtime?"

Race or National Origin. Examples of questions that are illegal include "What country are you from?" "What kind of name is that?" "Is English your first language?" "Were your parents born in the United States?" You may ask if the candidate can read or write English or another language if these skills are job-related. You may also ask whether a candidate has the legal right to work in the United States, since this is a requirement for employment.

Age. Federal law prohibits discrimination in employment against anyone over the age of forty, so employers should never ask applicants their age or ask any age-related question such as, "What year did you graduate from high school?" To determine a candidate's legal eligibility to work, an employer can ask, "Are you eighteen years of age or older?" Other improper questions include, "How long do you plan to work before you retire?" It is appropriate to ask about short- and long-term career goals.

Religion. Interview questions such as "What is your religion?" or "Do you go to church?" are prohibited. They are not job-related and can be considered discriminatory against candidates of different religious beliefs. Since employers are required to make reasonable efforts to accommodate religious observances, it is also inappropriate to ask, "Does your religion prohibit your working on Saturdays?" or "Are there any holidays on which you cannot work?"

Disabilities. Under the Americans with Disabilities Act, employers are prohibited from asking questions about an applicant's disabilities during the preemployment process. Employers cannot ask questions such as, "Have you ever filed a workers compensation claim?" or "Do you have any disabilities that would interfere with your ability to do this job?" If the candidate has an obvious disability or discloses a hidden disability during the interview process, you can ask how the candidate would perform a particular job or whether reasonable accommodations would be needed. You can also show a list of the job responsibilities to the candidate, followed by the question, "Are you capable of performing these duties with or without reasonable accommodation?" An employer can ask about a candidate's attendance record at previous positions, since absences can be caused by many reasons other than disability. Questions about attendance records must not include the reasons for absences.

*Arrest and Conviction Records.*Because most arrests do not result in convictions, questions about arrest records can be interpreted as biased against particular minority groups. If you consider a record of conviction in making an employment decision, you must be able to demonstrate a business necessity for the requirement. When in doubt, refrain from asking about convictions during interviews. (See the section on Preemployment Testing and Screening, later in this chapter, for information on conducting background checks.)

Credit History. Questions about a candidate's finances, such as "Have your wages ever been garnished?" and "Do you own or rent your home?" are illegal. (See the section on Preemployment Testing and Screening for guidelines.)

Personal Questions and Other Inappropriate Inquiries. Personal questions that are totally unrelated to job requirements should always be avoided, even if there is no discriminatory intent behind them. "Do you have an active social life?" or "Do you belong to any groups, clubs, or societies?" are examples of questions that can be seen as having a sex, ethnicity, or other improper bias. Trick or cute questions are inadvisable, whether or not they are illegal. A trick question that is designed to mislead or catch a candidate off-guard—such as, "You were only at your last job six months. Why were you fired?"—may unnerve and annoy the prospect and is unlikely to add to the discussion. Also avoid "cute" inquiries such as, "If you could be any animal, what would you be and why?" There are certainly better ways to elicit information.

As a rule, if you design your questions with the purpose of bringing out information about the candidate's work experience, judgment, character, and maturity, you will be best equipped to make sound hiring decisions.

"I've planned for the interview. Now what?"

After you have adequately prepared for the interview, it is time to meet the candidate. There are four distinct parts to a successful interview.

Part 1: Welcoming the Interviewee. Begin by making the candidate comfortable and the setting productive for a conversation. Have a prepared, genuine welcome statement, which can be as simple as a making a comment on the weather, thanking the candidate for finding your office if it was a difficult trip to make, or remarking on a common alma mater. It is important to keep the welcome brief and not to let it evolve into a lengthy discussion that eats into the interview time.

Conduct the interview in a quiet, private location without interruptions. Nothing makes a candidate feel more unwelcome or unimportant than to have the interview interrupted by telephone calls, pagers, or knocks on the door during an interview.

Part 2: Asking Questions to Determine Qualifications. After you develop rapport with a candidate, turn the conversation to specifics about the candidate's background and qualifications for the position. This is the time to ask the questions that you prepared in accordance with the guidelines earlier in this chapter. Tell the candidate that you may ask additional questions at other points in the interview, which you will do if you realize that you need additional information or clarification.

Avoid a "halo effect" that limits the questions you ask. A halo effect occurs when some characteristic, shared experience, or qualification of the candidate so overwhelms the interviewer that he or she assumes the candidate is perfect and does not follow through with enough questions to determine the candidate's appropriateness for the job.

Part 3: Allowing Time for Candidate Questions. When you have asked all the questions you feel are necessary, offer the candidate time to ask questions. A candidate for a management position who does not have questions obviously has not prepared and may lack business acumen. If you cannot answer a question, respond honestly. If the answer to the question can be determined from another source, tell the candidate that you will get the information and follow up later.

This is the time to "sell" the candidate on the company. The individual should leave the interview with a basic understanding of the company and the position and the sense that the organization will be a good place to work. Never do all the talking. When an interviewer dominates a conversation, it is likely that the candidate will not have the chance to provide the information you need to make a sound hiring decision.

Part 4: Concluding the Interview. A proper close to an interview is just as important as an appropriate opening. This is your opportunity to ask any additional questions. Explain the next steps in the interview process. Next steps may include determining the candidate's availability for further interviews, or just stating that the company will review results of the interview and get back to the individual by a specific date.

An interview may provide job candidates with their first impression of your company. Remember that when people are treated inconsiderately during the interview process, word spreads rapidly throughout the employment community. Strive to make a favorable impression on all candidates, whether you hire them or not.

Better Forgotten: Don't Put the Candidate in the Hot Seat
While conducting an interview in a conference room as part of a college recruiting trip, an HR executive nixed a candidate who did not maintain eye contact during the conversation. For the next candidate, the interviewer changed seats only to find that the previous candidate had been staring straight into strong sunlight. This applicant was too inexperienced and eager to point out the problem to the recruiter. Check your environment before making a mistake that puts a candidate at a disadvantage.

PREEMPLOYMENT TESTING AND SCREENING

The hiring process does not end with the interview. As a responsible employer, you may want or need to take additional steps to assist in the hiring decision. These steps include doing preemployment testing, background checks, reference checks, and any medical screening.

"Should I require candidates to take a skills test?"
Many employers require a candidate to complete one or more preemployment tests. An extensive range of tests is available, and they can be helpful as long as you select an appropriate test.

- *Basic skills tests.* Employers have administered basic skills tests for years, most commonly to measure typing and computer abilities. These tests are easy to define and administer. They can be designed in-house, requiring the candidate to complete all or part of a typical assignment, or purchased from a vendor and administered in-house or online. For certain technical positions, a math or use-of-tools test may be appropriate.

  If you conduct a skills test, it is essential that the components of the test are relevant to the job and that the test be administered uniformly to all candidates for the position. Uniform administration must extend to the location and format of the test, including any technology used.

- *Soft skills tests.* Tests have also been developed to measure "softer" skills that are required for a job. For a service environment, the test may include questions or specific examples of situations that you want the candidate to respond to, or it may be targeted toward determining whether the individual uses polite, positive language in responding to requests.

  Less specific are psychological tests designed to target personality types determined to be best suited for an occupation. For example, an individual applying for a position that requires completion of inventory and record keeping might be tested for attention to detail. Before using psychological tests, make sure that they are actually relevant to and useful for your candidate evaluation. It could be difficult to justify the use of this type of test for all employees in an organization where there are a variety of positions and a range of interaction with others.

- *Validation of tests.* For any test to be a useful measure and to be considered nondiscriminatory, it should be validated. Validation means there is a demonstrated correlation between people's performance on the test and their performance on the job to the standard measured by the test.

  With the growth in availability and use of tests, the Equal Employment Opportunity Commission has issued updated recommendations concerning employment testing.

  The guidelines state that:

  - Employers should ensure that employment tests are properly validated for the applicable position. The test or selection procedure must be job-related. A test vendor's documentation supporting test validity may be helpful, but the employer is responsible for ensuring validity.

- If a selection procedure results in screening out a protected group, the employer should see if there is another effective selection procedure that has less adverse impact, and, if so, adopt the alternative procedure.

- To ensure that a test or selection procedure remains predictive of success in a job, employers should keep up to date on changes in job requirements and should update the test specifications or selection procedures accordingly.

- Tests should not be adopted casually by managers. No test should be implemented without an understanding of its effectiveness and limitations for the organization, its appropriateness for a specific job, and whether it can be properly administered and the results evaluated.

Any test or procedure that has an adverse impact on any protected class is considered discriminatory. For example, if more men than women are selected based on the results of a test, it is discriminatory and therefore illegal.

The cost of testing can vary widely. Some test providers charge for administering and scoring each test; others train employers to do so and charge user fees. Your cost analysis should include how much time you will spend on testing, as well as the potential reduction in turnover and recruitment costs resulting from using an effective test. Check a variety of references including, if possible, individuals who took the test and were hired based on the results. Request sample tests and a trial period from any third-party test provider.

In some situations, a testing company will provide additional research and customization if your company volunteers as part of a test site for a new product. This is a good way to get a targeted test, as long as validation is built into the process.

"What do I need to know about preemployment drug testing?"
Drug testing is more fully discussed in Chapter 8. If you decide to do preemployment drug testing, select a reputable company. Ask how the test will be conducted and determine specific drugs to be screened.

"Can I require applicants to take preemployment physicals?"

If you require a candidate to take a preemployment physical, you must ensure that the recommendations, results, and subsequent decisions made about the applicant do not violate the Americans with Disabilities Act (ADA). Generally physicals are conducted after an offer is made. These exams are costly and time-consuming and should only be considered for employment situations that require specific information related to performance and the potential need for reasonable accommodations. (See Chapter 7 for more information on ADA compliance.)

"How do I conduct an effective reference check?"

Reference checks seek to obtain written or verbal verification of information and/or opinions about qualifications and past performance. Almost anyone in your organization can conduct a minimum reference check to verify information from previous employers or educational institutions. Someone comfortable asking open-ended questions to obtain information should conduct reference checks that seek opinions. Do not merely contact the human resources department of the candidate's previous employer for a reference. This is especially true when hiring a manager, salesperson, or other key employee, when it will be important to speak with supervisors, subordinates, peers, and sometimes even customers, depending on the nature of the job responsibilities.

As in an interview situation, ask questions designed to elicit specific information. Instead of asking, "Was Tom a good performer?" ask, "What results did Tom produce?" This is also a good time to gain a different viewpoint on the candidate—such as the individual's relationships with subordinates, management style, and other perspectives. Write up the results of all reference checks in a consistent format, including the date, the name of the person spoken to, and the details provided.

Often, a candidate will offer written letters of reference. While these letters are sometimes helpful, they are typically form letters lacking in details that will aid your decision-making process. Letters of reference are not a substitute for good reference checks. If a candidate is employed, do not call the current employer without explicit permission. If you feel you must have information relating to this job, ask for the name of a former employee of the company.

"Isn't it quicker to just plug the candidate's name into an Internet search?"

Type a candidate's name into the box of your favorite search engine and within seconds you are likely to find at least a minimum amount of information. Facebook and LinkedIn results may provide some helpful professional information, but you may also discover personal information that is irrelevant to the candidate's ability to perform the job, which could lead to discrimination and other charges if used in connection with the employment decision. In addition, while an Internet search may help you verify some dates and facts, it is no substitute for a thorough reference check.

"What is a background check, and do I need to conduct one?"

Background checks provide history about a potential employee from sources outside of previous employment. Criminal records, motor vehicle records, and credit reports may be part of a background check. The law requires that the extent of the preemployment background check be appropriate in relation to the specifics of a job. If a position requires someone to drive a vehicle, conduct a motor vehicles department check. You may want to retain a background check company because such companies may have quicker access to information than you would.

When information about a criminal record is used to make a hiring decision, the use must be based on a business necessity. You should consider the nature and seriousness of the offense, the time elapsed since conviction or incarceration, and how the offense relates to the job. Criminal record checks can be complicated because they require access to multiple jurisdictions. When contracting with companies to conduct these checks, ask how they obtain the information and how long the check will take to complete. State laws vary when it comes to whether an employer can deny employment based on a previous conviction, and the law may prohibit employers from asking certain questions. Check with counsel before acting.

Some employers also conduct credit checks when hiring for a position involving financial or cash-handling responsibility. If you conduct any background check, credit check, or reference check through a third party (i.e., someone other than a company employee), you will be covered under the Fair Credit Reporting Act (FCRA). The FCRA has specific guidelines for the use of credit checks and other defined "consumer reports" that require that the employer obtain the prior consent of the candidate. Under the FCRA, you will also be required to make certain disclosures to the applicant if the information contributes to your making an adverse decision. Because employers that violate the provisions of the FCRA may suffer significant legal consequences, it is important that you understand your responsibilities before allowing any outside parties to perform any investigations regarding a candidate. You can obtain more information about your obligations under the FCRA through the Federal Trade Commission. A number of state laws also limit employer use of credit data in the employment process.

A Side Note: Negligent Hiring

Companies that fail to conduct adequate reference or background checks on potential employees may be liable in court for negligent hiring. Negligent hiring is a legal concept that holds an employer responsible for injuries caused by its employees if the employer failed to make reasonable inquiries into employees' backgrounds and their suitability to hold a position. Most negligent hiring lawsuits are based on the premise that an employer hired an employee without obtaining available information about that individual's criminal, violent, or other dangerous tendencies, and placed the employee in a position where he or she could harm coworkers, customers, or members of the general public. An employer can be held responsible for negligent hiring whether or not its employees are acting within the scope of their jobs.

MAKING THE JOB OFFER

"How do I decide on a candidate and make a job offer?"

All too often, hiring decisions are made without thorough review and analysis. Studies have shown that interviewers frequently make up their minds during the first few minutes of an interview and use the rest of the conversation to validate their decisions. They may not check references and instead go straight to a job offer. The total cost of replacing an unsuccessful hire can be as high as several times the individual's annual earnings, depending on the level of responsibility of the position. Time spent making the correct hiring decision is decidedly cost-effective.

When you have completed the steps in the hiring process, review all available information before making your decision. Rank the candidates in order of preference. Obtain detailed feedback—not merely a yes or no—backed by clear information from everyone who met the candidate.

If you are hiring for a position that is paid an hourly rate, you can extend an offer to the candidate as soon as you have reached a decision. Think of the job offer as an opportunity to welcome an employee to your company. Congratulate the individual and provide details about the rate of pay, date, time, and location where they are expected to report to work, and name a person the new hire can contact with additional questions.

"How do I negotiate a job offer?"

If you are hiring for a salaried position, especially a key position in the company, you should expect to negotiate the job offer with the candidate. Before you begin, you must understand all the potential parameters of the compensation that will be offered. Employers typically make offers at 80 percent or 90 percent of the maximum they are willing or able to pay. The individual making the offer should understand all the forms of compensation, including base pay, bonuses or incentives, and the value of additional benefits. Decide in advance issues such as the potential availability of sign-on bonuses, relocation assistance, and reimbursement for any other expenses.

Sign-on bonuses are paid to attract a candidate and/or to compensate a candidate who has the potential to lose bonuses or incentives when accepting a new position. They are typically paid out over a specified period of time. Some organizations require employees who leave within a year to return a part of their sign-on bonuses.

If you are offering relocation expenses, state specific guidelines. Your company may have an existing policy detailing exactly what is covered, a maximum dollar amount allowable for the move, or even a single payment of a specified amount.

Before you offer or agree to any variations in benefits, inquire whether changes are allowed under your benefits plan. For example, your benefits contract may not permit you to move up an eligibility date for medical coverage. In this situation, you might offer to reimburse COBRA costs to continue benefits up to the eligibility date.

> **Better Forgotten:** *"Did you read the offer letter?"*
> A senior manager in financial services eagerly awaited an offer letter
> after a verbal negotiation about a new position. When the letter arrived
> it included a base salary that was 20 percent less than the verbal offer.
> The hiring manager had not carefully checked the offer letter.

"I know what I want to pay. Why should I negotiate?"

If your company is not willing to negotiate a job offer, you must realize
that you are setting the tone for a working relationship. A candidate for
a sales or marketing position or any senior role should be expected to
ask for more than the offer. This is a good opportunity to assess the individual's negotiating skills. Do not give an immediate answer during a
negotiation, and don't expect an immediate response to an offer. A
career change is an important decision; you do not want to pressure job
candidates before they have had the opportunity to carefully consider
your offer.

"Should I put the offer in writing or have the employee sign an employment contract?"

Employers commonly follow up verbal offers with written offer letters
that confirm details. It is essential that these letters accurately reflect the
verbal offer. When promised or requested, provide offer letters promptly. Never send an offer letter by e-mail to a candidate at work. Even if
the candidate prints out the letter and deletes the file, it is still retained
on the employer's server. Any offer letter should specifically state that it
is not a contract for employment. The effectiveness and defensibility of
employment contracts and noncompete agreements vary widely. If you
are considering the use of an employment contract, it should be drafted and reviewed by legal counsel.

"The selection process sounds like a lot of work. Do I really need to take all this time?"

The employment process is very time-consuming. It is impossible to
expect a positive outcome by cutting corners. You cannot speed through
an interview or reference check and hope to gain the information
needed to make a decision.

A good interview and selection process is an investment. It is the first impression for a future employee, and the process will set the tone for the working relationship. And taking care in this investment will greatly increase the chances that you and your new employee will have a mutually beneficial relationship over the long term.

HR Policies

Why Do We Need Them and
What Should They Look Like?

ALL ORGANIZATIONS HAVE SOME TYPE of policies and procedures. There are practices regarding what time to report to work in the morning, how much vacation time an employee may take, and the days when paychecks are released. Without these rules, it would be virtually impossible to run a business efficiently.

Although all organizations have policies, the manner in which they are documented and presented to employees varies considerably. There are companies with extensive policy manuals and those in which nothing is formalized in writing. Some businesses write their procedures in great detail, leaving nothing to individual interpretation; others present only broad, general provisions. Other than practices specifically required by law, there are no specific rules on how to document and implement the principles and practices by which a business is run. Therefore, the form, substance, and tone of an organization's policies and procedures are totally within your discretion as a business.

This discretion presents both a challenge and an opportunity for a business. The challenge is deciding among almost infinite choices on how to define, structure, implement, and communicate the company's rules of operation. As for the opportunity, a sound and appropriate set of policies will lay the groundwork for supporting the company's business objectives, providing employees with the necessary guidance, and achieving the desired organizational culture.

"Should our company policies be in writing?"

Having a set of written policies enhances employee understanding of company rules and expectations and encourages communications between employees and supervisors and among workers in general. It is neither necessary nor desirable to have *every* rule and practice documented, but it is advisable to take the time to formalize the important ones. In addition, having certain policies in writing—such as rules prohibiting unlawful discrimination and harassment—may save an organization a lot of time and money in the event of a lawsuit.

THE EMPLOYEE HANDBOOK

The employee handbook is the most common way of documenting policies and procedures. If you have worked for several employers, you have probably seen a variety of handbook types and styles, or even worked without a handbook.

"Should our company have an employee handbook?"

Some organizations pride themselves on informality. They believe that an employment or policy handbook only adds needless bureaucracy. Other businesses, fearful of lawsuits, are afraid that they will "say the wrong thing" in the handbook and unwittingly encourage employee lawsuits. While it is true that a poorly crafted handbook may create legal troubles, the advantages of having an employment handbook far outweigh the negatives.

A good handbook serves a variety of useful purposes. The document informs employees about company policies, procedures, and practices and can communicate expected standards of performance and conduct. The handbook is a reference guide to help managers and supervisors take appropriate actions in a given situation. Without the handbook, supervisory employees are left to their own devices, which can lead to uninformed, inconsistent, and possibly illegal decision making. A well-designed handbook can positively influence employee morale and promote employee loyalty. It can introduce a new employee to the organization, providing information about company history and facilities and helping the individual to fit in more easily. In addition, a manual can create a sense of consistency of practice that will enhance the employee's feelings of being treated fairly.

If the employee handbook is carefully drafted, it can be an important tool to *avoid* liability in employee lawsuits. The employer that clearly states policies against discrimination and harassment based upon race, color, gender, religion, sexual orientation, age, or other protected status; outlines grounds and procedures for termination; and follows these guidelines over time will be in the best position to defend against charges in these areas. While state and federal laws sometimes require that certain policies and procedures be posted on employee bulletin boards or other public places, distributing a handbook to all employees ensures that the company's critical standards are accessible to all and that each employee will have a reference when questions arise.

"Where do I begin in developing an employee handbook?"

The task of preparing an employee handbook can seem daunting to smaller organizations or to employers without large human resources staffs. But keep in mind that the basis for most of the material in the handbook already exists in your organization. Even if you have never before had an employee manual, you are already operating under a system of informal or unwritten policies and procedures. You may even have previously documented some of them in internal office memos. Think of your handbook as a formalization of standards and practices that, to a large extent, are already in use.

There is no single way to write a handbook and there are no established rules regarding the inclusion of policies and procedures. Some organizations choose a formal writing style; others choose a more friendly, conversational tone. Many of these decisions are up to you, the employer, and they depend on the unique culture of your organization.

Whatever you do, avoid the temptation to merely copy another organization's handbook. Laws vary widely from state to state, and practices differ depending on the industry or labor market. What may be applicable to one employer may not be relevant to your organization. In addition, if you do not take the time to develop your own employee handbook, your organization will miss out on the opportunity to convey to employees the elements that make your organization unique.

*"What policies should the employee handbook contain,
and how should I organize it?"*

In general, an employee handbook should contain answers to the questions most frequently asked by employees. Furthermore, the employee
handbook should have information pertaining to basic employment
matters that all employees should be aware of.

The best employee handbooks are organized logically, with the
policies grouped into sections. The pages should be numbered and there
should be a good table of contents so employees can find specific topics easily. Here are examples of frequently used sections and the policies
and procedures that might be contained in each.

Introductory or "Welcome" Section

This section of the handbook serves as a welcome for new hires and an
orientation for existing employees. It generally includes information
about the history of the organization and its mission and values, as well
as an explanation about the purposes of the employee handbook. Many
handbooks begin with a letter of welcome and appreciation from the
head of the organization.

Because the introductory section is usually the first part of the
handbook that people read, it will influence employees' impression of
the employer and their willingness to continue reading the policies.
Make sure the tone you set in this section is consistent with the way you
want your employees to view your organization and its leadership.

Better Forgotten: *"Lost in translation"*

A hotel chain introduced a new employee handbook to its staff, appropriately hiring an outside service to translate the document into
Spanish. However, when the company reviewed and revised the handbook during the two following years, it neglected to create Spanish
versions of the revisions. Keep all employees up to date on changes in
policy and procedure.

Equal Employment Opportunity (EEO) Policies

Begin this section with a statement that the organization is committed to equal employment opportunity and a healthy work environment that's free of discrimination and harassment of any kind. After this initial statement, the section should detail the individual policies, including:

- EEO policy (affirming the organization's commitment to providing equal employment opportunities to all, regardless of gender, race, religion, sexual orientation, age, marital status, and other protected status, and to following the law in all respects in connection with providing a fair work environment)

- Antiharassment policy (prohibiting harassment based upon gender, race, religion, sexual orientation, age, or any other protected category)

- Americans with Disabilities Act (ADA) policy

Employment and Compensation Policies

This section contains the policies regarding the day-to-day nature of an individual's employment and compensation. Topics can include:

- Hours of work
- Meal/break times
- Attendance policy
- Overtime policy
- Time records
- Pay periods
- Transfers and promotions
- Performance appraisal system
- Personnel records
- Introductory/probationary period
- Standards of conduct
- Dress code

- Solicitations, distributions, and use of bulletin boards
- Confidential information policy
- Theft of company property
- Smoking policy
- Employment of relatives
- Computer, e-mail, and Internet use policy
- Facebook and social media policy

Time-Off Policies

This section contains the organization's policies related to time away from work, both paid and unpaid. Policies and procedures covered here can include:

- Vacation time
- Personal days
- Sick days
- Holidays
- Bereavement leave
- Jury duty
- Military leave
- Family and Medical Leave Act
- Unpaid leave of absence

Employee Benefits

The handbook should describe general information regarding benefits offered to employees, including the availability of:

- Health and dental insurance
- Life insurance

- Short- and long-term disability insurance

- 401(k) plan

- Pension plan

- Flexible spending accounts

- Tuition reimbursement policy

- Workers compensation benefits

Employee Safety Policies

In this section, emphasize the organization's commitment to the safety of its employees and include those policies reinforcing that commitment, including:

- Safety rules

- Procedures for reporting an accident

- Emergency procedures

- Procedures for responding to and preventing violence in the workplace

- Policies prohibiting workplace substance abuse

- "Guns at Work" regulations (Several states have recently adopted legislation prohibiting employers from preventing employees from keeping guns in their locked vehicles on company premises. If your state has such a law, create a policy that clearly defines applicable employee rights and restrictions.)

Corrective Discipline/Termination Policies

This section is particularly important from a legal perspective. While progressive discipline and termination policies can be helpful in defending against wrongful termination lawsuits, courts will closely scrutinize these policies when these suits arise to determine whether they were (a) reasonable and (b) consistently followed by the employer. Avoid inflexible, highly detailed disciplinary and corrective action procedures, because there is a good chance that your managers will not follow them to the letter. Corrective action policies should include language that allows the employer the discretion to skip any or all of the steps of the disciplinary process. Policies covered under this section might include:

- Open-door policy

- Internal complaint procedures

- Forms of potential disciplinary action

- Internal investigations and searches

- Dismissal

- Resignation

"Should I have a severance policy in the employee handbook?"

To retain the maximum flexibility in your company severance policy, we recommend that you do not formalize this policy in writing in the handbook. If you do not have a written severance policy, you will have more freedom to offer individualized packages to terminated employees that take into account the specific facts of the termination (see Chapter 9). If you publish a set policy in the handbook, such as "Employees terminated for reasons other than cause will receive two weeks' severance for every year worked," you may create legal problems should you pay a specific employee more or less than that amount.

"Are there any stylistic considerations in writing the handbook?"

Keep in mind that a diverse population of employees will be reading this manual. Write in clear and simple language so that all employees will be able to understand the intent of the information presented. Avoid ambiguity. Draft policies carefully so that they will be interpreted the way you mean them to be. Do not use excessively small print, and leave plenty of white space on each page, so that the material will be easy to read and won't intimidate the reader.

Avoid words or phrases that commit you to act in a certain way in all instances, such as "will," "must," and "employee rights." Instead, use words such as "may," "can," and "generally." For example, in your internal complaint policy, instead of saying, "The human resources department will respond to complaints within five days," you might say, "The human resources department will try to respond to complaints within five days."

Use a positive tone throughout; do not adopt a punitive posture. As an example, consider the wording for a simple vacation policy:

> In order to properly schedule vacation time and assure that the organization meets its staffing requirements, employees should submit their vacation requests at least thirty days in advance.

Now compare the previous example with the following wording:

> Vacation requests not submitted at least thirty days in advance will be denied.

Both provide the same notice requirement, but which do you think employees would view more favorably? If possible, explain the reasoning behind certain policies, especially those that are likely to be seen as controversial.

"What legal issues do I need to look out for in creating the handbook?"

Many employers resist the notion of adding legal language to the employee handbook. Understandably, most organizations want an employee-friendly document, not a legal instrument that could alienate and frighten employees. However, in creating your handbook, the most important legal consideration is ensuring that your policy manual will not be interpreted as an employment contract or a guarantee that employees can remain employed as long as they follow the policies described in the handbook. For this reason, you will need to add legal disclaimers to the document.

Disclaimers should appear prominently within the handbook—in large and/or bold type—and they should be repeated several times if the handbook is particularly lengthy. Examples of possible disclaimer language are as follows:

This handbook is not intended to create an employment contract, express or implied, and in no way serves to modify the "at
will" employment relationship between the employee and
employer. Either party may choose to terminate the employment relationship at any time, with or without cause or notice.
(This disclaimer emphasizes that nothing written in the handbook
creates a guarantee of continued employment for the employee and
that either the employer or the employee can end the employment
relationship at will.)

This handbook is intended as a guide only and is not intended
to be a complete description of the employer's policies and procedures. (This allows the company to have policies and procedures
that are unwritten—such as severance practices, as discussed previously—or in writing, but not contained in the handbook.)

This list is intended as an example only and is not intended to
include all acts that could lead to employee disciplinary action.
(This statement allows you to discipline or terminate an employee for
a reason that is not specifically mentioned in your progressive disciplinary policy.)

This handbook supersedes all previous information concerning
the subjects discussed herein, whether oral or written. The
employer reserves the right to modify the policies and procedures contained herein at any time. (This disclaimer indicates that
earlier versions of the policies contained in the handbook no longer
apply and that the company is free to make changes to the information in the manual at its discretion.)

This handbook can only be changed in writing, by [the head of
the organization]. (This disclaimer prevents employees from claiming that their supervisor, or other member of the company, authorized
a deviation from the written policies and procedures.)

"Do I need to get an attorney involved in the process?"

Although you can save a considerable amount of money by drafting the
handbook yourself, it is advisable to submit a draft to an attorney for
review and fine-tuning before releasing it to employees. In this way, you
can ensure that the policies comply with all applicable laws and that
your disclaimers are adequate to protect you when the need arises.

"If we have facilities in more than one state,
do we need multiple handbooks?"

Yes, you probably do. Although federal laws and your fundamental employment policies will remain constant no matter where you operate, individual states may have specific protections, notice requirements, or other laws that are particular to that state alone. Or you may have different policies across locations if, for example, one state houses corporate offices and another a warehouse or manufacturing site. While you can use the same basic handbook across the board, the handbook for each facility should include the individual variations required by law, or specific policies or procedures not applicable to all locations.

Better Forgotten: *"What state are we in now?"*

A medium-size appliance company acquired a competitor in another state and doubled in size overnight. The human resources manager did not hesitate to immediately distribute the current handbook to its new employees. The handbook was not compliant with the state laws of the acquired business, and the safety procedures described had no relevance to the new facility. Mergers, acquisitions, and other major changes require a reassessment of policy materials.

"Is there anything else I should consider as
I'm writing an employee handbook?"

Remember that the handbook is intended to outline the organization's significant policies and procedures, not to cover every situation that may arise in the course of the employment relationship. Focus on those issues that are most relevant to you as an employer, not situations that seldom, if ever, arise or apply to only a small group of employees. Address the document to the majority of well-intentioned employees who wish to understand and abide by the company's policies, not the errant few who will inevitably violate them.

✓ Do not duplicate details that are covered in other employee publications. For example, while you may want to include a brief statement of employee benefits and an outline of eligibility for coverage, there is no need to address at length information that is provided in the organization's benefits information package. In these instances, the handbook should simply tell employees where they can obtain further information.

✓ Avoid including information that is subject to frequent change, because this will quickly render a new handbook out of date. For example, a detailed description of the use of the company's time clock system may require updating if you should purchase another model or type of system. It is advisable to omit these instructions from the handbook and post them elsewhere.

✓ Because employees are likely to take the handbook home and show it to friends and family members, be careful not to include confidential information or other details that you would not want outsiders to know.

"How do I get employees to read, understand, and follow the policies in the handbook?"

If you have created your company's first employee handbook, or if you have substantially revised an old one, you will want to take special care to properly present the new manual to employees. Initially, workers may feel overwhelmed when a volume of "rules" is handed to them. You can help to allay their concerns by taking a personal approach. Call a meeting for employees to introduce the handbook and allow individuals to ask questions about the policies. Explain that in general, the handbook does not constitute a change in policies, but merely serves to put into writing the policies, practices, and standards that the organization has always had. If the handbook includes any elements that do, in fact, constitute a change from past practices, consider including a summary sheet outlining any significant changes.

You need to notify employees that it is their duty to read and understand the policies contained in the handbook and that they are responsible for requesting assistance if they do not understand a particular policy provision. Distribute along with the handbook a Receipt of Handbook Acknowledgment Form that each employee should sign and return to the HR department or other person in charge of employee records. (A sample form is provided in the Tools and Templates at the end of this book.) The form states that the employee has received and read the handbook and agrees to abide by all the policies contained in it and to seek clarification from supervisors when needed. The form should also restate any important legal disclaimers. Keep the Receipt of Handbook Acknowledgment Form in each worker's employment file. In the event there are any legal disputes surrounding the policies contained in the handbook, you will have proof that the handbook was distributed and that the employee acknowledged his or her understanding of employer standards and practices.

Worth Repeating: *"These policies aren't 'boring' at all!"*
A large equipment maker made learning about company policies fun for employees. During new employee orientation, the employees would participate in creative quizzes, role plays, and games that centered on company policies and procedures. Participants remembered much more of what they had learned than had they just been asked to sit and read the handbook.

"Once I have created and distributed the handbook, is there anything else I should do going forward?"

It is critical to review the handbook periodically to ensure that it accurately reflects changing policies and practices of the organization, as well as changes in federal, state, or local laws. Establish a review procedure at the time you develop your handbook. The procedure should include:

- A time frame for review (preferably annually)

- The designation of the individual(s) responsible for conducting the review

- A method for notifying employees of any changes to the handbook

Notify employees of any changes either by issuing a revised version of the handbook or a periodic "supplement" to the existing manual. Have employees sign a new Receipt of Handbook Acknowledgment Form every time you issue a revised handbook or supplement.

"How about an electronic handbook?"

For most employees, your company intranet is the best place for the employee handbook and other relevant policies. It is easier to update than paper and is certainly more friendly to the environment. If you dispense with a paper handbook, you will need a system that records receipt and tracks employee acknowledgments. Don't forget any employees who do not use computers on the job; have a paper handbook available for them.

You may also use the company intranet to publish policies and procedures to guide managers. You can restrict access to managers by building appropriate access levels into the system. Whatever format you choose, your handbook should reflect the quality of your organization. Handbooks need not be highly stylized, bound books, but they should not be faded, crooked photocopies or electronic documents that are difficult to navigate. With the range of electronic and publishing resources available today, you can create a document that is professional and represents your own style.

Performance Management

How Do I Evaluate Performance and Conduct Meaningful Performance Reviews?

ASK EMPLOYEES ABOUT performance management and their experiences giving or receiving performance appraisals and you are likely to hear griping or humorous or scary anecdotes. Companies' approaches to performance management vary widely. There are organizations with elaborate performance-management systems that combine frequent feedback with documentation, those that use simple forms for one annual discussion copied from other businesses or forms books, and others that use no system at all.

Meaningful ongoing performance management helps both individual employees and the business as a whole. Effective performance management is a key for the motivation, retention, and development of employees, because individuals learn how they are performing and where they are going in the organization. Managers learn more about their subordinates in the process, strengthen relationships through discussion, and develop their own coaching skills. The entire organization benefits from a system that aligns performance to company-wide goals, provides a structured format for measuring results and giving feedback, and establishes a record for each employee that can be used for individual development, to inform future supervisors, and to make sound employment decisions.

No matter what the size and culture of your organization, it pays to be attentive to performance management. Since there is no single correct approach for every business, you must take steps and adopt structures that fit with and work for your organization. Never just copy the approach of another company and assume that it will work for you. In this chapter, we will discuss some of the considerations involved in developing and implementing a performance-management system that will get you the results you want.

DEVELOPING A PERFORMANCE-MANAGEMENT SYSTEM

"What is 'performance management'?"

Performance management is a systematic approach to tracking individual performance against the targeted objectives of the organization and identifying strengths and opportunities for improvement. It involves more than giving an annual performance review. While a periodic formal review may be part of the performance-management process, good performance management is an ongoing process, not a once-a-year event.

"Where do I begin in creating a performance-management process for my organization?"

Set Your Expectations. You cannot measure performance unless you first establish the expectations. For professional sports teams, the expectations are clear and measurable. The team wants to win. Individual players are expected to score points, complete specific plays, increase speed, or keep the opposing team from scoring. Performance is monitored daily and progress is easily determined. When performance declines or goals are set at higher levels, players are coached for improvement in form, plays, strength, speed, strategy, or resilience.

Monitoring performance is not as straightforward for most employers, but the same principles apply. You need to set goals for the company as a whole. Include specific objectives, such as revenue targets, excellence in customer service, or development of cutting-edge products. Once you have established your goals, you can set team and individual objectives to meet your goals.

Individual expectations for employees can be divided between specific results and the attributes, attitudes, or behaviors that lead to those results. For example, you may expect your vice president of sales to achieve target annual revenues of $1 million. To sell $1 million worth of products, she must perform a series of activities and actions that perhaps include hiring and managing a sales force, planning and forecasting, customer development, etc. For you to determine whether your vice president has been successful, you must continually evaluate whether her skills, attitudes, and behaviors are producing the results you want.

Worth Repeating: *"Thanks, now I know what I have to do!"*
A multi-location service employer gives new employees a job expectations sheet that lists their rate of pay, major responsibilities, the name of their manager or supervisor, the other positions and departments with which they will interact, and their measures of success. Expectations are crystal clear from the onset.

Fit the Program to Your Company's Culture and Philosophy. If you have articulated precise goals to your employees, emphasize these goals in your program. If you are in the process of significant business growth and need information on which to base promotions, design a process that will elicit the information you require. A well-thought-out performance management system that meets your needs, fits your culture, and can be adapted when the business changes will improve morale and retention and become an integral part of your operation.

Facilitate Solid Communication. Performance management requires solid two-way communication about expectations and the individual's progress against these expectations. The best managers meet informally, one on one, with their direct reports on a regular basis to share updates on activities and projects, business direction and goals, philosophy, and feedback on results and expectations. The managers comment on performance status and suggest improvements; the subordinates tell the managers if there are any process problems or other obstacles to meeting the objectives.

"What is all this I hear about coaching?"

Coaching—or developing individual performance—is central to performance-management discussions. Scheduled meetings can provide an opportunity for coaching, but the most successful managers coach their subordinates all the time. The best employees consistently seek out direction and coaching. Coaching can consist of a variety of activities, including:

- Giving and clarifying direction

- Jointly identifying and developing goals

- Giving and listening to feedback

- Acting as a source for guidance and advice

- Actively helping people do the work

- Suggesting improvements in concepts, process, or outcomes

- Building self-confidence by providing encouragement and reinforcement

- Maintaining morale through motivation

- Breaking down barriers and providing resources to achieve results and change

- Developing skills, knowledge, and abilities

- Giving guidance on advancement

- Providing guidance on interpersonal relationships as they affect the employee's work

"Do we need a formal mentor program?"

It depends on your organization. Mentoring on some level exists in all organizations. Strong managers will act as mentors to those they supervise, and mentor situations will evolve naturally and informally outside of the reporting structure, whether as an outcome of the recruitment process, a special project, or a friendship. Mentors may coach, but in addition they provide practical advice on how to get things done within the organization, or how to navigate company politics and plan a career strategy. The most successful employees often credit a strong mentor with helping them to prosper and advance within the company.

One complaint about informal mentoring is that mentors tend to seek these special relationships with people just like them. If you find that only a narrow segment of your employees are benefiting from mentoring relationships, you may want to adopt a more formal mentor program. These can be simple approaches, such as pairing new employees with a more senior manager or structured programs with significant training requirements for individuals who volunteer to be mentors.

Worth Repeating: Mentor Up

Many companies have found success with reverse mentor programs that encourage learning relationships up the hierarchy. Senior managers can find out firsthand about new technologies and learn from the experiences of millennials entering the workplace. This multigenerational approach also helps bridge the gap and foster understanding.

"How do I deal with unacceptable performance within my performance-management structure?"

When faced with unacceptable performance, such as a project riddled with major errors or disruptive behavior at a staff meeting, give immediate feedback rather than waiting for a "better time" or, even worse, the annual review date. If you fail to address the issue, the employee will either not know of the problem or will think she can get away with poor performance. And you, the manager, may continue to seethe inside. When addressing performance deficiencies, don't bring employees into your office, tell them what they are doing wrong, and threaten them that they are never to do it again "or else." Instead, plan for a two-way discussion where both sides understand the problem and agree on a solution.

Recommended action steps include:

- Explaining the nature of the deficiency and asking the employee why it occurred.

- Listening to the employee's response.

- Asking the employee for ways to correct the problem or prevent a recurrence.

- Agreeing on a plan of action, which may include identifying additional resources or obtaining more information.

- Expressing support and confidence in the employee's ability to improve.

- Documenting the plan of action in a memo or e-mail to help track follow-up. This documentation should not be a disciplinary action, but rather an agreement on expectations.

If performance does not improve, then begin the disciplinary process. Employers often use the term "progressive discipline," which refers to escalating corrective steps as problems and infractions occur. Progressive discipline does not mean that once an employee problem comes to light, discipline speeds up. The idea is to correct performance problems, not to "catch" employees and build up a record against them.

Your disciplinary process should make clear to employees that corrective action will not always be progressive, following the same steps. The level of discipline should be appropriate for the type of infraction or performance problem and consistent with actions taken in similar situations. Disciplinary decisions may also take into account the employee's length of service and previous history of infractions. The procedure may vary for hourly and managerial employees. For hourly employees, disciplinary action will often follow this progression: verbal warning; first written warning; final written warning or suspension without pay; and termination. Managerial discipline is usually handled by means of discussions, which are documented by memos or letters, and ultimately, if appropriate, termination. There are some serious circumstances that require immediate termination without progressive discipline. They include theft, fraud, possession or use of illegal drugs in the workplace, and physical violence.

Documentation of disciplinary steps is very important. In written warnings, state the reason for the action and the consequences for future infractions or continuation of the problem. Both the manager and the employee should sign the documents, with copies retained by the employee and placed in the personnel file. When developing a disciplinary policy, give yourself the leeway to skip some or all of the disciplinary steps in appropriate situations.

THE PERFORMANCE-APPRAISAL PROCESS

"Does performance management have to include formal performance evaluations?"

The great majority of organizations use performance evaluations as part of their performance-management process. Some companies limit their performance-management activities to appraisals alone. Many of the same people who use performance evaluation as a tool dislike and criticize the entire process, citing reasons such as poor communications, lack of training, and the discomfort of a potentially negative conversation. Some critics fault the hierarchical approach of traditional top-down feedback, believing that it de-emphasizes entrepreneurial talent and individual input.

There are organizations that have successfully eliminated formal, structured evaluations while maintaining a performance-management system. Some have replaced the once-a-year evaluation with informal and formal processes that revolve around providing better and more frequent feedback.

You are not required by law to conduct formal evaluations (with the exception of limited government standards for certain licensing arrangements). In fact, a poor evaluation process and format may do more harm than good. If you have a system in place that is not helping you achieve the performance results you want, take a break from the process, review it from start to finish, and introduce a new evaluation system if you feel it will help the company.

"What are my first steps in developing a performance-appraisal system?"

First, identify what you are trying to measure. Typically, the evaluation process will:

* Identify gaps in performance or competencies and recommend strategies for closing the gaps

* Capitalize on strengths

* Use a combination of the above approaches

You will also need to determine whether the review will be tied to compensation decisions and, if so, how. Surveys and focus groups with managers and employees are excellent ways to gather information about the measurement approach and techniques that will work best in your organization. Ask questions designed to identify goals, previous positive and negative experiences with performance reviews, roadblocks to effective reviews, preferred rating scales, timing and levels of evaluation, best practices, and training needs. Soliciting input will also help you get early employee buy-in regarding a changed or a new process. Your program must have full support from top management for success. Management should participate in your development and training process.

"How often should performance reviews occur?"

Use an evaluation schedule that fits with the goals of your organization. Some employers have one set due date for all evaluations, with the discussions conducted up to eight weeks before the deadline. This universal date makes record keeping and tracking very easy and, if tied to compensation practices, can facilitate budgeting. It also provides a set time frame for managers to concentrate on the process and allows them to easily compare members of their teams. A single review date can, however, create a logistical nightmare for larger departments or managers with a large number of direct reports. They may be forced to complete dozens of appraisals within a short time frame.

You may find that it's more realistic to set up more than one review date during the calendar year. Think about assigning different review dates for hourly and salaried employees, or dividing employees based on factors such as hire date, last promotion, or geographic location. Spreading the review dates can alleviate time pressures, but it will increase record keeping and tracking requirements. Some businesses perform evaluations on or about the worker's employment anniversary date. The anniversary date system allows managers to review performance over consistent one-year increments, but it can be time-consuming to track due dates and collect documentation.

Once you choose an appropriate review schedule, it is important to devise tracking procedures that will ensure that appraisals take place as planned. Human Resources Information Systems (HRIS) and payroll systems can track due dates automatically and generate reminders. Special software, with or without performance-management tools, can help track the process. Strictly adhere to your stated timetables. Even an outstanding performance review can dampen the morale of an employee if it's conducted six months after the due date. If you fail to provide negative reviews in a timely manner, you may risk legal liability should you decide to terminate an employee and he argues that he was never notified of his shortcomings or given the chance to improve.

"What does a good review format look like?"

Keep it simple. A twenty-page performance review document will look daunting to most managers. Simpler reviews are more likely to result in greater consistency among ratings. You may decide to have more than one review format, such as separate appraisal documents for managerial and support staff or technical and nontechnical employees, but be sure that employees in similar job categories are measured similarly. Effective performance evaluation forms contain the following elements:

- *Clear standards by which the performance will be measured.* List the specific competencies or skills being measured, with examples of success. If you have job descriptions for your positions, the abilities listed in these documents can serve as good starting points. There are also many standards that apply to all positions, such as timeliness, accuracy, ability to prioritize, and a positive attitude, among others.

- *An appropriate rating scale.* The purpose of the rating scale is to provide an objective way to determine whether an employee is meeting performance standards. Some organizations use a numerical system (e.g., a 1 through 5 scale); others prefer descriptions such as Excellent, Good, Fair, and Unacceptable. Most businesses provide between two and five tiers of achievement within the rating scale. Having more tiers can allow you to draw finer distinctions among candidates, but it can also lead to inconsistencies when people have varying understandings about the difference between a rating of 3 and one of 4. Whichever measurement you choose, clearly specify which ratings constitute acceptable performance and which fall below company standards. If you distribute a form to your customers asking them to rate their satisfaction with the company, using the same rating scale for your internal performance reviews will promote consistency in language and expectations when you talk about performance.

- *Space for written comments by the supervisor.* Encourage specific comments and require them in situations involving superior or very poor ratings. You do not want managers to mechanically check boxes without thinking through their responses. Explain on the form that the reviewer should carefully select examples that concentrate on performance, not personalities or trivialities, with an eye toward helping the employee understand the assessment.

- *A section for an employee self-appraisal.* Employees should be able to assess their own performance. A designated space can be provided on the evaluation form or employees can be asked, prior to the review meeting, to complete the same form their supervisors complete. Self-appraisals (see Tools and Templates) increase employee buy-in to the process, assist supervisors in their focus, and identify any blind spots workers may have about their performance.

- *Suggestions and specifics for employee development.* This may include in-house or external educational or training programs or on-the-job experiences recommended for the worker's further professional growth.

- *Objectives set by the employee and manager at the last appraisal and rating of their results.* Comparing last year's goals with actual performance provides continuity of standards from evaluation period to evaluation period.

- *Objectives to be met by next appraisal date.* These can include new goals as well as prior objectives that were not completely met.

- *Approval by all the levels necessary for the company's process.* Approval requirements will vary, but all appraisals should be reviewed by at least one person in the organization who is familiar with the goals of the appraisal process. When supervisors submit reviews that do not meet the organization's performance-management objectives, they should be coached on the proper way to complete the appraisal and required to redo the document.

"Where do I get my form?"

While another organization's appraisal form will rarely be entirely adequate for your needs, you may be able to customize documents from other companies, or you can pick and choose elements from several different forms. Alternatively, you may want to work with a consultant to develop an original form or purchase an off-the-shelf software program with built-in performance evaluation templates or wizards. If you choose an off-the-shelf product, look for one you can tailor, and evaluate the training materials, rating guides, or other support materials available.

> **Better Forgotten: Right Logo, Wrong Information . . .**
> An HR director responsible for the opening of a new national location took with her a copy of the company's performance evaluation form. She carefully changed the logo on the top to reflect the new location, but she did not look at the body of the form. As a result, the form contained confusing references to functions and priorities not relevant to the new location.

There is no need to rush to select a product or grab someone else's forms. A quickly developed program that doesn't reflect your organization or meet your needs will cost more money in the end and cast doubt on the integrity of the entire review process. Before purchasing an expensive product, test the system with a small group that includes members of senior management. Even if you then decide it is a perfect product, make sure it allows you to make changes, and make sure you have not spent so much money on this one product that you can't make any other changes in your process for at least five years! Performance review should be a dynamic process that grows and changes with the company.

"Can I just use the Internet to automate the whole process?"
There are a variety of online solutions available to automate the performance-management process, but take care not to eliminate the human element. Integrated Web-based and other software programs can include data from new hires, training, competencies, reminders, and customized materials. You can also purchase stand-alone performance evaluation products in a myriad of formats and price ranges. When reviewing any product, look for the ability to customize the software to reflect the positions in your organization and include specific terms and jargon. With an automated process at your fingertips, it can be tempting to e-mail your review off to the recipient, seek an electronic signature, and skip the per-

formance-management conversation altogether. Don't fall into this trap, as you will increase the potential for miscommunication and discontent and will miss the opportunity for productive, relationship-building discussions.

Streamline the basics by using simple spreadsheets and putting all forms and procedures on a company intranet or shared file drive. Whether you purchase a program or use existing resources, train users to avoid inputting subjective judgments or potentially discriminatory statements in electronic formats (see Chapter 8 for more on electronic communications). A Web-based review that states that "Bob is certainly slowing down since he turned sixty. I don't know how he will ever make quota at his age" is just as damaging as a paper-based one.

"I have the forms . . . now I just send them out and wait for the reviews to come in, right?"

Wrong. The biggest mistake employers make in performance evaluations is setting calendars and sending out forms, and then sitting back and expecting them to be completed effectively. You cannot assume that all managers will read the instructions on the form and proceed to write insightful appraisals. Whether you are implementing a new system or maintaining an existing process, training is critical to give managers the knowledge and motivation to provide meaningful feedback. Whether you conduct the training in-house or through outside providers or educational institutions it should include information about:

- Why the organization values performance appraisals and how individual performance benefits the organization

- The structure of the process and its relationship with compensation

- The meaning and application of the rating criteria

- How to develop goals that are specific and measurable

- How to give feedback, both positive and negative

- How to coach an employee

Training should also provide managers with the chance to practice their written and verbal appraisal skills before their first review discussion. Managers have the most difficulty giving constructive feedback that focuses on objective measurements, using specific examples. Instead of telling an employee he has a "bad attitude," the reviewer using effective feedback techniques might say, "I have noticed that you often fail to cooperate with your coworkers. You did not show the teamwork we expect of our employees when you started an argument with Mary just because she asked to borrow your scissors."

Better Forgotten: *"Nobody's perfect!"*
We have all worked for, or heard of, managers who state that they never give the highest ratings available on evaluations because "no one is perfect." Why have the highest levels on the form then? Train managers about the meanings of the various ratings and the standards of performance that qualify an employee for a particular ranking.

Every manager's own appraisal should include a section rating his timely and comprehensive completion of subordinates' evaluations. Managers will come to understand that providing accurate, prompt, and constructive feedback is an organizational priority and an important criterion of acceptable performance as a manager.

Alternative Appraisal Methods

There are numerous other evaluation methods that come in and out of vogue that you may wish to consider. Usually these approaches will supplement, and not substitute for, the traditional one-on-one performance review.

"Will 360-degree feedback make me dizzy?"
The concept of 360-degree assessments, feedback, or evaluations is based on the assumption that an organization can cull more information from a variety of sources than from managers alone. This process replaces the traditional top-down rating with anonymous performance feedback from peers, subordinates, managers, and in some cases, even customers and suppliers.

Before even investigating 360-degree assessments, identify your goals and the results you expect. Will you use the information for development purposes only, or will it become a factor in pay and promotion decisions? What will be your timeline and training needs, and how will you communicate the results to participants? A 360-degree assessment can be administered using paper and pencil, on the Web, or even by telephone. The method you choose will depend on your goals and your participants. When selecting appraisal forms for 360-degree reviews, you'll want to look for flexibility, costs, and support services that meet your needs.

The evaluations will generally contain four or five rating scales with space for comments, with between eight and fifteen respondents assessing each employee. It is important to use at least six evaluators to preserve anonymity, to train participants on the system, and to communicate the timetable.

If used properly and under the right circumstances, 360-degree feedback provides honest information and different perspectives, and during growth and change periods it can be a perfect tool to gain a picture of the entire organization. It can be especially useful in work situations that involve many cross-functional teams or relationships. However, this appraisal method will not work for every organization. It may not work in companies with a distinct hierarchy of management and reporting structure or where there is a low level of trust among employees. Furthermore, it may not be effective over the long term. Studies have indicated that when you solicit ratings from the same group over a long period, the evaluators tend to be less honest and more flattering. In addition, implementation of the process can be daunting because of the number of people involved. Do not cut corners to minimize costs.

"Who's keeping score on a balanced scorecard?"

The balanced scorecard is a method of evaluation that uses four specific, balanced perspectives to measure performance: financial, customer, internal business processes, and learning and growth. On each scorecard are goals and ratings at each level of achievement. While the balanced scorecard approach can be adapted to rate individuals, it is really a tool for understanding overall organizational performance. Balanced scorecards can take different forms based on the results you want to measure, but the system is best used in an organization where there is a highly developed existing structure or means for process improvement.

"Should I rank my employees through a forced ranking system?"

Forced ranking systems place employees along a curve of performance or in categories of percentiles for performance. The best performers would, for example, be placed in the top 20 percent, with a large group in the middle at 70 percent and the worst performers dwelling in the bottom 10 percent. The ranking is "forced" because there is a requirement that 10 percent of employees be given the lowest rating regardless of whether their reviewers would have rated the workers that way on their own.

Forced ranking is rarely the sole component of performance management, but rather a result of some form of review. The system has been used to provide greater rewards for top performers and specific deadlines for performance improvement for the lowest-ranking employees. Some employers have used a "rank and yank" philosophy under which the bottom 10 percent of employees are automatically terminated each year, allowing the organization to consistently purge the lowest performers. Although this process can aid an organization by reinforcing goals and objectives and rewarding the best employees, it can be demotivating for the rest of the workforce and can promote competition and individual performance over teamwork. In some major companies, forced ranking has resulted in well-publicized discrimination, disparate impact, and class-action lawsuits.

Probationary Periods

"How do I evaluate new employees?"

Some new employees seem to fit seamlessly into their new jobs and surroundings and others take more time to get acclimated, but you have probably also faced the situation where a recent hire is performing far below expectations and shows a lack of desire or ability to improve to an acceptable standard. You will want to have flexibility built into your policies so that you can terminate these clearly unsatisfactory relationships before they adversely affect other employees or your bottom line. A well-defined probationary, introductory, or "tryout" period will enable both you and the employee to determine if the job is a good fit.

Generally, a probationary period will range anywhere from sixty days to six months. Inform new employees of the terms and duration of the probationary period, whether in a written offer letter or the employee handbook. Your explanation should state that either you or the employee can terminate the employment relationship at any point during this time, with or without cause or notice.

When you have a new employee who is not performing, first ask yourself whether you have established and clearly communicated your expectations. If your new IT technician is completing a substandard six repairs a day, did you inform her that the expectation is ten repairs a day? Also look at whether there is another significant problem with a working relationship or with communications and whether the employee does in fact have the necessary skills and knowledge to complete the job. Let her know that her performance is unacceptable, then set a brief period of time within the probationary period for her to demonstrate change. Workers who begin the employment relationship violating basic rules of conduct such as attendance or punctuality are unlikely to be good employees. New hires should be expected to demonstrate their best behavior, and those who come in with bad attitudes or behavior problems should be terminated.

Worth Repeating: *"Thanks for the form!"*
A start-up company gave all new hires a blank copy of the new employee evaluation form during the orientation program, explaining when and how it would be used. This took some of the mystery and potential for fear out of the process.

The completion of the probationary period is a good time for a first performance evaluation. You can use a basic checklist that summarizes what the employee has accomplished or learned, reinforces expectations, and measures adherence to generally expected outcomes, such as good attendance and an ability to work with other departments. The same evaluation form can be used prior to the end of the probationary period to provide the framework for a discussion when the employee is not performing at expected levels.

Do not make the mistake of extending a probationary period to give an employee another chance. The purpose of a probationary period is to set a time frame for early review to predict success. In addition, extending probationary periods for one employee but not for others can raise concerns about inconsistent treatment. Complete the introductory evaluation as soon as possible after the end of the probationary period. If you wait too long, the employee will likely believe either that everything is great or that you just do not care. Don't limit introductory reviews to lower-level employees. Even the most senior executive will benefit from early, structured feedback. If you find that the term "probationary" creates a negative impression, simply call the first discussion a 90- or 120-day review.

CONDUCTING THE PERFORMANCE APPRAISAL

"Who should conduct the appraisal?"

Generally, the employee's immediate supervisor should conduct the performance appraisal. If the supervisor does not have the experience to conduct a proper review, the manager at the next level can communicate the evaluation. While more than one manager may have input into the content of the review, select only one person to actually participate in the appraisal meeting. A lone employee sitting in a roomful of managers is likely to be put on the defensive.

"How should I plan for the in-person appraisal discussion?"

The best performance evaluations are conducted when both the employee and the manager are well-prepared. Use a structured approach for planning and conducting the review.

✓ Set the date, time, and location of the review and communicate this information to the employee.

✓ Request a self-appraisal and designate a due date.

✓ Review previous performance-appraisal documents for this employee, especially the most recent. If another manager prepared the last review, you may want to contact this person if you have questions.

✓ Review any other goals or incentives, both individual and team-based.

✓ Review the individual's personnel file or your own notes and records concerning any recognition received or conversations about performance.

✓ Complete a draft of an evaluation form once you have received and read the self-appraisal.

✓ Submit the review to any parties who need to authorize the document or any related salary actions.

"How do I conduct the review?"

Choose a quiet place, free of interruption. If you select an off-site location such as a restaurant or coffee shop, choose one where you and the employee will be comfortable. Do not start the meeting by reading the form out loud and reviewing it line by line. The best reviews focus on discussion of performance, not completing a form, and you want to set the scene for a conversation. Begin by welcoming employees and asking them about their overall experience at work since the last appraisal. You can also gain insight by soliciting their perceptions about the department. Then proceed to the body of the review. Summarize results from the previous appraisals, including specific goals and development activities; cover the ratings of the specific competencies or job requirements, skills, or knowledge; and set out the new goals and development plan. Sometimes the insights you gain from the conversation may lead you to change some of your prepared ratings.

The evaluation should be an interactive process, giving the employee the chance to participate, ask questions, respond to feedback, and offer suggestions. The worker may not always agree with all comments in the review, but he or she should be allowed to express concerns and request clarification—although you should not let the meeting disintegrate into a complaint session. You may wish to split the review into more than one session, with the latter meetings focusing on goals and development plans that require further thought. Once the review document is completed, whether during or after the review meeting, the employee should sign it and retain a copy.

"Can I use the evaluation to tell the employee to shape up or ship out?"

The performance review is not the place to have your first discussion about an individual's unsatisfactory performance. A review—positive or negative—should never come as a surprise, but should be a reinforcement of your continuing communications with the employee in accordance with your total performance-management process. If you have had previous discussions about performance problems, you may appropriately use the review to put the employee on a performance improvement plan (PIP), outlining the performance standards that the employee must meet as a condition for continued employment. When structuring a PIP, be sure it includes:

- Specific, measurable improvements that the employee must demonstrate. Instead of using vague language such as "We expect better attendance," you might say, "We expect no unauthorized absences within the next ninety days."

- A defined, reasonable time frame during which improvement must occur (generally sixty to ninety days, but no more than six months).

- A written statement that if the employee does not make the improvements within a designated time, disciplinary action will be taken, up to and including termination.

If a performance evaluation discussion gets nasty or the employee is too defensive or argumentative to hear you and respond clearly, do not hesitate to reschedule and get advice on how to continue.

Better Forgotten: *"Don't put anything negative in writing!"*
A mid-level manager worked in the field for a company where the managers conducting reviews wrote summaries to ensure that nothing negative ever went in the form sent to the corporate office. They said that only positive items belonged on the permanent record. As a result, employees did not get helpful developmental suggestions in writing.

"What do I do with the final written evaluation?"
Once the evaluation is completed and signed by all necessary parties, place the document in the employee's regular employment file. Retain all previous evaluations in the file as well, so that you have a history of the individual's performance and growth.

"Are there any other rules about
maintaining the employment files?"
Because an employee's file is generally available for inspection by the employee and his superiors in the organization, it is important to limit documentation in this file to materials that *relate to the individual's employment*. It is proper to put the following documents in the employment file:

- Job application

- Resume

- Offer letter

- Employment contract (if applicable)

- Performance evaluations

- Disciplinary reports

- Company awards

- Training record

- Compensation history

Keep information that is sensitive in nature and not directly related to the employee's qualifications, compensation, or performance in separate files, in order to protect the employee's privacy rights and avoid allegations that the information was used improperly. Strictly limit access to this information to those with a need to know. The types of information in question include:

- *I-9 documentation*. While the law does not require that these forms be kept apart from the basic employment file, the Bureau of Citizenship and Immigration Services recommends keeping them separate. (See Chapter 7 on regulatory issues for more information about maintenance of I-9 records.)

- *EEOC records.* Because these records cannot be used for determining employment status, they should be stored separately (see Chapter 7).

- *Grievances, discrimination complaints, and responses.* Since these documents do not relate directly to the individual's employment status, store them separately from general employment files in an "employee confidential" file. This will help to avoid potential retaliation claims.

- *Employee assistance.* Documentation concerning whether an employee has sought help through the employer's employee assistance program is confidential and should be kept in a confidential file.

- *Medical records.* The Americans with Disabilities Act (ADA) requires that medical information be kept apart from personnel records. Therefore, benefits enrollment information, documentation on preemployment physical exams, workers compensation, disabilities, Family and Medical Leave Act (FMLA) requests, reasonable accommodations, insurance claim specifics, and physicians' notes should be kept in confidential medical files, protected from access by other employees. You may inform managers and supervisors about necessary work restrictions or accommodations, but only to the extent necessary to enable them to implement appropriate actions.

- *Results of preemployment criminal background or credit checks.* While this information may be used in the employment process, it should not be included in personnel files, where it may be viewed by a manager who has no reason to access the results.

Finally, never collect or retain information that is not directly related to an individual's employment. Examples of such inappropriate material include documentation related to an employee's personal life, religious or political beliefs, social club memberships, or sexual orientation.

Employee Relations and Retention

How Do I Keep Good Employees and Maintain Working Relationships at All Levels?

YOU HAVE MADE THE EFFORT to find and hire the best candidates. You have oriented them to your company culture and spent time and resources training and developing them. Now you want to keep them—keep them working for your company and not the competition, and keep them content, motivated, and focused on the business.

When employees are unhappy in the workplace, when morale and productivity lag and turnover is high, the root problem is usually not compensation. Generally, these difficulties will be people-driven, stemming from poor communication, a perceived lack of appreciation and recognition, lack of clear paths for career growth, and unresolved grievances and conflicts.

This chapter discusses ways you can open and improve lines of communication, resolve conflicts before they become crippling, and let your employees know that they are valued.

FOSTERING EFFECTIVE WORKPLACE COMMUNICATION

Ask executives and managers what is standing in the way of better effectiveness in their businesses, and more often than not they will mention the need for "better communication." And they are usually correct. Poor communication does account for a multitude of workplace woes, including interpersonal conflict, wasted money and effort, poor productivity, legal exposure, low morale, and high turnover.

Whether your organization has five, five hundred, or fifty thousand employees, the way it communicates will directly affect worker focus, morale, and commitment. What is good communication? It is providing the right kind of information and delivering the right message to your employees clearly and in the appropriate manner. Good communication is also about encouraging—and having adequate mechanisms in place to allow—employees to deliver information to management.

"What types of information should I be sharing with my employees?"

You should pass along information that will better enable employees to do their jobs, as well as news about the company's progress, business changes, and other matters that affect the workforce. Be sure to communicate information to employees at all levels of the company, and don't forget individuals who telecommute or work at remote locations. Types of information to share include:

- *Vision, mission, and goals.* It doesn't matter what term you use, but you should let employees know what the company stands for, where it is going, and the progress it is making toward fulfilling its objectives. Employees want reassurance that management has a clear direction. Even if your company does not have a long-term business plan, talking with workers about where you would like to be in a year—or within the next six months—will help instill confidence and increase focus.

- *Business results.* Make it a practice to inform employees how the business is doing financially. Whether or not you share this information, your workers will likely know if the company is doing well or is faltering. However, communicating in greater depth on this subject will make employees feel involved and will help them better understand the reasons for management actions. Communicate financial results in a fashion that you are comfortable with and that your employees will understand. The information you share can range from complete profit-and-loss statements to percentage increases in revenue to cost of supplies.

● *Triumphs and disappointments.* People who know that their work has contributed to a successful enterprise will be more motivated and fulfilled. So it is confounding that some organizations will report a large new customer or long-term contract to a newspaper but not their own employees. Do not be afraid to report on disappointments as well as successes. By disclosing information about situations that have not worked out so well, you can pass along what you learned from the experience and increase the chances of improving the next time.

● *Organizational and business changes.* If your organization is going through major changes such as a layoff, restructuring, office move, or sale of a line of business, tell employees sooner rather than later. You'll help to quell rumors and speculation, and your employees will feel flattered that you respected them enough to share this information. If your organization has recently gone through a merger or acquisition and you now have a group of new people on board, prompt and honest communication of postmerger procedures and the vision for the organization going forward will help deter the best employees from both companies from jumping ship.

Worth Repeating: *"Show off those clippings!"*
Successful companies keep employees well informed by displaying copies of ads in prominent locations or by circulating e-mail updates. This helps to reinforce the company message and demonstrate the company's role in the industry and local community.

"How open and honest do I have to be?"

There are some situations where you will not be able to pass on information because you are legally restricted from disclosure. Examples are pending mergers or acquisitions, securities transactions, or situations where you have signed nondisclosure agreements. Barring these restrictions, give workers the information they need to understand the business and direction of the company and to be successful themselves. Never lie to employees or tell them half-truths. If people ask you questions that you are unable to answer for reasons of confidentiality, don't falsely tell them that you have no information on the subject. When they find out you have been untruthful (and they always do!), you will lose credibility in the long run. Instead, you might answer that you are not in a position to share the information at this time.

"What are the best methods of communicating to employees?"

Regardless of the astonishing range of communications technology available today, the best method of communicating most important information is in person. Depending on the circumstances, it may be better to communicate to people individually, in small groups, or if practical, to all employees at once. Some companies hold quarterly employee meetings at which the president and key executives report on business results and new developments. In other businesses, the president will meet with small groups for breakfasts or pizza luncheons where employees can ask questions and share their concerns. When you have employees at remote locations, regular visits from the president or other senior staff members will decrease their sense of being isolated from the company as a whole. The more critical the information you have to share, the more important it is that you communicate the news in person.

Letters from the company's president or owner or a senior executive are good ways to provide general information that employees can share with a spouse or family member. A letter mailed to the employee's home can summarize organizational performance, thank employees for their efforts, provide forecasts of upcoming business, or reinforce important workplace matters that would be strengthened by home discussion, such as the company's response to press about the business.

Newsletters or "e-newsletters" are easy to produce and can be used to inform, reinforce company culture, announce company contests, and celebrate birthdays, new births, or service milestones. Gone are the days in most workplaces where paper memoranda are circulated around the office. E-mail has become the chosen way to communicate, but it often falls short as a method of primary communication. Though e-mail is convenient, it lacks the personal touch, and it should never be used to tell people about vital or controversial matters or news that is likely to arouse employee emotions. Also, since employees get numerous e-mails every day, they are more likely to accidentally delete the message or overlook its urgency.

If you have a very important message to communicate, get it out repeatedly, through a variety of formats.

"What are the best methods to get information from our employees?"

Since communication is a two-way process, establish ways for your workforce to communicate with you. Employees will feel empowered and valued, and you will be able to glean important data that will help you run your business more effectively and act on those matters about which your workers are concerned. Never assume that you know what your employees are thinking. Instead:

- Encourage employees to ask questions in company, small group, and individual meetings. When holding small group meetings, try mixing employees at all levels to get a variety of perspectives.

- Conduct employee focus groups and surveys about attitudes and opinions. You may be surprised by what you learn.

- Have a procedure for employees to express grievances, and make sure you follow up promptly and consistently with your policy.

- Establish a suggestion box where employees can submit questions or voice concerns. Devise a response format, and respond promptly and consistently to let workers know that you take their input seriously.

- Consider establishing an employee hotline run by an independent provider, or setting up in-house confidential voice mail boxes, so employees can report problems that they might be afraid to report otherwise.

- Walk around informally and talk to your people. Casual conversations can yield a lot of information. Managers should not sequester themselves in their offices.

Better Forgotten: *"What were those survey results?"*
A mid-size employer hired an outside consultant to design and administer an employee opinion survey. The results were compiled in a comprehensive form and sent to all key managers. The company sent a summary to all employees and formed a committee to create action plans. Nothing else was done. One year later when the company distributed another survey, only 5 percent of the employees even bothered to respond.

"Can poor communication on the part of individual managers create retention problems?"

Absolutely, and this problem is exacerbated because many managers think they are better communicators than they actually are. There is an overused, yet true, saying that people do not leave their jobs, they leave their bosses. In employee exit surveys, the most frequent employee complaints about former supervisors involve poor communication skills. This isn't surprising, because businesses do not always hire and promote managers based on their communication and management skills. Many individuals possess a wealth of knowledge in their fields and are highly skilled in the technical aspects of their jobs, but they fall short when it comes time to assign projects, convey expectations, and make employees feel good about working for the team.

There are certain common manager communication problems that, if identified, can be addressed. Do you recognize yourself or anyone in your organization in these descriptions?

- *Managing by e-mail.* Far too many managers use e-mail as a substitute for personal interaction. Would you try to build a relationship with an important new customer via e-mail? Would you hire a key executive without meeting this individual? Of course you wouldn't, and neither would most experienced businesspeople. However, the same managers who know that personal contact is key to interpreting a person's character and reactions and establishing commonality often choose to "manage by e-mail"—even when workers are in offices a few steps away. While no one should seek to discuss sensitive or delicate matters electronically, even everyday business is better handled through personal contact when possible. More direct contact helps create better rapport and trust.

- *Lack of clarity.* Many managers assume that when they give instructions or discuss a business situation, everyone understands them and is ready to take action. Then they are amazed and upset when the resulting project bears no relation to the outcome they had in mind. Often, different people make different deductions from the same information, and they proceed in good faith to do the opposite of what the manager expected. Clear communication results from asking the right questions, gaining clarity, and confirming what we have heard. Only then can people achieve a common understanding of a business issue or course of action. Managers need to be aware of and facilitate this process. When giving assignments or instructions, ask open-ended questions to make sure the employee understands. Instead of saying, "Do you understand?" you might ask, "What steps will you take to complete this task?" Never make employees feel inadequate for asking questions.

- *Poor listening skills.* Since every communication involves at least two people with differing priorities, needs, and perspectives, it is just as important for managers to listen to their staff as it is to be heard. In addition to giving assessments and instructions, solicit feedback from employees. Ask if there is anything you can do as a manager to make their jobs easier or more satisfying. Consider their suggestions and treat seriously the concerns they raise.

- *Failure to give consistent feedback.* Some managers don't tell employees what they are doing right or wrong during the course of the year, and then, at annual review time, they drop a bombshell on the unwary. While a well-considered annual performance evaluation is a valuable communications tool, employees resent when feedback is a once-a-year event. They also miss the opportunity to learn from their successes and mistakes. People do not like surprises, and they want an opportunity to develop and improve throughout the year. Provide continuing, constructive, on-the-job evaluations focusing on situations as they arise, while they are still fresh in everyone's memory.

- *No tact and empathy.* Some managers have no problem giving feed-back, as long as most of it is negative. They can pick away at the most minute details of a worker's perceived problem areas or announce mistakes and deficiencies in front of others, but never offer a word of thanks or praise. Constant criticism is demotivating. Highlight the positive as well as the negative, correct mistakes without getting personal, and treat people as you would wish to be treated. Others will be more inclined to listen and respond.

- *Too busy to manage.* It's true: Managers are busier than ever with their own heavy workloads, but many forget that an important part of a manager's job is managing. It is critical to carve time out of your schedule for regular one-on-one and group employee meetings. While it is totally appropriate to make employees aware of your time pressures, offer your undivided attention during these meetings. Taking telephone calls or allowing other interruptions conveys to employees that you do not consider their concerns a priority.

"Once I have identified an interpersonal communication problem, what can I do to fix it?"

Improving communications involves a multifaceted approach, depending on the situation and the individuals involved. Since many people are not aware of their limitations in communicating, sometimes merely making them aware of their actions will be enough to bring about positive change. Most of the time, however, a bad communication style will be deeply ingrained in the manager.

You can use coaching and mentoring to effectively attack interpersonal communication issues. The coach can be someone within the organization or an outside consultant. For executives and senior-level managers, you will likely have more success with an outside coach or consultant. When coaching managers to improve their communication skills, keep in mind the following guidelines:

✓ Be explicit and use concrete examples. Instead of saying, "You are not a good listener," you might say, "I noticed in the staff meeting that you talked right over Jane when she had questions about the deadline."

✓ Show the negative impact *on the manager* of the bad communication. It is human nature that self-interest is the factor that most effectively generates change. For example, don't simply tell the manager that he is not clear in his instructions. Try saying something like, "Because your staff had to redo their work so many times, you missed your project deadlines. If you take the time to explain your assignments at the outset, you and your team will have a better chance to earn the full quarterly productivity bonus."

✓ Remove poor communicators, if necessary, from managerial responsibilities. Some people, no matter what you do, will not develop into good communicators. After unsuccessful coaching, you may rightly determine that they should not be managing others. Often, they will be just as relieved as you are when they are free of these responsibilities.

✓ Small group training is an excellent way to teach your executive or management team to improve their management and communication styles. There are myriad fine outside and in-house training sessions on communication, management, and leadership.

STRUCTURING REWARD AND RECOGNITION PROGRAMS

You may be able to lure new hires through the door with an attractive compensation and benefits package, but if you don't maintain a positive working environment they will leave to work elsewhere—sometimes for jobs that pay less. While it is important to provide fair pay, the key to creating an outstanding work environment is making people feel appreciated and recognized for the work they do. No one likes to feel unnoticed or taken for granted. Reward and recognition programs let workers know that their efforts count.

An employee recognition program is different from an incentive program. Under an incentive system, you pay money or other valuable compensation for meeting specific performance goals. If a salesperson meets her sales targets, she will get a specified bonus, or if a development team gets a new product to market on time, each member will receive a certain amount. Recognition programs, on the other hand, appreciate people for their efforts as individuals, often for positive contributions that do not directly affect the bottom line. Recognition programs can be a way to thank the receptionist who always greets visitors with a warm smile, or to acknowledge the financial analyst who puts forth the extra effort to make new department members feel welcome. Unlike incentive programs, reward and recognition programs can be inexpensive. While you may not be able to provide significant incentives in difficult times, it is easy and desirable to maintain a continuing program of employee recognition and appreciation.

"How do I develop strong reward and recognition programs?"

The biggest mistake businesses make is assuming they know how employees want to be recognized and structuring programs that do not reflect the real needs of their workers. As your workplace is made up of a variety of diverse individuals, one type of recognition effort will probably not work for everyone. Create a system that reflects both individual and group needs and the type of culture you want to develop or maintain.

✓ Determine the types of behavior and performance you want to reward. Do you want to encourage good attendance? Team efforts? Creativity?

✓ Solicit employee input. If you want to get an accurate perspective on the types of recognition your employees would value, ask them! You can distribute surveys or hold individual or focus group meetings to attain this information. Get input from people at all levels of the organization. Different levels of employees may have different needs and motivations.

✓ Survey supervisors and managers who will be responsible for selecting the individuals who receive rewards. They will have some valuable feedback concerning how decisions should be made.

✓ Organize a committee to review employee feedback and make suggestions for activities going forward.

✓ Communicate the program clearly and consistently to employees. If you are implementing a formal program that has specific eligibility and performance requirements, explain them fully. Misunderstandings generate bad feelings.

✓ Be prepared to be flexible and to inject novelty and variety into the program. While employees may initially enjoy receiving a mug with the company logo for their efforts, when their desks are cluttered with company mugs over the years, this reward will not seem very special. Your goal is to inspire enthusiasm.

✓ Be genuine. If your managers shell out empty praise or you implement programs by rote or out of a perceived obligation rather than a real desire to reward and inspire, your employees will spot your insincerity. In the end, they'll feel insulted and patronized rather than rewarded and inspired.

Worth Repeating: *"Don't forget the night people!"*
A twenty-four-hour hospitality company holds regular midnight dinners for the overnight staff. Senior managers who come in late at night host the employees. The overnight staff appreciates the recognition and that they can get answers from the source. Don't leave your night workers in the dark.

"What types of recognition programs should I consider?"
Your efforts should include both formal and informal recognition. The possibilities are limited only by your imagination, but the concepts that follow can serve as a starting point.

Praise. Praise doesn't cost a dime, and there are few people who don't appreciate a sincere compliment or word of acknowledgment. Instill in your managers the importance of praising employees both for outstanding effort and positive results. Praise is most effective when it is specific and delivered at the time when workers do something right. Rather than saying, "You have a good attitude," say, "Several customers have praised your responsiveness on this project." This statement gives the employee direct reinforcement and will encourage him to continue that behavior.

Small, Informal Reward Items. These include inexpensive symbols of gratitude that are usually presented spontaneously, by the employee's manager. These modest "on the spot" tokens are very effective, but should not be given so often that they begin to seem routine or arbitrary. Examples of these rewards are thank-you notes; T-shirts, mugs, or other trinkets; plaques and certificates; impromptu, informal luncheons; parking spaces; gift certificates; or movie and sporting events tickets.

Awards Luncheons or Dinners. These meetings are more formal than impromptu pizza parties and are usually held periodically to celebrate milestone service periods. Awards luncheons and dinners are also excellent methods of recognizing exemplary employees in front of their peers. Don't just stand up and hand your outstanding workers plaques or pins at these events. Build camaraderie and motivate employees to strive for the reward by publicly explaining why the recipient's work mattered, sharing stories and humorous anecdotes.

External Rewards. Consider nominating outstanding employees for outside rewards. Chambers of commerce and other business associations, trade organizations, and other professional groups frequently request nominations for people with noteworthy business accomplishments. Community or industry recognition for a job well done is extremely flattering.

Larger Merchandise Rewards. As merchandise awards are more costly, they are usually reserved for service awards or the achievement of a significant goal. As a rule, it is not the value of the gift that is important but the recognition itself, and awarding items of substantial value on a frequent basis can result in employees focusing more on the prize than on their work. Some organizations successfully award employees "points" for designated behaviors or achievements, which they can accrue and redeem for merchandise in the future.

Internet-Based Reward and Recognition Programs. While online programs lack a personal touch, they can be a fast, convenient, and inexpensive way to administer and track reward programs. There are many online vendors that offer software packages and record-keeping services that allow employees to track the status of their awards and redeem them for merchandise online.

> **Worth Repeating: *"Give them a tour!"***
> A start-up energy research company held an open house and invited employees to bring friends and family for a tour. Senior management acted as tour guides and met attendees, who enjoyed light refreshments. Employees loved showing off their workplace and the cost was minimal.

"Is it safe to hold a holiday party for my employees?"

A holiday party is a common way to thank workers for their efforts during the year and to thank customers for their support. However, it is important to plan these events carefully. As an employer, you may be held legally responsible if an intoxicated employee gets into a car accident on the way home from your event. Other inappropriate employee behavior can result in harassment charges, workers compensation claims, and other legal liabilities for a company.

Most companies still find that the benefits of a party outweigh the risks, so they hold some type of holiday festivities for their workers. You can minimize risks by observing the following standards:

✓ Hold the party off company premises and outside of normal business hours.

✓ Notify employees that attendance is optional and avoid negative actions or comments when an employee does not attend.

✓ Circulate a memo to all employees, before the party, emphasizing the importance of moderation in drinking (if you are serving alcohol) and reminding them that the company's policies regarding sexual harassment and discrimination apply to company parties.

✓ Take precautions if you do serve alcohol. Hire bartenders or caterers—don't let company employees mix drinks. Have plenty of non-alcoholic beverages on hand, and provide entertainment or some other activity for attendees besides drinking. You might consider providing vouchers to limit the number of drinks served, or limit the hours during which alcohol is served. Instruct bartenders not to serve minors and to stop serving individuals who seem intoxicated. Designate employees to circulate during the party to spot those who do not look sober. Provide transportation home by means of designated drivers or company-paid taxis for those who request it or are deemed unable to drive safely. If you are holding the party at a hotel, negotiate reduced-rate hotel rooms for employees.

✓ Encourage employees to bring spouses, significant others, and children, if appropriate and financially feasible. This practice increases the likelihood that the occasion will be festive but professional. Misbehavior is much less likely to occur in a family environment.

✓ Take any employee complaint about harassment or any other improper conduct at the party seriously and investigate it just as you would complaints about regular activities during business hours. Don't write off an allegation just because the behavior occurred at a party.

Better Forgotten: *"Was that entertainment?"*
A well-intentioned marketing company hired a comedian for its employee holiday party without thoroughly checking him out. The comedian regaled the group with off-color stories and offended several employees. This was embarrassing for the company and could have led to serious complaints. Choose entertainment that will engage employees, but be appropriate for the occasion.

MAINTAINING WORK-LIFE BALANCE

A significant amount of an employee's waking hours are spent at work. Not long ago, for most people this meant showing up at their workplace for a defined time period each day and, depending on the organization, putting in additional hours or "face time" after regular hours or on weekends. Increasingly, employers are finding that helping workers create and maintain a balance between their home and work lives is key to retaining the best employees. Through alternative work and scheduling arrangements and other life- and family-friendly programs, employers that help employees reduce stress and gain personal satisfaction reap the benefits of a more loyal, motivated, and productive workforce. These programs can make your company more desirable to prospective employees and have even been shown to help decrease absenteeism among existing workers. There is no "one size fits all" approach to flexible scheduling. Whether a particular program will work for you depends largely on the specific needs and characteristics of your workforce. Before creating and implementing any plan, survey your employees to determine their needs so that you don't spin your wheels developing something that will not be seen as a benefit.

"What types of alternative work arrangements can I consider?"

Flextime. Flextime is a term for variable schedules that allow employees to vary the start and end times of their workdays while still working a standard number of hours within a given workweek. Employers designate a set of core hours during which all employees must be at the workplace, as well as the hours that are "flexible" for the employee. For example, you might designate the core hours as 9:00 a.m. to 4:00 p.m. and permit your workers to start their day between 7:00 and 9:00 a.m. and leave between 4:00 and 6:00 p.m., depending on the time they start. Flextime is an attractive option to help employees deal with family issues, commuting patterns, and educational, volunteer, and wellness activities. Flextime programs can be structured on an ongoing basis or occasionally as needed by an individual. These programs are also attractive to employers because they can generate significant goodwill at virtually no cost to the organization.

Telecommuting. Telecommuting, or telework, which allows employees to work from their homes or other locations outside of the office either occasionally or every day, is becoming a mainstay in American business. These arrangements help employers to attract and retain excellent workers no matter where they live, help save on office overhead, and can boost productivity when employees spend less time commuting and suffering the frequent interruptions of an office setting.

Job Sharing. Job sharing allows two or more employees to share the responsibilities of one job. It is a way to attract and keep qualified individuals who, either because of conflicting priorities or lifestyle choices, do not desire to work full-time. Usually, the employees who wish to share a job will present a proposal to management that outlines the job coverage schedule and how responsibilities will be divided. Compensation is agreed between the company and the job sharers, but employees working less than full-time hours may receive reduced or part-time benefits.

Compressed Workweek. A compressed workweek allows full-time workers to complete the minimum weekly required hours in less than five full days. For example, to meet a required forty-hour workweek, employees might work four ten-hour days a week and get the fifth day off, or work eighty hours within a nine-day period and get the tenth day off. There are no specific legal requirements for structuring compressed work-weeks, except that you must comply with any state or local overtime regulations applying to workdays of longer than eight hours.

While compressed workweeks are usually best suited to manufac-turing businesses, hospitals, or positions where contact with customers is prearranged (e.g., doctors, lawyers, accountants, etc.), if this type of program fits in well with your business, there is no reason not to con-sider implementing it.

"What should I consider in determining whether these work arrangements are appropriate?"

Not all positions are appropriate for alternative work arrangements. Some jobs require a physical presence in the office during normal working hours. A telecommuting arrangement will not be successful unless the individual has the discipline and focus to work independent-ly and achieve specified goals. When considering job-sharing arrange-ments, decide whether both employees are equally qualified to do the job and whether the nature of the position is such that it makes busi-ness sense to divide the work. You have the discretion to be selective about extending these benefits to workers, as long as you do not dis-criminate. If you deny individuals the flexibility they request, explaining your reasoning will help to diffuse resentment.

In addition, just because an employee works at home doesn't relieve you of the obligation to comply with minimum wage or overtime requirements, nor are you exempt from all responsibilities to provide a safe workplace. Workers can and have filed workers compensation claims for injuries that occurred while telecommuting. Train workers on how to avoid foreseeable job-related injuries, such as repetitive motion or carpal tunnel disorders, and recognize that harassment and discrimination can still occur involving workers not present in the office.

"How do I implement these alternative work arrangements in my organization?"

Once you have determined that your workers and your organization could benefit from alternative work arrangements, develop clear written plans or policies and communicate them to employees. While the plans will vary according to the details of the arrangement, you will want to include:

- A detailed description of the parameters of the program (e.g., the core and flexible hours included in a flextime program or acceptable work schedules for a compressed workweek, the types of positions suitable for the program, and other eligibility issues)

- Instructions for submitting employee requests under the plan or policy

- Criteria for managers to use in deciding whether to approve or reject requests, or for creating a new position specifically designed for a nontraditional work arrangement

- The consequences for misusing the program

- A statement that the organization has the right to change, suspend, or terminate the programs at any time and for any reason

Upon approving an individual employee for participation in a flextime, telecommuting, or job-sharing program, it is helpful to draw up a written agreement signed by both the manager and employee with specific details of the situation. You can use this "contract" to evaluate the success of the arrangement or as documentation in the event of a future employee problem.

PROVIDING MEANINGFUL CAREER GROWTH

While you may have some excellent employees who are content to remain in the same job for years, many workers will outgrow their jobs and feel the urge to move to new challenges. It is tempting to resist moving capable workers when they express interest in a new role, focusing on how difficult it will be to replace Jane as the shop foreman or Joe as the office manager and the normal disruption that transitions bring. And business conditions will not always allow you to approve a requested move. However, employers who do not routinely encourage their good performers to take on new responsibilities within the organization, or who do not allow for career growth, risk losing their most ambitious and valuable workers.

Career advancement can involve moving up in the ranks of management, but not everyone can have a management job, and some people don't even want the stress that goes along with one. Savvy companies will also develop career growth strategies that involve meaningful opportunities for lateral movement to keep employees loyal to the organization, stimulated, and motivated to succeed.

"How do I foster career growth for employees at my business?"

A good career path program is one that benefits both employers and employees, where there is some synergy between what the employee wants from his career and what the employer can offer in light of specific business needs. The variety of available career options will generally depend on the size and nature of your business. Smaller firms may have fewer open positions across a smaller range of job functions than large companies, but they may be able to offer employees more responsibilities and the opportunity to create a larger role for themselves. Growing companies may have more opportunities for advancement than businesses that are stagnating or are experiencing hard times. Analyze the needs of your business and determine what types of career growth you can and cannot offer your employees.

Large companies will commonly develop clearly defined career structures, with set criteria to progress from level to level. Small and mid-size employers are less likely to have this type of formal program. However, all companies can take certain steps to creating practices that encourage opportunities for advancement and growth.

- *Find out what your employees want their careers to look like.* Their answers may surprise you. Programs or practices that sound great on paper mean nothing if they are not meaningful to employees. You can get an overall view of how your employees view their careers through group surveys, but nothing beats one-on-one discussions. Develop a plan with the individual regarding the path for achieving her goals. If you believe the employee's goals are not realistic, either due to the company's business circumstances or your perception of her abilities, be honest and let her know what you can provide.

- *Tie development to your business plan.* Look at your company's short- and long-term business goals to determine what skills you will need in the future. Communicate these goals to employees and provide training opportunities, both internal and external, to enable them to acquire the knowledge and skills that will be critical to future growth.

- *Promote from within.* Advertise job openings and promote from within whenever possible. Some employers automatically assume that the only qualified candidates for new openings come from outside the company. This attitude is dispiriting to the workforce. For open positions, clearly state the requirements and the level of performance the employee must attain and maintain in the current position in order to be considered for a new one. If you believe an individual is not qualified for a desired position, explain your reasoning so that there is no misunderstanding.

- *Provide training and development opportunities on a regular basis.* Whether this training involves learning new skills, keeping a worker current on knowledge needed in his current position, or providing mentoring to facilitate professional development, employees appreciate your commitment to their careers. Some companies are ambivalent about providing "too much" education or training, fearing they will lose employees with company-financed expertise or recently acquired degrees to other companies, especially if appropriate advancement is not available in their own organization. While you can't prevent every defection, just remember that these former employees can be great ambassadors for your organization, often becoming customers or referring business.

- *Stress the employee's responsibility for career growth.* Emphasize that while the company will provide opportunities, individual employees must be proactive in taking advantage of these opportunities and proactively managing their own careers. Explain that advancement is dependent on performance and results, not just seniority. Encourage employees to make their career aspirations known, to seek feedback, and to be on the lookout for new opportunities to take responsibility, learn, and grow.

RESOLVING WORKPLACE CONFLICTS

No matter how well-run your organization is, disputes, conflicts, and grievances will inevitably arise. As individuals, we have our own ideas and goals, and it is only natural that in pursuing our own agendas we will sometimes be at odds with others with differing objectives and viewpoints. Life in business organizations is no different. In fact, today's businesses are especially vulnerable to conflict. They employ an increasingly diverse workforce, operate in a complex global economy, and navigate pressures to deal with rapid change and increased productivity requirements.

While all businesses contend with conflicts and disagreements, some are able to turn their experiences into learning and growth opportunities, while others let the animosities devolve into anger, low morale, high turnover, and employee lawsuits. The difference between positive and crippling results is directly connected to the organization's ability to identify healthy versus unhealthy conflict and to manage and resolve disputes and grievances before they get out of hand.

"Isn't all organizational conflict undesirable?"
Some amount of conflict is not only desirable, it's also necessary. Without a broad range of ideas presented by persons with diverse backgrounds, experiences, and points of view, innovation is virtually impossible. Conflict can also present an opportunity for personal growth. When we learn the skills to work out our differences and to develop approaches that take into account the needs of others, we become more effective and aware businesspeople.

The difference between "healthy" and "unhealthy" conflict is this: While healthy conflict revolves around the vigorous exchange of ideas in the best interests of the organization, unhealthy conflict is based on anger, frustration, and personal animosity. The key to effective conflict management is to create an environment that encourages workers to challenge ideas and forbids them from attacking people.

"Are there systems we can implement to prevent and resolve workplace disputes?"

While it is tempting to ignore a problem and hope that it resolves itself, conflicts rarely do. Instead, they fester and spread. By taking a proactive approach, you will be able to uncover and address problems before they escalate into full-blown feuds or lawsuits. There are several practical techniques for preventing and resolving differences in the workplace. Some organizations have formal conflict-resolution programs; others resolve differences through less structured means. Larger companies will often use internal ombudsmen or independent negotiators or mediators to facilitate communications among the parties, but in smaller companies, the success or failure of conflict-resolution efforts will depend on the conflict-management skills of the managers. Every business must select the methods that best fit the culture of the company and its resources.

The most common conflict-resolution program is the "open-door policy," which gives employees the opportunity to resolve problems with their managers or coworkers. Traditionally, these programs provide that employees first bring the problem to their supervisors (or the next level in the hierarchy if the problem is with the supervisor). If the supervisor is unable to resolve the issue, the employee may elevate the grievance to the next higher level of supervision, and then to successively higher levels until the problem is satisfactorily addressed.

While open-door policies give workers a defined, structured way to have their issues heard, there are limitations to the process. An open-door policy is only as effective as the conflict-resolution skills of the managers addressing the issues. Additionally, these policies rely on employees to initiate the issue-resolution process. Often, individuals will not come forward, and it will be up to the manager to recognize the problem and take steps to resolve it. Whether or not you have a formal issue-resolution procedure, it pays to train managers and supervisors to build awareness about conflict management and to enhance intervention, mediation, problem-solving, negotiation, and other conflict-resolution skills.

Provide individual coaching for executives and managers who require special assistance with conflict management, either as an element of their career development or to help them deal with special situations. Executives must set a standard from the top. If middle managers feel disrespected, attacked, or stifled by senior management, chances are that they will pass this negative attitude down to the employees they supervise.

"Are there basic conflict-resolution skills we all can learn?"
Yes. When a conflict arises in your workplace, consider these guidelines:

✓ *Call the disputing parties together in a neutral area, such as your office or a conference room.* Treat the meeting as a serious occasion. Do not take telephone calls or allow other interruptions. Tell them that you have observed or been informed that there have been difficulties between them, and ask to hear each person's side of the story. Listen carefully and empathetically. Commonly, people will interrupt each other to argue their side of events. Firmly state that you will hear only one person at a time, that you expect everyone to listen to each other, and that everyone will get a chance to speak.

✓ *Do not show a bias toward any individual's point of view.* If you show sympathy with one of the parties, the other will invariably lose trust in the process and stop sharing openly. It is not your job to be the judge of who is right and wrong. You are there to help the parties accept their differences and work toward a meaningful solution.

✓ *Keep the discussion focused on the issue at hand.* If the participants begin to ramble or drift off topic, gently guide them back. Focus on the present and the future, rather than letting parties bring up old, unrelated gripes. Never permit personal attacks such as "John is an idiot" or "Mary is lying." Do not interject your own opinions or experiences. This dispute is not about you.

✓ *Probe until you understand the root cause of the conflict.* Even substantive disagreements are often fueled by interpersonal differences. John and Mary may be appear to be arguing about setting a project timetable, but the problem could have roots in John's perception that Mary disrespects him. Address the interpersonal issues before attacking the substantive ones.

✓ *Do not ignore emotions.* Behind every dispute there are real emotions, such as hurt, anger, and betrayal. While you should not dwell on the emotions involved, it is important to acknowledge that they exist. Expressing their emotions will help the parties obtain closure and move on.

✓ *Work with the parties to find a way they can both come out "winners,"* focusing on common goals. If John and Mary are fighting about the details of a project timetable, remind them that while their approaches may differ, they both have an interest in seeing that the project is successful and if the project fails both of them will suffer. Ask each of them about the compromises they would be willing to make and those that they would like to see from the other to ensure the success of the project. The plan does not have to be a complete compromise, but the result should be acceptable to both individuals. Sometimes early efforts to resolve the conflict will be fruitless. In this event, be prepared to stop the meeting and resume it at another point, giving the parties the opportunity to think through the points discussed. When you have reached an agreement, put the plan in writing so each person has something he or she can refer to and work with.

✓ *Follow up periodically.* If the conflict is significant, don't expect miracles overnight, but look for indications that the individuals are acting on the plan as agreed and taking steps forward. Tell the participants that it is okay to take small steps, and recognize their accomplishments as they attempt to work through their differences.

WHEN EMPLOYEES LEAVE:
CONDUCTING THE EXIT INTERVIEW

Even if you have made every effort to create a positive work environment, employees will leave the organization. Sometimes the reasons can be completely personal, such as relocation or the desire to stay at home with a child. Other times they stem from the employee's dissatisfaction with the company. Conducting structured exit interviews with departing personnel is an excellent way to identify causes of turnover. Employees leaving the organization are likely to be more honest with you than those you currently employ. You can use the results of exit interview surveys to determine whether there are underlying problems that are causing people to leave, and to build a strategy for improved retention.

"Who should conduct the exit interview and what should they ask?"

A member of the human resources department or other neutral person will typically conduct the interview. The employee's manager should never conduct the interview because the employee would be reluctant to be completely honest, especially if the manager's behavior or style contributed to the decision to leave. Interview those employees who have voluntarily resigned from the company. Fired employees are less likely to give you objective information. You may choose to use a written questionnaire, but with verbal interviews you can ask follow-up questions. Conduct the conversation in a quiet place where it will not be overheard, or on the telephone, and assure the employee that all responses will be kept confidential.

Ask questions that will elicit information about the perception of your company as a place to work and will help you to identify trends developing in any specific area or with an individual manager. (See the sample exit interview questions in the Tools and Templates section.) To maintain confidentiality, keep exit interview data separate from the employee's personnel file.

Worth Repeating: *"I'm in the club now!"*
A large regional law firm established an "Alumni Club" for attorneys who leave the firm. The firm distributes a semi-annual alumni newsletter communicating business and personal news about the firm and its members and holds a barbecue or cocktail party for the club every year. The "alumni" retain a sense of attachment to their "alma mater," and they regularly refer clients to the firm.

"What happens if the employee reports harassment or other illegal conduct in the exit interview?"

Occasionally, employees will report in the exit interview that they resigned because of to a supervisor's sexual harassment or commission of fraud. Even though the employee is leaving and did not file a complaint during the course of employment, you are still obligated to treat the matter seriously. Ask employees for full details of the conduct and why they chose not to report it earlier. Conduct a full investigation, and if you find the complaint to be justified, take appropriate corrective action regarding the offending party. (See Chapter 8 for more information on how to conduct employee investigations.)

Sound employee relations are important in all phases of the employment cycle, including departure. You may feel inconvenienced or upset when workers leave, but do not try to make them feel uncomfortable about their decision or treat them as the enemy. A former employee can be an ambassador for your organization to potential employees and customers, and you may end up hiring this person again in the future.

5

Compensation

How Should Employees Be Paid?

IF YOU WANT TO ELICIT STRONG EMOTIONS from a group of workers, ask them about compensation. Everyone has an opinion about the subject, most of the time relating to something they believe their organization could be doing better. Yet certain aspects of compensation are shrouded in secrecy and discomfort. Employees often fear requesting raises or are reluctant to ask questions about pay. Similarly, many managers hate responding to requests for raises or cannot answer even the most basic compensation inquiries. When compensation issues are not addressed head-on, they lurk behind the scenes and become sources of rumors, misinformation, and discontent.

The problems organizations and individuals face when communicating information about pay stem from the very personal nature of compensation and the complexity of wage and hour laws. Some companies face additional challenges because they do not have, or fail to inform employees about, an organizational compensation philosophy or policy. In this chapter, we will discuss the relevant wage and hour laws and other considerations involved in developing, implementing, and disseminating a total compensation strategy.

WAGE AND HOUR LAWS

Compliance with federal wage and hour laws begins with your obligation to prominently post the federal wage and hour compliance poster in your workplace. Many companies sell wage and hour posters, but you can get them for free by calling your local Wage and Hour Division of the Department of Labor or by downloading them directly from their Web site.

The next step is to make certain that you, or the company that completes your payroll, keep proper employee payroll records that include:

• Name and Social Security number

• Address (including Zip code)

• Date of birth (if under eighteen)

• Gender and occupation

• Time and day of work and when work begins

• Hours worked each day

• Total hours worked each workweek

• Basis upon which wages are paid (e.g., hourly or weekly rate of pay)

• Regular hourly rate of pay

• Total daily or weekly straight time earnings

• Total overtime earned for the workweek

• All additions or deductions from employee's wages

• Total wages paid each pay period

• Dates of payment and pay period covered

If an outside vendor completes your payroll, it maintains this information and can provide it to you in an easy-to-understand format.

"What do the minimum wage laws mean for my business?"
The wages you pay your employees are not determined by legislation, but there are laws that establish minimum hourly rates. The Fair Labor Standards Act of 1938 (FLSA) sets a federal standard for the lowest rate of

> ### Worth Repeating: Don't Forget to Audit
> A manufacturer with multiple locations performed selected audits each pay period, closely reviewing paper checks and direct deposits from a different department each time to make sure they matched employee addresses and Social Security numbers. One audit uncovered extra vacation payments that had been requested by a manager who was using the money to support a gambling habit.

pay per hour of work for most jobs. Many states also have their own minimum wage laws. In situations where federal and state laws are different, you must comply with the law that is most generous to the employee.

There are some very narrow exceptions to the federal minimum wage requirements. You do not have to pay minimum wage to tipped employees who earn at least the minimum wage when their tips are added to their direct wages, or to workers under twenty years old during their first ninety days of employment. You can get information about these and other exemptions from the U.S. Department of Labor.

No more than 5 percent of all U.S. employees receive the federal minimum wage, because in most locations it is not a competitive rate of pay. There are states and localities that require that area standards or prevailing wages be paid to contractors performing work for municipal agencies. Some municipalities have also adopted a minimum wage called a "living wage." Living wage campaigns are generally driven by coalitions of community groups, religious leaders, and unions with the aim of requiring private employers that benefit from government contracts or funding to pay their workers at rates at least at the local poverty level. There are more than a hundred living wage ordinances with varying requirements in locations throughout the United States.

"When do I have to pay my employees overtime?"
Under the FLSA, employees working more than forty hours a week are entitled to overtime unless they qualify for certain specified exemptions. Employees who are legally eligible for overtime are often referred to as "nonexempt," as opposed to "exempt" workers, who fit into one of the excepted categories. Exempt workers receive their full salaries for each workweek regardless of the number of hours they work. However, you

cannot avoid your overtime obligations merely by classifying workers as exempt and paying them salaries. The FLSA sets strict guidelines for determining whether a position qualifies for an exemption.

In August 2005, the Department of Labor issued revised regulations governing overtime eligibility for executive, administrative, professional, outside sales, and computer employees. These regulations describe what are commonly called "white-collar exemptions." As an employer, you are responsible for determining which positions in your organization are exempt and for defending your reasoning if challenged.

Executive Exemption

To qualify for the executive exemption, individuals must:

* Regularly direct the work of two or more full-time employees or the equivalent

* Have the authority to hire, fire, and promote employees, or such individuals' suggestions about the employment status of others must be given particular weight

* Regularly exercise a high degree of independent judgment in their work

* Receive a salary of at least $455 per week

* Have as their primary duty the management of the enterprise, or management of a customarily recognized department or division

Administrative Exemption

This category is often overused, but should be limited to those who:

* Have the primary duty of performing office or nonmanual work that is directly related to the management or general business operations of the employer or its customers

* Have a primary duty that includes exercise of discretion and judgment with respect to matters of significance

* Receive a salary of at least $455 per week

Professional Exemption

The professional exemption recognizes those positions requiring special skill and training. Employees in this category of exemption must:

- Have the primary duty of performing work that requires advanced knowledge (defined as work that is primarily intellectual in character and requires consistent exercise of discretion and judgment)

- Have advanced knowledge in a field of science or learning

- Have advanced knowledge that is customarily acquired by a prolonged course of specialized intellectual instruction

- Receive a salary of at least $455 per week

Outside Sales Exemption

The outside sales exemption applies to employees who:

- Have the primary duty of making sales or obtaining orders or contracts for services or for the use of facilities for which payment will be received from a client or customer

- Are customarily and regularly engaged in making sales or obtaining orders away from their employer's place of business

Computer-Related Occupations Exemption

In order to qualify for the exemption for computer-related occupations, employees must:

- Receive a salary of at least $455 a week or, if compensated on an hourly basis, a rate of at least $27.63 an hour

- Be employed as a computer systems analyst, computer programmer, software engineer, or other similarly skilled worker whose primary duty includes:

  - The application of systems analysis techniques and procedures, including consulting with users to determine hardware, software, or other system functional specifications

- The design, development, documentation, analysis, creation, testing, or modification of computer systems or programs, including prototypes, based on and related to user or system design specifications

- The design, documentation, testing, creating, or modification of computer programs related to machine operating systems; or

- A combination of the duties listed above, the performance of which requires the same level of skills

"How can I avoid mistakes in classifying positions?"

You can minimize your risk by carefully reviewing your current wage and hour practices. In your analysis, pay attention not only to job descriptions of exempt employees, but also to the way each job is actually performed, to ensure that only those employees who are legitimately exempt are classified and paid that way. A position is not automatically exempt just because the job has a managerial-sounding title or because the employee has a professional degree that is not applicable to the job. It is the actual primary duties of the worker, not the occasional responsibilities, and the level of judgment and discretion required by the position that matter.

Better Forgotten: *"But they volunteered to work!"*
When wage and hour investigators responded to a complaint made against a national retail chain they learned through interviews that employees were consistently encouraged to begin work before punching in for their shift and to stay "to help out the boss" after the scheduled day ended. Employees cannot legally volunteer to work overtime without being paid the premium pay, much less without being paid at all.

Pay exempt employees strictly on a salary basis. Generally, you must pay exempt workers their salary for each week they perform work, regardless of the quantity of work performed or availability of work. With limited exceptions, you cannot take deductions from their pay because of sickness, partial day absences, or jury service. If you take deductions from the salary pay of exempt employees, they may lose exempt status and you may be obligated to pay them for back overtime.

"How do I calculate overtime payments?"

The FLSA-mandated overtime rate is 1.5 times the nonexempt employee's "regular" hourly rate of pay for all hours worked over forty hours during the week. Employers frequently make the error of calculating the amount based on the worker's "base" hourly rate of pay. When workers earn a flat hourly rate, the regular and base rates will be the same. When employees work at two or more different rates or earn commission, bonuses, payments for good attendance, or other forms of compensation during the week, you must include these variables when determining the regular hourly rate.

Here is an example of this calculation: An employee works forty-five hours in one workweek—thirty hours at $15 per hour and fifteen hours at $20 per hour—and also earns a $40 commission for the week.

Step 1. Multiply the hours worked by the hourly rate for those hours:

30 hours × $15 per hour − $450

15 hours × $20 per hour − $300

Step 2. Add the totals from step 1, plus the $40 commission, to get $790 total base pay.

Step 3. Determine the regular rate by dividing the total base pay by the total hours worked (i.e., $790 / 45 hours − $17.55). This is then the regular rate for this week. So for forty hours of work, this employee would earn $702.

Step 4. The overtime rate of time and a half is calculated on the rate determined in step 3 (i.e., $17.55 × 1.5 − $26.33). Five hours of overtime equals $131.65.

Step 5. Add the forty hours at the regular rate plus the overtime: $702 + $131.65 − $833.65

Had there been no commission involved, you could have avoided the calculations by paying all the overtime based on the higher rate of pay, because this rate will always be higher than any regular rate that was calculated as a weighted average. In any week where the employee has earned a commission or other extra payment, always do the calculation, since the regular rate may be higher than the highest of multiple hourly rates.

You are obligated to pay nonexempt employees for time worked, whether or not the work was on the clock and whether or not any off-the-clock work was voluntary. It is not enough to have a policy stating that managers must approve all overtime—if your employees were working, with or without manager permission, they are entitled to pay. Wage and hour claims related to off-the-clock work have skyrocketed. Be sure you do not pressure employees to record only regularly scheduled hours on their time sheets, or work additional unpaid time early or late. Company-sponsored meetings and training sessions also count as hours worked for overtime purposes. It is critical to develop accurate methods to keep records of actual time worked by your nonexempt workforce and to ensure compliance with company overtime policy.

You may be subject to additional state or local laws regarding the payment of overtime or setting working hours or break times. There is no federal requirement to pay overtime for hours worked on Saturday, Sunday, or holidays, but some state or local governments require employers to pay premiums to those who work on these days. In some jurisdictions, you must pay overtime to nonexempt employees if they work more than eight hours in one workday, regardless of the number of hours they work in a week.

Wage and hour investigations are most often triggered by a complaint from a disgruntled current or former employee, or one who hears about the success of a claim filed by a friend, or reads about high-profile class actions. Once state or federal investigators begin an audit, they are likely to continue their work until they find a violation, and the number of claimants is likely to grow in the process. Because audits are time-consuming, and penalties for violation can be significant, it is best to be proactive in understanding and complying with the laws. If you have questions regarding interpretation of any of the wage and hour regulations, seek the advice of an experienced professional. Your local department of labor can be helpful in answering inquiries and will not use the information you provide to seek out potential violations.

THE COMPENSATION SYSTEM

Since it is unlikely that you will be paying your entire workforce the minimum wage, you will need to determine what to pay them. You will make better decisions if you take the time to determine your compensation philosophy. Compensation decisions guided by a sound framework or philosophy will result in practices that make sense for your business.

"How do I figure out my compensation philosophy?"

Start by answering the following questions:

- What can you afford to pay and continue to earn the profit margins you expect?

- How should pay compare to similar positions in relevant markets?

- Will you offer bonuses or incentives?

- How much will you spend on benefits, and how will this influence pay rates?

- Will you follow the same philosophy in different parts of the business or different geographic locations?

- Who will make decisions regarding pay and raises?

- How and when will raises be given?

- How often will you review your compensation philosophy?

- How will you communicate this philosophy to employees?

There is no right or wrong answer to any of these questions. If you are a small company with limited opportunity for growth and promotion, you may believe you should pay higher wages than other companies in your area or industry. Alternatively, you could decide that your wage rates will be average but you will offer an incentive plan linked closely to company financial performance.

Whatever decisions you make, put them in a written format you can share with employees. This may take the form of a policy, a statement in an employee handbook, or notes or minutes of a senior management or owners' meeting. Be prepared to review this philosophy or policy at least annually. Changes in your business, including growth, acquisitions, new products, economic conditions, available talent pool, and competition, can trigger revisions.

Now that you've laid the foundation, it's time to build the framework!

Armed with your compensation philosophy, the next step is to implement a system to help you make decisions and resolve problems about pay. The most effective compensation systems are those that are relatively easy to understand and administer.

Unless both internal equity and external competitiveness are present in your compensation practices, you will have a difficult time attracting and retaining employees and keeping up morale. Internal equity relates to whether the compensation structure reflects the relative value of jobs and people within the organization. External competitiveness ranks compensation alongside competitors or comparable positions in different industries.

Setting Rates of Pay

"What are pay grades and how do I use them?"

Pay grades, sometimes called rate ranges or steps, are the basic element underlying the majority of formal compensation structures. Under these systems, organizations group jobs of similar values into grades. Each rate range reflects a distinguishable pay difference from others and will include a variety of jobs. Within every grade, there is a salary minimum, a midpoint, and a maximum, with the minimum and maximum salaries generally about 15 to 20 percent lower or higher than the midpoint. People with little or no experience typically begin at the bottom of the rate range. The midpoint of the range is generally the "going rate" for the position.

Structuring a wide salary spread within each grade allows businesses the flexibility to recognize differences in individual performance and accommodate salary growth. However, if the salary spread is too wide you will have less control over your pay rates. Usually, the higher the level of position, the broader the salary range. There are no set rules regarding how many grades an organization should have. It depends on the size of the company, the complexity of the reporting structure, and the range of jobs.

Some organizations use a variant of pay grades called "broad banding," a concept that employs fewer grades and much wider salary spreads.

There are several approaches to slotting positions into grades. Some companies perform job analyses using such factors as the level of skill, education, and experience required; responsibilities such as number of reports and fiscal oversight; and market wages. Some will use a formal job points system that assigns a point value to each component of a job description. The point total for each position determines its place in the grade system. Job points systems are very time-consuming and expensive when done correctly. It is easier to use labor market comparisons to set rates and ranges.

Review your rate ranges at least every two years. There is no need to adjust your entire grade structure just because the relative values of one or two jobs have changed. You can always regrade a position or make changes to salary spreads within individual ranges. Competitive pressures, area wage fluctuations, or changes in job requirements may trigger range adjustments.

"We don't have formal job descriptions. Do we need them?"

While it is not necessary to have job descriptions for your employees, these documents are helpful. Job descriptions can be used to inform employees about their responsibilities, guide supervisors when evaluating work distribution and departmental organization, and help determine appropriate pay grades and classifications. They can also be an important part of the process of identifying overtime-exempt positions by providing clear identification of actual primary duties. However, too many companies spend inordinate amounts of time writing job descriptions, only to put them away on a shelf, never to be seen again. The most helpful job descriptions are living documents that are short and easy to understand, tied to company goals, reviewed regularly by both the employee and the company, and modified as needed.

When you write job descriptions, do not focus on the history of the job. Instead, think about the position as you want it to be and how it is actually performed, related to the current needs of the organization. Describe the position's duties and not the individual in the position. Include:

- The job title

- A short, general summary of the job

- The title of the person the position reports to

- The departments the position interacts with

- The primary responsibilities and job functions

• The minimum education, experience, and training needed for the position

"How do I set rates of pay?"

While pay grades promote internal equity, pay rates establish external competitiveness. The amount you pay employees will be an important factor in determining whether they work for you or for someone else. Businesses commonly start developing their rates of pay by looking at market rates or at what competitors pay for the same job. This is easiest to do for hourly, nonexempt positions. If you wish to hire a clerk and know that the other companies in your area or industry pay clerks between $12.00 and $13.00 per hour, you can decide to match that average or pay more or less, based on your compensation philosophy.

Using market rates for salaried, exempt positions is more complicated. It is often difficult to identify a "going rate" or even a narrow range of pay for key positions. If you are hiring a sales manager, you cannot accurately conclude that "sales managers earn $80,000 a year because that is what XYZ Company pays." You will usually factor individual experience, education, compensation history, and industry expertise into your analysis.

Include geographic differences in your market rate analysis, especially for salaried positions. According to the 2009 Culpepper Geographic Pay Differential Practice Survey, more than 70 percent of employers with workers in more than one location provide geographic differentials or adjust pay based on location. Geographic differences may not be as striking at higher salary levels. If you have multiple locations where the market rate varies greatly, allow for these differences and make adjustments either in base salary or otherwise when you move employees between locations. In a move from a lower to a higher market rate, there are creative ways to pay the employee more without raising base salary. For example, you can add a separate "cost-of-living allowance" to the worker's paycheck. If this person subsequently moves back to the lower market rate area, you can discontinue the allowance without having to reduce salary. If the move is to a city where the rate is significantly lower, it is difficult to ask someone to take a pay cut, but you will want to achieve greater equity between this employee and new coworkers. You can attain this goal by taking away a benefit or perk to which other workers are entitled.

You can get wage market data from a number of sources. The federal Bureau of Labor Statistics (BLS) compiles this information in a number of different formats. The Occupational Employment Statistics division of the BLS releases statistics broken down in a number of ways, including by state and metropolitan area. When looking at information for specific positions you may see reference to the "SOC" code. This is the Standard Occupational Classification System that the BLS uses to identify jobs.

Chambers of commerce and trade organizations produce market data through wage surveys, which they generally provide free or for a reasonable fee to members or companies that participate. You can also buy compensation surveys from a number of large national consulting firms. Web-based salary search tools such as www.salary.com and www.payscale.com post free survey information, with more detailed data available for purchase. The big job posting boards publish salary information that is designed for use by the job seeker but can be used by anyone. The Web-based tools are generally not as comprehensive as the surveys produced by large consulting firms.

Pay Increases

"When should I give employees raises?"

Companies give raises on set dates in the year, on anniversary dates, and for employment milestones. The best timing for your company will depend on your philosophy, your budgeting process, your compensation system, and what your competitors in your geographic area are doing.

Better Forgotten: *"What's this extra money for?"*
An industry association required many levels of internal approval to authorize a salary increase, and by the time all approvals were in, managers forgot all about telling employees about their raises. Commonly, employees first learned about their raises when they found a larger amount in their bank deposit records. Communicate the timing and action taken on any raise.

"What criteria should I use to determine raises?"

Merit Increases. Merit increases are the most common form of pay raise. Many organizations tie the raise directly to performance evaluations, with a set percentage pegged to each performance rating. You may also choose to allocate a specific dollar amount or percentage for raises in each department and allow managers to determine the amount for each employee based on performance and contribution. This gives individual managers the discretion to give greater rewards to star performers as long as the total of all raises does not exceed the department's budget. Competitive forces have caused a sharp decline in the amount paid for merit increases. From the 1980s to the 1990s, average salary increases dropped from between 7 and 10 percent to between 3 and 4 percent. Since the beginning of the new millennium, average increases have continued to decline. According to the 2009 U.S. Salary Increase Survey conducted by the consulting company Hewitt Associates, the average merit increase for salaried exempt employees dropped below 3 percent for the first time since the survey was initiated in 1976. Employees sometimes incorrectly refer to these low increases as cost-of-living increases. Cost-of-living increases actually reflect the changes in the consumer price index compiled by the BLS and are more popular during periods of high inflation.

"Does this mean that more employers are skipping raises altogether?"

Due to the challenging economic environment of recent years, many employers have announced salary freezes, and some have even required employees to take pay cuts. Employees are never happy to hear this type of bad news, but they are rarely surprised. Before making the announcement, clearly identify the reasons for the decision and analyze whether such a move is appropriate across the board. Certain positions in the organization may be in high demand and may therefore require increases to allow you to remain competitive in the market to retain these employees. However, a pay action that affects all employees, including senior management, will send a message to employees that "we are all in it together for the good of the company."

When you lift the salary freeze or reinstate pay after a pay cut, you are not required to do this retroactively or make employees whole for amounts not paid during the salary action. Never promise that a pay freeze is a temporary or one-time event, as you will lose credibility if you find you must take similar, or more drastic, steps in the future.

"How do merit increases work within the structure of my pay grade system?"

You have substantial flexibility with individuals who are at lower points in the pay grade. People who start out at the minimum for the rate range usually do so because they were promoted into the job or otherwise had little experience in the area. Good workers will improve rapidly as they gain experience, allowing you to move them up quickly within the range toward and eventually beyond the midpoint.

When an employee reaches or exceeds the maximum pay point of the grade, your choices become more difficult. You can opt to "cap" or "red circle" this person's pay and not award further raises until you increase the salaries within the range or until the employee changes positions. Some companies that do not want to risk losing solid performers by freezing salaries will instead give them token raises or bump them to the next pay grade, if appropriate. The decision is entirely up to you and should be based on the individual circumstances involved. You can apply the same principles when a restructuring results in position changes and salaries are above the maximum for the new grades.

"Does a promotion always involve a huge raise?"

Not unless the job is a true promotion and not a lateral move. A true promotion involves significant additional responsibilities and the elevation to a new pay grade, in which case you should increase the employee's salary to fall within the new range. If the promotion is such that it justifies a very large increase, you can split or stagger the increase over the subsequent months. Since a new position is probably a stretch for many people, they will have the time to get their feet wet and grow into their responsibilities. Giving a very large increase all at once can set unrealistic expectations for future increases.

Better Forgotten: *"New suit? I guess you don't need a raise!"*
A young manager was overdue for an increase and was anxiously
awaiting corporate approval. A senior executive, well aware of this situation, complimented her on a new suit, adding that based on how
well she dressed it was clear that she was well paid and did not need
a raise. Personal comments have no place in salary discussions.

"Are merit increases the only way to give raises?"

Pay for Performance. A pay-for-performance system directly rewards individual productivity. Employees are given a specific set of objectives, with
certain tasks to complete or certain outputs to achieve, and pay increases are based on how well they meet their objectives. While some people claim that pay for performance aptly rewards the best employees and
fosters competition that improves performance standards, others say the
emphasis on individual efforts hurts teamwork and overall productivity.
Pay for performance has also been criticized because it does not take
into account the influence of process, materials, or machinery or other
factors beyond an employee's control that may impact attainment of
goals. Since pay for performance can involve subjective standards, the
system has also raised questions of bias.

Before implementing pay-for-performance raises, thoroughly
research the parameters and communicate the ground rules to affected
employees and their managers to avoid misunderstandings. As with any
pay structure, there should be no mysteries.

Raises for Single-Rate Jobs. If you have a few "single-rate jobs," where you
are paying a number of people the same wage, it is often effective to give
the same flat dollar amount of increase to all people in these positions on
a set schedule. However, if you have a number of single-rate jobs, it may
serve you better in the long term to give increases as a percentage of the
hourly rate, so that you don't compress the differences between rates of
pay and overtime. If you decide to implement merit increases for single-
rate job employees, the criteria for individual increases should be very
clear, communicated well to employees, and applied consistently.

Across-the-Board Increases. Across-the-board increases are raises given to all employees to deal with nontypical economic factors. You may, for instance, award this type of increase if you discover that your rates of pay are significantly lower than those of your competitors.

"What happens when employees complain about the system?"
No matter what pay and increase structure you choose, some people will be unhappy. But remember that there is no perfect method of compensation, and any approach may create problems. It is more important that you are comfortable that your approach fits in with your overall philosophy and that you communicate your system to the workforce.

In a common scenario, an employee will march into the manager's office, announce that she was offered a new job, and request a substantial raise or ask that the employer make a counteroffer to get her to stay. Before automatically succumbing to this ploy, consider the entire situation. If she is at the low end of the rate range or the competitive rate has changed significantly, it may be reasonable to grant the increase. Sometimes it is better to refuse. Remember that she has already interviewed elsewhere and received a job offer. She may already have "emotionally resigned" and be more interested in the new position. Once you grant the raise, she may continue to use this tactic into the future.

Never let your salary structure drive a decision that does not seem to make sense. You can create a "special case" to meet market demand for a position or to acknowledge an individual's unique or desirable background. Document these exceptions to show that the differences were not the result of any discriminatory motives.

Better Forgotten: *"Stay put and you'll get a bigger raise."*
A mid-level manager in a manufacturing facility was offered a transfer to the corporate office in a distant location, along with a larger salary as an incentive to make the move. He turned it down because he did not feel the raise was sufficient to relocate. Two months later, he received his regular merit increase, which brought his salary to a higher level than if he had accepted the transfer. When he asked why he had received more money by staying in the same job, he was told "it's based upon the points in the system." Don't let a point system guide salary decisions that don't make sense.

"Why can't we ever seem to keep salaries confidential?"
Despite publicized rules about the confidentiality of salary information
and the general reluctance to share information, salary details inevitably
seem to leak. Predictably, salary leaks create disgruntled employees, especially in circumstances where workers discover that a new employee
performing the same or a similar job is being paid more than they are.
When employees ask questions about perceived salary disparities, it is
best to answer honestly. Without discussing specifics, you should explain
that you are paying the higher rate because of market forces or the individual's different work experience or educational background.

Often employees may realize significant increases only by changing
jobs. But job changes can entail a loss of job security, seniority benefits,
and general comfort level that comes with knowing your employer.
Some of your employees will take that risk and others will not; it is
inappropriate to adjust everyone's salary every time you hire a new
employee for more money.

"What about those perks?"
Auto leasing, country club memberships, or clothing allowances may fit
into your compensation philosophy and policy—that is your decision.
Perks should be considered part of the total compensation package.
Before instituting any perks, survey eligible employees to determine
whether they perceive value in what you plan to offer. Also consider
that when you offer perks to only a selected group of employees, others may be resentful and morale may suffer.

VARIABLE PAY: BONUSES AND INCENTIVES

Variable pay is different from base pay in that employees are not entitled
to these payments but must continually earn them anew. Incentive
structures are divided into two categories: short-term programs that
reward behavior or performance over periods of a year or less, and long-
term programs that foster attainment of goals over a number of years.
Short-term programs are usually based on cash payments, while long-
term incentives typically involve stock or other equity arrangements.

Tailor your organization's incentive program to your individual
financial situation, business objectives, and employee demographics.

Calculate the potential total cost before implementation, and if there is a possibility that you will be unable or unwilling to pay the bonuses earned, change the plan or do not implement it at all. A plan with a bad payment history is not a motivational tool. If you already have a plan with a poor reputation and you want to continue to pay bonuses or incentives, discontinue it and create a new one.

"What are some of my bonus and incentive options?"

Flat-Rate Bonuses. The simplest and most common bonus is the flat dollar amount paid out once a year. This could be a holiday bonus, a special payment to recognize a company milestone or achievement above financial goals, or a payment under an annual bonus plan. Bonuses are generally given across the board or to specific categories of employees; they can include variable amounts based on criteria such as level of position or length of service, or payments as a percentage of the employee's base salary.

Short-Term Bonuses. Short-term bonuses are effective tools to recognize performance or spur improvement. Companies give these bonuses to reward achievements such as upselling, outstanding customer comments, measurable increases in production, quality improvements, or safety suggestions. These incentives have the biggest impact when you set a specific, short (usually one to three months) measurement window and tie awards to a publicized, company-wide promotion. Continuing these plans indefinitely dulls their effectiveness, can result in poor monitoring, and may create the misimpression that the bonuses are a regular part of pay.

Sales Incentives. Sales incentives can range from payments of flat percentages of sales to more complex systems comprising factors such as lead generation and performance against a specific sales target or plan. Commissions are payments made as a percentage of sales and are usually paid out on a regular schedule shortly after the completion of the sale. Choose a schedule that best fits your particular type of sales. If you sell a product with a high potential for returns or significant changes in the order before delivery, you may choose to "hold back" a portion of commissions until product acceptance. If you pay your salespeople on a commission-only basis, you may provide them a "draw" against a commission or incentive. Under this structure, you will deduct the amount of the draw from earned commissions or incentives prior to payout.

While your sales incentive structure should be driven by the results desired by the company rather than copied from a competitor, it is important to consider competitive factors as well. Give ample notice of any changes you make to payout or target amounts. Items to consider when designing a sales incentive plan include:

- How often will the plan pay out? Each pay period? Monthly? Quarterly?

- Who will maintain and review data concerning payout entitlements?

- Is the plan based on sales targets or total sales?

- If a plan is based on targets, what happens when employees exceed their targets?

- What incentives, if any, are paid if an employee leaves?

- Will there be holdbacks (payments that are delayed to enable the business to reconcile amounts due with cancelled sales or reduced customer payments)?

- How does the competition pay their salespeople?

- Will this plan reward individual performance, team sales, or both?

- What kind of records are salespeople required to keep?

- What time period does the plan cover?

Goal-Based Bonus Plans. Goal-based programs reward the achievement of company objectives, team performance, individual results, or a combination of the three. You can use individual payments as an award for successful completion of a project or for coming up with an outstanding cost-cutting suggestion. Company and team bonuses are typically paid for meeting financial, productivity, or cost-cutting objectives. Payouts under the plan can be a flat sum or based on a percentage of the profit made or the gain attained. When designing your program, carefully select those goals that are most important to your business, since eligible employees will naturally focus on performance that will help them earn the bonus. If your program provides annual payouts, enable eligible employees to track progress toward the goals throughout the year.

Sign-On Bonuses. The subject of sign-on bonuses is covered in Chapter 1 on recruitment.

Retention Bonuses. When a company goes through a merger, acquisition, or downsizing, employees begin to get nervous, lose focus, and leave for other employment, especially if they know that their jobs will be eliminated. Retention bonuses are predetermined amounts paid to those employees who continue in their jobs to a set date. They are valuable tools for keeping key employees during transition periods and other times of change and uncertainty.

Worth Repeating: *"I understand the incentive plan now."*
A consumer products company with a layered incentive plan gave new hires a spreadsheet with sample outcomes based upon a variety of variables within the program. Each year employees eligible for incentives also received individualized spreadsheets. The reports clearly demonstrated the level of compensation connected to specific results.

"Should we issue stock options?"

Stock options are a long-term incentive that gives the employee the right to purchase company stock in the future at the stock price on the date the options were granted. To exercise the right to purchase options, individuals must usually remain employed by the company for a specified period of time. Stock option plans are based on the theory that having options will encourage employees to produce more, so that share prices will increase and they can realize greater profits when they exercise their options and subsequently sell their stock. Options have traditionally been the compensation form of choice for start-up companies that were short on cash but projected huge earnings.

Volatility in the stock market and the scandals surrounding account-ing procedures and corporate accountability have caused many organiza-tions to rethink their stock option plans or to turn to other forms of equity-based compensation altogether. Although you may elect to grant equity incentives across the board, it is not fair to make them a major part of the compensation of all workers. These, and most other long-term schemes, should be geared toward executives and other key employees with greater control over the future direction of the company.

Stock-based incentives have significant tax consequences and com-plex legal requirements. Do not attempt to structure and implement such a plan without professional assistance.

"Now that I have decided which incentives to offer, how can I make the plans effective?"

How you administer the plan is just as important as the type of plan you choose. Employees must perceive that the plan is fair and provides value and incentive, and that the bonuses and incentives are paid as promised. These guidelines will help you:

✓ Document the plan in writing and distribute it to employees eligi-ble to participate. The document should include the reasons the organization is offering the incentive; details such as timing, eligibil-ity, and criteria for payouts; reasons for any variation in payouts; and whether amounts of payments will be capped. If the plan does not provide a specific end date, include a provision that the organization has the right to modify or terminate the plan at any time. The sim-pler the language, the better.

✓ Train the people responsible for administering the plan so that there is a single understanding of payment eligibilities and calculations. Also train the managers who will be making decisions about who will receive payouts and how much they will receive.

✓ Make payouts when promised under the plan, and plan your payouts to occur as soon as possible after the rewarded performance occurs.

✓ Evaluate the effectiveness of the plan on an ongoing basis. Analyze whether the incentive produced the intended results or improve-ments. Did it cause employee confusion or resentment? Were employees continually motivated or did they lose interest? Be pre-pared to change the programs to make them more effective, or develop new ones to help the organization attain new goals.

"Didn't you forget executive compensation?"

No, we left it out on purpose! Executive compensation is a term used to describe the special pay packages given to CEOs and senior manage-ment. These are limitless in variety, ever-changing, and have been subject to intense scrutiny, particularly in publicly held companies. Executive compensation should be structured by compensation experts, with assis-tance and administration by highly trusted investment professionals.

Benefits

What Makes a Benefits Package Competitive?

THE PATIENT PROTECTION AND AFFORDABLE CARE ACT (PPACA), signed into law on March 23, 2010, created a seismic shift in the employee benefits landscape. Deciding on an employee benefits package had already been an intimidating process for any employer. The mind-boggling array of choices—HMO, PPO, LTD, EAP—identified by an array of confusing acronyms combined with mounting costs and the demands of offering a competitive program have been taken up another notch with the addition of federal legislation and the fact that the law is still in flux.

Without minimizing the difficulty of wading through the options and requirements, we can tell you that it is possible to make intelligent and informed decisions that will help you to attract, retain, and improve the effectiveness of employees. This chapter covers the elements of an effective benefits process and explains ways to develop a comprehensive program that works for your organization.

"What are employee benefits?"

Employee benefits are all benefits and services, other than wages, provided to employees by the employer. These include legally required social insurance programs, health and life insurance coverage, retirement plans, payment for time not worked, subsidized assistance, and any other program an organization may offer to help its workers.

"Where do I begin?"

Begin by articulating your organization's benefits philosophy, similarly to how you developed a compensation philosophy as discussed in Chapter 5. Using your benefits philosophy as a guidepost will enable you to make decisions that will fit your company's culture and overall business plan. Start by answering these questions:

- What level of benefits can you afford?

- What will you expect employees to contribute toward the costs?

- How do you want your benefits to stack up against those offered by companies that compete for your employees?

- Will your benefits reward longevity and encourage retention or focus on short-term expectations?

- How will your benefits match the demographics of your workforce?

- Is it important for your organization to have benefits that encourage professional and/or personal growth?

- Are there specific or special benefits that you must offer because of senior management needs or the nature of your workforce?

- How do your plans, now and in the future, meet potential PPACA requirements?

"What do employees look for in benefits?"

It depends on the age and family status of the employee. While a worker with health problems or with a family might place health insurance at the top of the list, a young or single employee may be more interested in the amount of vacation available. If you do not already know what your employees value, ask them!

LEGALLY REQUIRED INSURANCE PROGRAMS

"Are there minimum benefits I have to provide?"

Yes, you are required by federal law to provide Social Security contributions, unemployment insurance, and workers compensation coverage.

Employers in California, Hawaii, New Jersey, New York, Puerto Rico, and Rhode Island must provide short-term disability (STD) coverage that replaces an identified minimum income in the event of a non-work-related injury or illness. In Hawaii, most employers are also required to provide a specified level of health care coverage to employees.

"Doesn't PPACA mandate employer-provided health benefits?"

PPACA does not require employers to offer health coverage, but beginning January 1, 2014, employers will be subject to "pay or play" and affordability penalties designed to encourage expansion of coverage. The smallest companies will not be affected by this "employer responsibility," which covers only those with an average of fifty or more full-time employees.

The potential penalty calculations are quite complicated and include consequences for both employers that do not offer health benefits and those who offer benefits considered unaffordable. The legislation assumes that by January 1, 2012, there will be Health Benefit Exchanges and Small Business Health Options Programs in place to make affordable coverage available to individuals and small businesses. The core components of the new law are presently under legal challenges that could result in further changes to PPACA.

An introduction to PPACA health plan regulations is included in the health insurance section of this chapter. In addition to these plan details, PPACA includes some programs to assist employers in providing coverage and adhering to other rules, such as:

- Small-business tax credits available through 2014

- Break time to be offered to nursing mothers

- An independent appeals process for participants of plan decisions

- Grants for small employer (up to one hundred employees) wellness programs

- Simplified cafeteria plans to allow tax advantages to small employers.

- Excise tax on high-cost plans

Many of the components of PPACA include definitions and regulations yet to be issued or clarified by the Department of Health and Human Services, Internal Revenue Service, and/or Department of Labor. Even as of this writing, some definitions have been issued while other effective dates have been delayed as the legal challenges continue.

Social Security Benefits

All nongovernment employers must contribute a designated percentage of each employee's pay toward Social Security, up to a maximum amount determined periodically by the federal government. You are obligated to make Social Security payments whether a worker is full- or part-time, temporary or newly hired—although there are some very limited exemptions, such as foreign students working temporarily in the United States. While employees pay a percentage of their wages for Social Security, many do not realize this is also an employer-paid benefit. Let your employees know that you are making this contribution as part of their total benefits package. The Social Security Administration can provide a wealth of additional information to both employers and employees.

Unemployment Insurance

Unemployment insurance was established by the federal government to provide individuals who are out of work through no fault of their own with temporary cash assistance to help tide them over while they actively look for work. Each state administers its own program under the federal guidelines. Employers are required to contribute a percentage of their payroll toward federal taxes under the Federal Unemployment Tax Act (FUTA) and toward state unemployment taxes. Your contribution rate will vary based on your claims experience—that is, the historical record of unemployment benefits charged.

Your state will determine both the size of the employer contribution and the duration and amount of the benefit paid to the employee. Employee benefits are generally based on a percentage of the employee's previous earnings, up to a state maximum. States will set payments for new employers at the industry average, an assigned rate, or the state average. Each state has its own timetables for reviewing unemployment claims experience and adjusting rates.

Employees who are terminated or laid off for a reason other than misconduct are typically entitled to unemployment benefits if they have worked for a minimum period designated by the state. Workers subjected to temporary layoffs or reductions in hours may also be eligible for payouts. While employees who voluntarily resign usually cannot collect benefits, some states make exceptions for people who leave their jobs under extenuating circumstances, such as to relocate to care for a sick family member. When you receive any requests for information from your local unemployment office, it is important that you respond in a timely manner, because you can incur considerable fines for missed deadlines.

You can reduce your unemployment tax rate by contesting appropriate claims and monitoring terminations. There are service providers, often affiliated with payroll service companies, that work with employers at reasonable cost to respond to unemployment claims and reduce or stabilize contribution rates. When selecting a provider, the size of the organization is less important than its unemployment claims processing knowledge and experience with the systems and procedures of your local unemployment offices.

Workers Compensation

"Why do I have to worry about workers compensation since no one gets hurt in an office?"

Workers compensation is a state-governed benefits scheme that requires employers to pay medical bills and partial lost wages that result from work-related injuries and illnesses. It is also a no-fault system that quantifies the extent of any permanent partial disability resulting from an injury or illness and provides monetary payments to the employee proportionate to the disability. Some employers purchase private workers compensation insurance, while others self-fund—meaning they pay their own claims. Self-insurance arrangements are typically administered by insurance companies or other third parties. Twenty states have their own workers compensation funds, to which some states mandate employer contributions. The cost of workers compensation insurance is based on the risk level of the industry and the claims history of the employer.

Too many employers accept high workers compensation premiums as a necessary evil, rather than working actively to monitor claims and rein in costs. You can dramatically reduce the risk of employee exposure to injury or illness through an active safety program. Work-related injuries are not confined to traditional manufacturing environments. Workers compensation costs have skyrocketed in all industries because of increased medical costs and rising claims connected with stress-related illnesses, repetitive motion injuries, and back problems. Work with your workers compensation carrier or state fund to identify potential hazards in your workplace, then take action and provide training to reduce these risks. Also, work with your carrier to reduce costs by actively reviewing claims. Ask your carrier to explain the way it processes claims and charges reserves and expenses. Find out if your state laws permit you to request second opinions for medical care or to designate a provider or network of doctors for covered injuries and illnesses. These methods will allow you to obtain more information about the course of treatment and avoid or contest spurious claims.

Keep in touch with your employees when they are out of work because of work-related injuries or illnesses. Regular contact will maintain their connection with the workplace, show that you care, and speed their return to work. Many employers make efforts to get employees back to work as soon as possible, even if they cannot yet return to their regular jobs. Providing employees with "light duty," "restricted duty," or "transitional duty" assignments can be very cost-effective. You will save on lost wage payments and aid workers in a rapid transition back to their regular jobs.

"Do I need a broker?"

Most employers purchase insurance benefits coverage and retirement plan services through a broker. Brokers can offer a good perspective on the range of plans available and help you choose appropriate options for your company. If you do not have your own internal benefits staff, a broker can provide much-needed assistance as a liaison with your carriers and keep you up to date on legislative requirements. You probably already use a broker for other types of business insurance; this person or company may or may not be appropriate for your benefits needs. Benefits brokers earn commissions from the benefit carriers and may charge additional fees for some services. A good broker will design programs to meet client needs regardless of commission structure.

Take the time to interview a number of brokers, asking them specifically about their experience in the applicable benefits area. Obtain competitive proposals to learn more about available options and select the best broker for your needs.

Better Forgotten: *"Why is my broker always in Europe?"*
An employer with more than two thousand employees across the United States was pleased to be assigned a senior VP at one of the largest benefit consulting firms to oversee health benefit plan negotiations. It did not take long to realize that this broker was clearly more interested in dedicating time to sizable global entities. Make certain that your broker fits your business.

BENEFITS THAT PROVIDE ECONOMIC SECURITY

Economic security benefits provide payments to employees and/or their families in the event that the employee dies or otherwise becomes unable to work.

Group Life Insurance

Life insurance is relatively inexpensive, but it offers employees and their loved ones a great deal of security. If an employee dies, the group policy pays a flat dollar amount to a designated beneficiary. The amount of the payment can be tied to the employee's position, annual salary, or a multiple of the annual salary, with a cap or maximum payout. Your premiums will be calculated based on the total dollar amount of coverage, the ages of your individual participants, or a rate determined from a census of the entire group. Unlike individual life insurance policies, most group plans require minimal or no prescreening to identify high-risk medical conditions. If your plan has prescreening requirements or limitations on benefits payouts, communicate these factors to your workforce.

"Do I have to worry about taxes and discrimination when I provide group term life insurance?"

If you pay for more than a specified amount of life insurance for employees, the IRS considers the value of the extra coverage to be a taxable benefit. Your accountant or payroll provider can perform this calculation. Ask also about rules to ensure that employers do not limit life insurance benefits to older, more highly compensated employees.

"What about the employee who wants more life insurance?"

Supplemental or optional life insurance is a popular voluntary benefit, providing employees a convenient way to purchase additional coverage at their own expense. Coverage is usually available in multiples of the employee's salary, up to a maximum amount. Employees may also be able to purchase limited life insurance coverage for a spouse or child. Individuals wishing to purchase supplemental benefits may be required to submit medical evidence of insurability, especially for higher levels of coverage. Your administrative responsibilities regarding supplemental policies will be the same as those for your regular group plan.

Worth Repeating: *"Don't tell my wife that my mom was still my beneficiary."*

A new HR director asked all employees to update their company group life insurance beneficiaries at open enrollment. During a file audit he had noticed that the company president still had his mother listed on the form, five years after he was married. Remind employees to update beneficiary designations when a life cycle event occurs, and collect updates from all employees on a scheduled basis.

AD&D Coverage

Group life insurance is often coupled with accidental death and dismemberment (AD&D) coverage that pays an additional benefit after an accidental death or the loss of a limb or eyesight. AD&D benefits are less expensive than life insurance, but they are not a substitute for basic life insurance benefits.

When problems arise under life or AD&D policies, more often than not they involve disputes as to the proper beneficiary. To avoid potential headaches, maintain up-to-date, signed records of employee beneficiary designations. It is good practice to ask employees to complete new beneficiary forms on a regular basis, perhaps annually or during open enrollment, and to replace the old forms with the new ones in your files. If you have employees who are out on disability leave, your insurer will probably waive life or AD&D premiums during the disability period, but will only continue coverage if you provide notice of the employees' extended absence. Consult with your insurance carrier to determine whether state laws require you to offer terminated employees the opportunity to convert their group coverage into individual policies.

Disability Insurance

"Should I consider a disability plan?"

Employees up to age sixty-five are statistically more likely to lose income because of extended absences. Short-term disability (STD) and long-term disability (LTD) insurance pay covered employees a percentage of their earnings when they are unable to work because of an illness or injury.

STD plans pay a percentage of the employee's weekly earnings for a fixed period of up to twelve months. The average policy limits coverage to six months. Employees are usually required to satisfy a brief waiting period before payments begin. Average payments range from 50 percent to 67 percent of earnings; more generous benefits could create an incentive for the employee to stay out of work. Your STD policy should clearly define the word *disability*, meet applicable state requirements, and cover disabilities arising from pregnancy in the same way as other disabilities.

LTD coverage replaces a percentage of income in more extreme situations, when the employee is unable to work for extended periods.

When you offer STD coverage, LTD will kick in after STD insurance runs out. Where there is no prior STD coverage, waiting periods for LTD can range from three to twelve months, or longer in situations involving preexisting conditions. Benefits are usually set at about 60 percent of the employee's base salary, with a plan maximum, either for a specified number of months or until the employee turns age sixty-five or seventy. The definition of a disability under LTD plans is generally more stringent than under STD plans. An LTD policy may limit benefits to people unable to perform any type of work at all.

Rates for both STD and LTD policies are based on your claims experience, but some companies choose to fund their own STD plans. Many organizations share the plan cost by requiring an employee contribution. You can help to control costs by requiring employees to use accrued sick and vacation time before receiving disability benefits and by reducing disability payments by amounts that the employee receives from Social Security or other sources. You can also contain expenses through an active return-to-work program, similar to the "light duty" plans described previously in the workers compensation section.

Alternatively, consider offering voluntary LTD plans, through which employees have the opportunity to purchase individual policies at attractive group rates through payroll deductions. Voluntary plans provide easy access to LTD for employees and portability if they leave the company. On the downside, these programs usually require a minimum percentage of employee participation, which can be difficult to reach and maintain. If you offer voluntary LTD benefits, you will have to continually communicate the benefits to employees if you expect them to participate.

"Who's going to pay for the nursing home?"

With the aging of the employee population and the availability of life-extending treatments and new options for care, long-term care (LTC) insurance has received increased publicity. LTC insurance is designed to cover the costs of care in nursing homes, assisted-living facilities, adult day care, or someone's own home. LTC is typically offered as a voluntary benefit, with employees paying all premiums. It is relatively expensive and complex and therefore requires very good communication in order to be successful and reach typical participation rates of 6 percent to 15 percent. While LTC options are more prevalent at large employers, increased awareness and the availability of a variety of policies make it a benefit worth exploring for employers of all sizes. PPACA includes the Community Living Assistance Services and Support Act (CLASS), which establishes a federally administered voluntary long-term care plan that can be paid for through payroll deduction.

BENEFIT DAYS: HOLIDAYS, VACATION, AND SICK DAYS

"I know Scrooge gave Bob Cratchit
Christmas off, but do I have to?"

Ebenezer Scrooge did not have to give Christmas Day off in London in the 1800s, and if you are a private employer, you are not legally required to recognize holidays, personal days, or vacation time. But you will likely find yourself with an unfortunate recruitment and retention problem if you do not offer some type of time-off arrangement. Return to your benefits philosophy and once again use it as a guidepost when devising a policy on benefit days that works for your organization.

Holidays

While public employers are required to give workers certain holidays off, private employers can devise their own holiday schedules. Your schedule will likely be influenced by your business cycle, industry standards, and practices in your geographic area. Start by deciding how many annual holidays you want to offer employees. Some employers set a fixed list of days on which their facilities will close, or they issue a new holiday schedule each year. Or you may opt for a shorter fixed list and set aside a given number of days as "floating" holidays that workers may use as desired. Floating holidays are an easy way to accommodate diverse religious and cultural observances. Some of the other questions to consider are:

- Will I pay a premium to employees who work on designated holidays?

- What alternative day will I give when the holiday falls on a non-working day?

- Are new employees eligible for paid holidays immediately, or will there be a waiting period?

- Will I offer part-time employees full or prorated holiday benefits?

Vacation Days

Employers typically encourage, or even require, employees to take vacation. Studies show that employees return from vacations rested, recharged, and ready to work. The two most important factors in a vacation policy are how much paid vacation time you will give employees and how the days are earned. You may elect to give all employees the same amount of vacation, to provide different benefits to exempt and nonexempt workers, or to offer more time to officers and executives. Most organizations provide increased vacation benefits as an employee's seniority grows.

You set the standard by which employees earn, or accrue, vacation time. If your policy allows twelve paid vacation days per year, you might decide that workers will earn one day per month. You may also set a waiting period, or a certain amount of time that employees must work for your company before they can earn or take vacation. You are permitted to place restrictions on employee use of vacation time. You can require advance notice for vacation scheduling or "blackout" dates during which employees cannot take vacation because of high business demand. You can set rules as to whether vacation can be taken in single days as well as multiple-day blocks. You may limit the number of unused vacation days an employee can carry over to the next year.

Most problems with vacation policies arise when an employee leaves the company and there is a dispute over the amount of accrued, unused vacation time that the employer must pay. Some states require payouts of unused days while others allow an employer to determine a policy. To avoid misunderstandings, prepare and communicate a written vacation policy that clearly explains the rules, especially concerning eligibility, accrual, and carryover limitations, and utilize an accurate tracking system.

Sick Days

With the exception of time off for work-related injuries or illnesses and STD as described above, there is no federal requirement to provide paid sick days to employees. But a handful of municipalities and at least one state have passed laws that mandate some form of paid sick days, and a growing number of legislative initiatives have the potential to gain passage in other locations. Where not required, the concepts and considerations for establishing sick days are similar to those for paid vacation: You determine eligibility, accrual rate, and whether you will allow carryover. Some employers allow workers to take sick time in partial-day increments to cover doctor's appointments and medical tests. Many employers are reluctant to give employees sick days because they believe they will take the time off whether or not they are sick. You can minimize the potential for misuse by paying workers for unused days at the end of a calendar quarter or year. Some companies retain unused sick days in a bank of "hospital days," to provide paid days for hospital stays or other disability situations.

"Is it better just to switch to a paid time-off policy?"

Many employers have moved away from separating sick, vacation, personal, and floating holiday time and are instead substituting a single bank of days called "paid time off" (PTO). Under the PTO concept, a business gives employees a specified number of paid days or hours to use however they wish, as long as they provide sufficient notice for planned absences. With PTO, employers no longer have to wonder if that employee who called in sick is really going to a weekday theater matinee. The reasons for absences do not matter.

PTO can discourage absenteeism. Instead of employees feeling that they have to use sick days or lose them, they can accumulate days to use for vacation or other pursuits. The system creates equity between those employees who traditionally use all their sick time and those who rarely use it. PTO also simplifies administrative record keeping, eliminating the need to track reasons for absences.

Worth Repeating: *"Thanks for making that clear."*
A larger company purchased a multilocation employer that had a significantly different vacation policy. The company transitioned employees to its vacation policy gradually, and affected employees were given written statements showing their own individual vacation benefits.

When creating a PTO policy, consider what types of absences you will include in your PTO bank, how many days off you will make available, whether you will differentiate between levels of employees or between full- and part-time workers, how time will accrue, what notice expectations are for scheduled leave requests, and whether you will allow carryover or will pay out unused days at the end of the year. You will also need to determine how PTO will interact with other paid and unpaid leave, such as disability and leave without pay under the Family and Medical Leave Act (FMLA). Since PTO does not distinguish between vacation time and other types of leave, depending on your state termination laws, you may be required to pay employees for earned, unused PTO at the time of termination. If you are shifting from a traditional days off program to PTO, develop a transition plan regarding unused days under the old system. It may take some initial effort to explain and sell the change to your employees, but most employees ultimately prefer the added flexibility of PTO.

HEALTH INSURANCE

Health care will undoubtedly be your largest employee benefit expenditure, and costs continue to rise at a staggering pace. Aging baby boomers, soaring prescription drug use, sophisticated and costly medical procedures, and fraud are key contributors to a cost structure that seems out of control. According to a 2010 study conducted by the Kaiser Family Foundation and Health Research & Educational Trust, between 2000 and 2010 the average annual health insurance premiums in employer-sponsored plans for family coverage rose from $6,438 to $13,770. During this same period the average employee contribution toward this premium has grown dramatically, but employers pay more than 70 percent of the total cost. While it is easy to fixate on health insurance costs, it is critical to remember that health benefits are a key tool for recruitment and retention. You will want to take the time to find a plan that both fits within your budget and meets employee needs. There are numerous types of plans available from a variety of sources. The key to finding a program that will work for your organization is understanding your real needs and shopping smartly.

> **Better Forgotten: *"When did that employee terminate?"***
> A large company with high turnover did not always notify carriers promptly of terminations and was, consequently, often charged for several extra months, or even years of additional premiums, sometimes adding up to thousands of dollars. The insurance company refused to provide full credit for these overpayments. Set up and maintain a good system for promptly notifying all carriers of terminations.

"Are there legal requirements for offering health benefits?"

Once you provide benefits, your plan will be subject to state insurance regulations. Many states have specific laws ranging from maximum copays for prescription drugs to parity for mental health coverage to minimum hospital stays after childbirth. If you have operations in several states, you can vary your coverage by state. In addition, all group health plans are covered by the federal Women's Health and Cancer Rights Act of 1998, which provides mandatory coverage for women who choose to have breast reconstruction connected with a mastectomy.

PPACA requires a series of changes that are to be phased in over a number of years beginning in 2010:

- Extension of coverage eligibility to dependent children up to age twenty-six

- Elimination of lifetime coverage limits and regulation of annual limits

- Prohibitions on rescission of coverage

- Ban on preexisting condition exclusions for children and later for adults

- Coverage of preventive services

- Parity in emergency room copayments for in-network and out-of-network service

- Primary care designation available for ob-gyn and pediatricians

- Auto enrollment into health plans for large employers

- W–2 reporting of the value of health coverage

- Requirement that employers provide uniform, clearly written summaries of health coverage

- Limitations on waiting periods for coverage to ninety days or less

- Coverage for routine costs for clinical trials

- Enhancement of rewards that can be offered for participation in wellness programs

Your best approach to become and remain knowledgeable and compliant regarding PPACA is to keep up to date on changes and implementation, with the realization that a great deal can change or will be undefined for some time. Your broker or carrier and employer associations will be good sources of information.

Better Forgotten: *"But I read the e-mail that said the costs of benefits would be taxed."*
During the summer of 2010 an e-mail campaign purporting to detail PPACA mandates incorrectly stated that the cost of benefits would be listed on future W-2 forms as taxable income. This false information caught employers and brokers off guard and added complexity to what are already confusing changes in the law. Don't believe everything you read in e-mails or on the Internet. Use only reliable sources for PPACA updates.

"Where do I begin looking for a health care plan?"
You may want to start with a broker. A broker will be able to present you with a range of options, provide clout when dealing with a larger insurance carrier, and give you leverage with claims issues once you sign on with a provider. Or you may want to contact carriers directly. Some insurance providers, particularly local managed care programs, prefer to

avoid paying brokers' commissions and work with the employer. Alternatively, many small employers purchase coverage at attractive prices through trade associations, chambers of commerce, or state-supported plans, and they may have the option of the exchanges when they are made available. Your state department of health can help you identify state resources.

"What factors will influence the cost of the plan?"

Your coverage costs will generally depend on the number of covered employees, whether they elect single or family coverage, and the level of benefits selected. Insurance companies will set their rates based on community ratings (i.e., the claims experience of a specific group or geographic area), or the organization's individual claims experience, or a blended rate. A community rating that spreads the risk will usually provide savings for small employers. If your employee population is young and healthy and does not incur large claims, an experience rating could work in your favor. You do not have a choice on how a particular plan is rated, but the rating could be one factor in your decision among providers. The higher the level of benefit, the more your plan will cost. Including a prescription plan, coverage for in vitro fertilization, and vision care will all add cost. If you join a group plan through your chamber of commerce or industry association, you will have a smaller range of benefit-level choices than if you establish your own company plan.

You can fully insure or self-insure your plan. Under a fully insured plan, you pay premiums to the insurance company that covers all expenses incurred by the group. Your carrier adjusts your premiums annually, depending on the claims experience of the group. Under a self-insured plan, you pay all the costs of health care and an administration fee, and purchase stop-loss insurance to cover very large claims. Self-funding your plan may save you money and, depending on the laws of your state, may exempt your plan from certain insurance requirements, but the approach also involves more risk. Larger companies are more likely to self-insure, and cover the potential of the largest claims with stop-loss insurance, because they are better able to absorb the risk. Other funding options may be available. Make sure you understand the specifics of your costs and potential risks.

"What type of health plan do I choose?"

Before making a decision, understand the different types of plans available.

Indemnity Plans. Thirty years ago, most employees with employer-sponsored health benefits went to the doctor, paid the bill, and then brought the receipt with a claim form to someone at work, who checked to make sure that all of the boxes were filled. The employer then sent the paperwork to an insurance company, which sent a check to the employee a few weeks later covering a percentage of the cost, typically 80 percent. There were low—or no—deductibles, and employees did not contribute toward the cost of this coverage. Employees visited any doctor they wanted and made their own decisions about when to visit a specialist.

This traditional indemnity plan sounds like science fiction today. Over the years, both insurance carriers and employers have made major changes to control costs. Some changes were administrative; employees now send claims directly to insurance companies for processing. Others affected the delivery of care, such as requiring precertification before all nonemergency surgery and medical management for chronic illness. Employees assumed increased deductibles and copayments, with caps on maximum insurance payouts. Insurers began to limit reimbursements to a percentage of "usual and customary rates" to discourage the use of high-fee providers. Yet all these changes failed to reduce the annual double-digit percentage increases in employer costs. Indemnity plans are in limited use today; most employers choose alternative arrangements.

Health Maintenance Organizations (HMOs). The HMO model is designed to cover a wide range of care and minimize out-of-pocket expenses by requiring that participants use specified providers for all medical services. An HMO may operate in a clinic-like setting, where all the providers are HMO employees, or it may provide participants with a list of providers in multiple locations that have contracted with the HMO to provide care at set rates. Under most HMO systems, a patient needs a referral from the primary care physician before seeing a specialist, hospital stays must be preapproved and are limited to in-network hospitals, and prescriptions are filled at designated pharmacies for preferred medications. The payout cap is usually high, with low employee copayment levels. These tight restrictions help to control and predict health care costs, but they severely limit options, especially for higher-paid employees who traditionally prefer to choose their own doctors.

Preferred Provider Organizations (PPOs). The PPO combines the HMO model with the features of an indemnity system to provide more options for employers and employees alike. Under a PPO, participants can either seek care from doctors in the PPO network or choose their own out-of-network care providers. To encourage use of in-network services, PPOs will typically require employees to pay a large deductible and make significantly higher copayments for out-of-network services. PPO plans cost more than HMOs, but they can be attractive for a diverse workforce, offering a range of benefit levels and provider options and allowing employees to set their priorities. Another variant of a PPO is a point of service plan (POS), which provides in-network discounts only if all services are directed in-network. For example, if a participant chooses an out-of-network provider, even if that provider directs him to an in-network hospital, he will not be eligible for in-network discounts.

High-Deductible Health Plans. High-deductible health plans (HDHP), the newest options designed to control ever-rising costs, have significantly expanded the alphabet soup of insurance approaches. Also termed consumer-directed or consumer-driven health plans (CDHP), these options combine higher annual deductibles with tax-advantaged savings, called health savings accounts (HSAs), that employees can use to pay for covered expenses and save for future medical expenditures. HDHPs create an incentive for better-informed decisions and cost consciousness when participants pay expenses from an account they control with the potential for rollover of unspent money into funds that can accumulate for future use.

There are three key features of HDHPs paired with HSAs:

1. The health benefit plan must have a minimum annual deductible at or above the annual rate set by the IRS; $1,200 for an individual and $2,400 for a family in 2011.

2. Each eligible participating employee has an HSA account set up with a trustee, typically a bank or insurance company, into which an annual maximum amount can be contributed as designated annually by the IRS. For 2011 HSA account maximums are $3,050 for an individual and $6,150 for family coverage. These can be interest-bearing accounts.

3. The IRS sets an annual limit, indexed each year, on out-of-pocket expenses that employees are responsible for, after which plans generally pay 100 percent of expenses. For 2011 the maximum annual combination of deductible and other out-of-pocket expenses for HDHPs is $5,950 for self-only coverage and $11,900 for family coverage.

Contributions into an HSA can be made by the employee, employers, or both, using a variety of formulas. Participants can use the accounts to pay for covered expenses or pay with out-of-pocket dollars and choose to allow the HSA to grow. Employees cannot make contributions into an HSA if they are enrolled in any other health coverage, including Medicare, that is not an HDHP. When spouses are enrolled in separate HDHPs with an HSA, the deposits in both accounts combined cannot exceed the annual family limit. HSAs create tax advantages for employers and employees. Much like 401(k) accounts, HSA balances roll over into subsequent years and are portable when an employee changes jobs or retires.

High-deductible health plans may also be paired with health reimbursement accounts (HRAs). These tax-sheltered accounts are funded only by an employer. Employers have significant flexibility in plan design and funding with an HRA. HRAs can allow rollovers and use in retirement but are not required to do so since they are employer-owned accounts.

HDHPs require extra attention to education and communications that must be tailored to the employee population. Additional time spent will translate into better benefits plan usage and employee satisfaction.

"Should I offer dental and vision care benefits?"

More employers than ever are offering dental benefits. Dental costs have remained relatively stable and insurance is widely available through indemnity coverage, PPOs, dental maintenance organizations, and national plans. Make sure that any network plan you are considering offers a good selection of dentists in your area. Dental plans are typically weighted toward preventive care and limit annual per-person reimbursements to about $1,000 or $1,500. While coverage for orthodontics is popular, you can limit eligibility to employees or children, or mandate the use of in-network providers to control costs. You can position your dental plan as a benefit separate from the medical plan, allowing employees to choose whether they want to elect coverage under medical, dental, or both.

Vision care is another popular health benefit offered through many HMOs, some PPOs, and a few national companies that maintain extensive networks of providers for eye exams, glasses, and contact lenses at either fixed or discounted rates. While these plans are easy to administer and do not cost much, many companies offer vision care as an optional benefit, with employees paying all or part of the cost. Those that choose the benefit are more likely to take advantage of the coverage. National retail eye care chains also promote employer discount plans, so you can offer discounts to your employees without providing a vision benefit plan.

"Our city government provides insurance coverage for domestic partners. Do I have to?"

No. Private employers that offer domestic partner coverage do so not for legal reasons, but for philosophical or competitive ones. Domestic partner provisions can cover same-sex and heterosexual partners and can require some form of recognized registration or proof of an ongoing relationship. Numerous studies have shown that the inclusion of domestic partner benefits has not caused cost increases.

"How do I make my final decision?"

Your decision will be based on a number of factors. There are your employee needs based on age, family, and income demographics. There are competitive needs, driven by the types of packages your industry and local competitors offer. Too many small companies design their plans around the needs of an owner or senior manager, which results in a higher-cost plan with fewer employee options. If the boss wants a plan that covers 100 percent of his Freudian analysis, look into purchasing an executive benefit plan. Executive plans can save money over providing costly benefits to an entire group, but some may create future violations of PPACA. Check the most recent regulations before instituting or modifying such a plan.

In addition to looking at the cost and benefit levels of specific plans, ask what services are included. Are there online solutions for billing and enrollment questions? Do customer service representatives speak languages other than English? Who will handle company questions and concerns? Can employees make benefit or enrollment changes on the telephone or online? One important measure of service is whether the carrier has a claims committee to objectively review denied claims. Finally, check the carrier's financial stability through a private, state, or local rating service.

You do not have to offer only one health plan option for employees. Offering differing plans, perhaps an HMO alongside a PPO, can meet different needs and potentially save costs over the long term.

"My insurance company is raising my rates. Should I change carriers?"

Not necessarily. Annual changes in health benefits carriers, levels of coverage, or employee contributions are quite common, but do not make this decision casually. When you change HMOs or other network plans, your employees may have to change most or all of their doctors. While you should not hesitate to change your plan if you and your employees are getting bad service, if your motivation is cost, first look at what you can do within your current plan to control your costs.

If your current copayment level for office visits is low, consider raising it. Higher copays reduce costs, give employees a greater understanding of the cost of care, and provide an incentive to limit doctor visits. You can also increase employee copayments for prescription medicine or offer preferential reimbursements for generic drugs. Many plans now include a list of generic prescriptions that are provided without any copayment at all. You may need to raise the rate of employee contribution. Employers generally require employees to pay from 20 percent to 40 percent of employer premium plan costs through payroll deductions. Many small employers pay for individual coverage but require an employee to pay the entire additional cost for family coverage. Contribution rates can be calculated as a percentage of total cost, a flat dollar amount, or as a percentage of earnings. Some companies steer employees to lower-cost plans by dramatically increasing the employee contribution rates required for the more expensive plans. Also consider reducing or removing certain benefits or increasing the eligibility waiting period for new employees.

Employees are likely to gripe when you ask them to make any extra payments or contributions, so it is important that you explain to them the big picture. They will be less likely to complain about paying $25 for an office visit if they are reminded that your plan will cover many thousands of dollars in expenses should they require major surgery and hospitalization. Single employees who feel that the $80 a month you deduct for coverage is outrageous probably have no idea that you are paying 80 percent of the cost. Preparing and distributing a breakdown of total cost and respective employer and employee contributions will help illustrate the magnitude of the figures involved.

"Is it true that I am obligated to offer insurance to employees after they leave the company?"

Yes, if you have twenty or more employees, you are covered under the terms of the Consolidated Omnibus Budget Reconciliation Act of 1986 (COBRA). COBRA requirements are discussed in detail in Chapter 9 on termination. COBRA mandates extensive employer notice and record-keeping responsibilities, but you can ease your administrative burden and minimize the risk of costly violations at a reasonable cost by hiring an outside COBRA administrator. The administrator keeps track of sending notification letters, billing former employees, and communicating with benefits carriers. Companies offering COBRA administration services include insurance carriers, payroll companies, and independent service providers. Choose an administrator that meets your communication and record-keeping needs; do not compromise your requirements to fit in with a third party's system.

"How do medical privacy laws affect our company?"

In 2003, the Department of Health and Human Services finalized new regulations under the Health Insurance Portability and Accountability Act of 1996 (HIPAA), giving patients broad protections over the privacy of their medical records. HIPAA rules are designed to control the use and disclosure of certain defined, protected health information. HIPAA laws are very complex, but in general, since it is the health plan and not the employer that is covered under the HIPAA rules, if you are not in a health care–related business, your most important consideration will be continuing to protect the privacy of employee medical records in your possession. Examine the flow of employee medical information in your organization (i.e., how the company obtains information, how much and what kind of data is normally received, and where the data goes once it's received). Ask yourself whether the company has a legitimate need for the level of information received and whether there are safe-guards in place for preventing improper access to the information. Keep employee medical benefit records confidential and separate from other employment records, and limit access to this data to those employees with a need to know.

Worth Repeating: Create Space in That File Cabinet
An employer with more than twenty years of records was running out of space for separate employee personnel and medical benefit files. One fat file contained health benefit plan enrollment forms dating back to 1985. There is no need to retain outdated information, particularly information about plans that are no longer offered through carriers that no longer exist! Make certain that all items with individual identifying information are shredded and not simply tossed in the trash.

"What is a cafeteria plan?"
Cafeteria plans, adopted under Section 125 of the Internal Revenue Code, are also known as Section 125 plans. Without a cafeteria plan, employees make payments toward their benefit plans on an after-tax basis. With a Section 125 plan, employees sign an acknowledgment and their contributions can be made as pretax dollars. A cafeteria plan provides tax benefits for employers as well. Check with an accountant to see whether this is a viable alternative for your company.

"Is a cafeteria plan the same as a flexible spending account?"
No, but a flexible spending account (FSA) is another way to offer employees a potentially valuable tax-exempt arrangement. Under an FSA, employees can set aside pretax dollars, up to a designated maximum, in an account to cover health or dependent care costs. As employees incur eligible costs, they submit proof of payment to the administrator and receive reimbursements from the account. Medical savings accounts reimburse expenses such as insurance deductibles, coinsurance payments, and other health-related payments, identified by the IRS, that are not covered under the regular medical insurance plan. Dependent care accounts reimburse expenses for child and dependent care (includ-

ing parents) for licensed day care, legal home care, preschools, some camps, and before- and after-school programs. You can establish FSA arrangements internally or through an administrator, with the employer paying the administrative fee for worker accounts.

Employees must elect to fund their FSAs at the beginning of the plan year, and at the end of the year they forfeit any money they do not spend. Therefore, workers should take a conservative approach in estimating their expenses. This is a great benefit for employees who understand how medical and dependent care expenses can add up and are interested in reducing their taxable income.

EMPLOYEE ASSISTANCE PROGRAMS

"What can I expect from an employee assistance program?"
An employee assistance program (EAP) helps employees handle non-work-related problems that can interfere with their performance on the job. The first EAPs targeted alcohol and substance abuse problems, but the plans have subsequently evolved into "broad brush" programs that respond to a wide range of issues, from domestic violence to aging parents. Under an EAP system, employees can confidentially contact a third party for assistance. The EAP will either provide short-term telephone or in-person counseling or refer the employee elsewhere for help.

An EAP can offer employees referrals that the employer would otherwise lack the expertise to provide. A good EAP will also advise an employer and its managers how to identify and properly handle employees who show signs of problems such as domestic violence or alcohol or substance abuse. EAP providers can be large or small, local or national. Select one that matches your style and philosophy, that provides service your employees will find accessible, and that will train your managers to refer appropriate employees to the program.

RETIREMENT BENEFITS

"What is the difference between a
pension plan and a 401(k) plan?"
Employer-sponsored retirement plans can be divided into two types: defined benefit and defined contribution plans. Defined benefit plans are

the traditional pension plans. Employers make 100 percent of the contributions toward these plans and, upon retirement, employees receive a specific monthly benefit. The benefit can be a flat amount or it may be based on a formula including age, earnings, and years of service. The plan is funded through employer contributions and investment of plan assets. Defined benefit plans are common in the public sector and in large companies, especially those with long-standing union contracts.

Defined contribution plans provide an individual account for each participant, and the value of each account is usually based largely on the dollar amount contributed by the individual, although there will also be investment gains or losses.

Because defined benefit plans are increasingly costly and burdensome to administer and have been the subject of much litigation in recent years, most employers are offering defined contribution plans. There is even a trend among employers who have long offered pension plans to employees to either freeze or terminate those plans in favor of defined contribution plans. The 401(k) plan is the most popular of these vehicles.

401(k) Plans

"What is a 401(k) plan and how do I set one up?"

A 401(k) plan is an employer-sponsored plan that helps workers save money for their retirement. Employees can put an elective amount, usually up to 15 percent of their annual earnings, into a retirement savings account on a pretax basis, up to a maximum set by the IRS each year. Employees age fifty or older may contribute at a higher level. Not all plans require employers to contribute, but most provide that employers either match or contribute a percentage of the employee contribution. All contributions are given to a third-party administrator or plan provider, who invests the funds as the employee directs. If employees withdraw their money before they reach age fifty-nine and a half, they have to pay tax on it, plus a 10 percent fine to the IRS. However, if allowed under the plan, individuals can take loans against their accounts and can always take a hardship withdrawal under specific situations defined by the IRS.

Because they offer many advantages, 401(k) plans are hugely popular. These plans allow employees to manage and check their own accounts, and employees like to be able to make decisions about and watch their investments. They appreciate the convenience of payroll savings, the opportunity to save pretax dollars at much higher levels than IRAs, and, when offered, the "free money" benefit of employer contributions. When employees switch jobs, they can roll over their funds to their new employer's 401(k) or other qualified retirement plan. A qualified plan is one that meets all the requirements of the IRS for favorable tax status. Employers save money, too, because they can fund contributions with pretax dollars.

Your provider may be an insurance carrier, an investment company, or a third-party administrator. When setting up a new 401(k) plan, do not assume that all plan providers are the same. Administrative services, fees, and investment options vary. In all cases, you will want to investigate and ask the following questions:

- What fees are assessed, and are they charged to the employer or deducted from plan earnings?

- What services does the plan offer, and is there an additional charge for services? For example, you have an obligation to your employees to educate them about your 401(k) offering.

- Will the provider help you educate employees or do you need to offer independent education?

- What material will the provider use to communicate plan details?

- What types of investment options does the provider offer? You have a fiduciary responsibility to provide a variety of investment options, not just your company stock and one or two others. Investments should cover the gamut, from conservative to higher risk investment choices, and optimally the funds should have offerings spanning a variety of investment management firms. Employers who do not offer a range of investment alternatives risk litigation from employees who are unhappy with the range of options.

- What are the customer service offerings? Can employees contact the provider directly, by phone or over the Internet, to change investment options or ask questions?

- How often can employees change their investments?

- How easy will it be for the employer to change investment options in the event of underperforming funds or new market trends, and what assistance will the provider offer in making recommendations regarding appropriate fund options?

If you are changing 401(k) providers or making fund changes, find out if there will be a blackout period during which participants cannot access their accounts. Also, identify how money will be moved from funds that are no longer offered into new options. Ask for changes that are most favorable to your employees and communicate these details.

When setting up your 401(k) plan, decide which employees are eligible to participate in the plan and whether you will require a waiting period for new employees before they are eligible to contribute. All 401(k) plans are governed by strict ERISA rules (see page 150) designed to ensure that the plan is fair to all employees and that it is not "top-heavy"—that is, it does not favor highly compensated individuals. You must run an annual nondiscrimination test to ensure that lower-level employees as well as key employees are taking advantage of the plan. If the plan does not pass the discrimination test, you must take steps to correct the problem that may include returning plan funds to the highly compensated employees, who will then have to pay income tax on these amounts. Repeated test failures can cause tax implications for all participants. Your plan provider or an accountant can usually perform these tests and will be helpful in suggesting solutions should you run afoul of the top-heavy provisions.

It is advisable to designate an "investment oversight" or "fiduciary" committee within the company to regularly review the performance of the plan, ensure that the plan complies with any new laws and regulations, meet with advisers to determine whether the current plan options are still appropriate, and resolve administrative questions that may come up from time to time. This committee is typically made up of senior finance, HR, and legal executives, and sometimes other members of the management team. Take minutes of all meetings that document important decisions regarding the plan. Demonstrating that the company has acted responsibly in protecting employee contributions will help to limit your liability in the event of a lawsuit.

"What happens to the 401(k) accounts when employees leave?"
The answer depends on the provisions of your plan and the employee's reason for leaving. There will be options for retirement, rollover, cash distributions, or remaining in a plan as an "inactive participant." Any money that an employee contributes into any plan is always 100 percent vested. An amount is considered vested if it belongs to the employee today. Subject to legal guidelines, employers may adopt a schedule that allows only a specific percentage of employer contributions to vest each year, so that the employee must work for the company for a determined number of years to be fully vested in the employer portion of the account. In these situations, an employee who leaves the company will be entitled to take away the full employee contribution and the vested percentage of the employer contribution.

Other Retirement Plans

"What are the other types of defined contribution plans?"

SIMPLE Plans. If you are a business with one hundred or fewer employees who each earned at least $5,000 in the previous year, you are eligible to adopt a Savings Incentive Match Plan for Employees of Small Businesses (SIMPLE). Your SIMPLE plan will allow both you and your employees to make pretax contributions under rules that are much less complicated than those for traditional 401(k) plans, with fewer administrative responsibilities and lower plan costs. An accountant, financial adviser, or independent plan administrator can provide you with the most up-to-date rules for SIMPLE plans and help you make decisions about setup and administration.

Profit Sharing. Many companies include some sort of profit sharing as part of their compensation structures, but you can also structure a profit-sharing plan as a defined contribution retirement plan. Employers can contribute a flexible amount based on individual salaries and company earnings. Employees do not make contributions to the plan and they do not receive payouts until they retire or leave the company. Profit-sharing plans can be strong incentives in companies where business fluctuates and participants can see and understand the results of their hard work. These plans are good options for smaller businesses because they allow employers to contribute in profitable years but not in tough times.

Money Purchase Plans. This is the simplest form of defined contribution plan. The employer makes a predetermined annual contribution to the account of each eligible employee, whether or not the company is profitable.

"What about nonqualified plans?"

A nonqualified plan is a retirement or deferred compensation plan that does not meet ERISA and IRS requirements for favorable tax status, but does provide a long-term investment vehicle for senior executives or owners. Nonqualified plans allow highly compensated employees to defer and invest more money than they can under a 401(k), especially those plans that have been determined to be top-heavy. There are numerous forms of nonqualified plans, all of which involve potential risk for both the employee and the employer. Retain a reputable investment adviser to design your plans. Understand and inform participants about how contributions will be invested and the consequences and availability of early withdrawals.

"Do I have any other reporting requirements?"

The Employee Retirement Income Security Act (ERISA) sets out detailed reporting and compliance rules to ensure that employee benefit plans are properly administered, well-funded, and do not favor owners and the highest earners in a company. You are required to complete a Form 5500 for each of your benefits plans at the end of each plan year. If you are offering health plans to employees through a chamber of commerce or trade association, you do not have to submit a Form 5500 for those plans. Form 5500 requests basic information about the number of employees covered and types of coverage. Your benefits carrier, plan administrator, or broker will often complete the forms for you or can send you the forms and filing instructions.

"Haven't we covered everything?"

While we have described the most common benefits, there are numerous others you may want to offer or consider. Tuition assistance can be a qualified plan or be limited to simple reimbursement for adult education. Employees of retailers and consumer products companies frequently enjoy employee and family discounts. Subsidized or paid meals may be a big benefit for your workforce. Child care referrals, subsidies, or nearby day care providers may enhance your retention. We could continue on and on with the possibilities, but these will be for you to decide, based on your company philosophy. For each benefit, identify who will gain and your goal in implementation. Communicate that the benefit exists and how to use it. You can then measure use and satisfaction and continually develop and maintain a high-quality benefits package that your employees will appreciate and value.

Regulatory Issues

What Are the Major Employment Laws and How Do I Comply with Them?

ONE OF THE MOST CHALLENGING TASKS you will face in human resources management is complying with employment-related laws. Not only are there countless federal laws governing all aspects of the employer/employee relationship, but there are also various state and local laws that expand upon federal employee protections or place requirements on employers in areas not covered by federal law.

Throughout this book, there are references to employment laws that relate to specific topics as they are discussed. In this chapter, we cover some of the other major federal laws. You will gain a sense of the broad reach of these laws and learn to spot potential problem areas within your company. Be sure to check with an attorney regarding the specific laws that apply in the state where your main business office is located, and in any other state in which your company employs workers.

LAWS PROHIBITING DISCRIMINATORY PRACTICES

In 2009 alone, there were more than 93,000 charges of discrimination filed with the Equal Employment Opportunity Commission (EEOC) under the various federal antidiscrimination laws, resulting in hundreds of millions of dollars in settlement costs to companies. This settlement amount does not even include damages related to claims that actually made it to court—where employers incurred countless additional millions of dollars in damages for engaging in discriminatory employment practices.

While there is no way to completely prevent employees from claiming that they were discriminated against, there are ways to greatly decrease your potential for liability. Among them:

- Understand the basics of federal, state, and local statutes regarding discrimination and seek counsel in specific instances when questions arise.

- Create strong antidiscrimination and harassment policies and communicate them throughout the organization. Employers are required by law to conspicuously post notices advising employees of their rights under the laws enforced by the EEOC.

- Train executives, managers, and supervisors regarding proper workplace conduct and how to deal with actual or suspected violations.

- Evaluate the underlying *business reasons* for employment policies, procedures, and practices that you institute to ensure that they are driven by legitimate and not discriminatory motives.

- Establish a work environment where discrimination, harassment, and retaliation of any kind are not tolerated. Investigate all discrimination complaints seriously and deal with wrongdoers appropriately and consistently.

"What are the primary federal antidiscrimination laws?"

The most significant laws affecting employers are:

- Title VII of the Civil Rights Act of 1964, prohibiting employment discrimination based on race, color, religion, gender, or national origin

- Age Discrimination in Employment Act of 1967, outlawing discrimination against workers age forty and older

- Americans with Disabilities Act of 1990, protecting qualified individuals with disabilities

- Fair pay laws, including the Equal Pay Act of 1963, mandating that men and women who perform substantially equal work for the same employer under similar working conditions receive substantially equal pay, and the Lily Ledbetter Fair Pay Act of 2009, which provides additional protections to victims of discriminatory pay practices

- Title II of the Genetic Information Nondiscrimination Act of 2008, prohibiting genetic information discrimination in employment

"What types of discrimination do the federal antidiscrimination laws protect against?"

Federal laws prohibit discriminatory practices that may arise in *all* aspects of the employment relationship, including:

- Recruitment, hiring, and firing

- Compensation, fringe benefits, assignment, and classification of employees

- Transfer, leave, promotion, layoff, or recall

- Testing

- Use of company facilities

- Training

- Any other term or condition of employment

The antidiscrimination laws also make illegal any *harassment* on the basis of an individual's membership in a class protected by any of these laws or association with a person in a protected class. They also prohibit *retaliation* against a worker for filing a charge of discrimination or participating in an investigation or taking actions that oppose discriminatory practices in the organization.

Title VII of the Civil Rights Act of 1964

"Who does Title VII apply to, and what types of discrimination do the laws prohibit?"

Title VII applies to all private employers, state and local governments, and educational institutions that employ at least fifteen workers. The laws prohibit employment discrimination on the basis of race, color, gender, religion, or national origin. While blatant, direct discrimination is usually easy to spot, it is often more difficult to determine whether certain outwardly "neutral" policies, practices, or decisions will have an unfair impact on specific categories of employees. You may be held liable for actions that have a disproportionate impact on one or more protected categories of worker unless you can demonstrate that the basis for the action is job-related and serves a legitimate business purpose.

- *Race and color discrimination.* Title VII makes it illegal to discriminate in employment against individuals of a particular race or color. For example, you cannot refuse to hire someone because he is Asian, or deny someone career development opportunities because she is Caucasian. The law also forbids discrimination on the basis of stereotypes about the characteristics of members of a specific race, such as assumptions that members of some racial groups do not work as hard or are less honest than others.

  In addition, Title VII prohibits discrimination based on an unchangeable characteristic associated with race, such as skin shade, hair texture, or certain facial features. Therefore, since African-American men are prone to a condition under which they develop severe shaving bumps, a "no beard" policy may be found to violate Title VII unless you can show a sound, job-related reason for having this policy—such as a restaurant adhering to local health codes.

- *Religious discrimination.* Under the religious discrimination laws, you cannot consider an employee's religion in making hiring decisions. In addition, when requested by employees, you must accommodate their religious practices unless doing so would cause an undue hardship for the company. Reasonable accommodations may include providing workers time off for religious observances or providing a place to pray. You do not have to accept the particular accommodation requested by an employee; you are free to substitute a different one if it would serve the same purpose. There is no set definition of what constitutes "undue hardship," but generally under Title VII, if the accommodation would cost you more than a minimal sum, you are not required to make the accommodation. Keep in mind, however, that some state laws hold employers to a higher standard to demonstrate undue hardship, such as showing that accommodating the employee would require significant difficulty or expense.

- *National origin discrimination.* National origin discrimination means treating someone less favorably or more favorably because of the place where he is from, or because she has a common ancestry with people from a particular place. There are several components of national origin discrimination to which employers should pay particular attention when setting rules or policies or making other employment decisions.

  - *Foreign accents.* Employment actions based on an individual's accent are permitted only when the accent affects the ability to perform job duties. You cannot discriminate merely because a person speaks with an accent—the accent must interfere with communication skills *and* effective communication skills must be necessary for the job. Teaching and telemarketing positions are among those that may require effective oral communication skills, but you should never generalize. Always look at individual circumstances to determine whether a worker's accent realistically bars her from doing an effective job.

  - *English fluency requirements.* Similar to rules regarding foreign accents, you can require employees to be fluent in English only if fluency is a real and reasonable requirement for the job. While English fluency may reasonably be required of a salesperson, it is harder to argue that it is needed for a janitorial position.

  - *English-only requirements.* Some companies choose to adopt policies allowing only English to be spoken at the workplace. These policies are allowable if they are not implemented for discriminatory reasons *and* the rule is needed for the business to run safely and efficiently. Therefore, while a policy requiring bank tellers to speak English to the bank's English-speaking customers is appropriate, a policy requiring the same tellers to speak only English during breaks is unacceptable. If you have an English-only policy, you must notify employees of the rule as well as the consequences for violation.

  - *Citizenship requirements.* Title VII does not specifically outlaw discrimination based on citizenship, but it does prohibit using citizenship as a pretext for discriminating on the basis of national origin. Because the line between citizenship and national origin is often quite murky, we do not recommend that you adopt such a rule.

> **Better Forgotten:** *"Paranoia is not a business justification!"*
> A casino was ordered by the EEOC to pay $1.5 million to its house-keeping staff for enforcing an English-only rule created because one of the non-Spanish-speaking employees believed that the others were talking behind her back in Spanish. Managers and others would shout, "English! English!" at Hispanic workers as they walked through the halls. According to the EEOC, there was no proper business reason for the rule, and the treatment of the Hispanic staff was humiliating.

- *Gender discrimination.* Gender discrimination covers gender-based employment decisions, sexual harassment, and pregnancy discrimination.

- *Sexual harassment.* Sexual harassment law can be complex because illegal harassment can take many forms and encompass a variety of subtleties. While sexual harassment claims are most frequently filed by women, the victim—as well as the harasser—can be either male or female, and there is no requirement that the victim and the harasser be of opposite sexes. According to the EEOC, the harasser can be the victim's supervisor, coworker, a supervisor in another area, or agent of the victim's employer. In fact, the victim does not even have to be the person actually harassed, but can be anyone who is negatively affected by the offensive conduct.

"What types of conduct do the sexual harassment laws prohibit?"

In general, behavior constituting sexual harassment falls into two categories: quid pro quo and hostile environment. The line between the categories is not always clear, and it is possible for both types of harassment to occur together.

1. *Quid pro quo* describes situations in which the victim's engaging in sexual conduct with the harasser becomes the basis of the employment decision. Examples of quid pro quo harassment are a supervisor saying, "Have sex with me and you will get the promotion" or "If you don't have sex with me you will be fired."

2. *Hostile environment* situations are those where sexual conduct is not a prerequisite for an employment decision, but the working environment is so pervaded by discrimination, insult, or abuse that it becomes unpleasant or threatening for employees to do their jobs.

Quid pro quo harassment is relatively simple to define and determine, whereas hostile environment harassment is often ambiguous and complex. Hostile environment claims make up the majority of sexual harassment complaints. Conduct that is considered sexual harassment comes in many forms, including:

* Sexual advances or requests for sexual favors

* Verbal or physical contact that is sexual in nature (e.g., pornographic pictures in the workplace, lewd or offensive jokes shared verbally or through office e-mail exchange)

* Blatant hostility toward an employee or group of employees because of their gender (a situation that often occurs when women work in jobs or environments that were previously occupied solely by men)

For conduct to be considered illegal sexual harassment, it must be unwelcome, severe, and pervasive in the workplace. Unwelcome behavior is that which the affected party does not solicit and finds offensive or undesirable. While true consensual sexual relationships are not harassment, just because an employee agrees to the activity does not automatically make the relationship consensual. If an employee voluntarily entered into a sexual relationship with her supervisor because she feared losing her job if she did not comply, she may have a valid legal claim. Even more problematic is the situation where a sexual relationship is initially consensual, but later one of the employees wants to end the relationship and the other persists in sexual conduct. Behavior that persists past the point where it is consensual for both parties is sexual harassment.

To be considered severe, the conduct must be serious enough that a "reasonable person" would find it offensive. This standard precludes the hypersensitive person from successfully claiming injury from an innocuous remark or action. "Pervasive" behavior means that it is persistent in the workplace rather than occurring in isolated instances. A male employee asking a female coworker on a date one time is not harassment, even if the woman makes clear she is not interested, but repeated requests can develop into a harassment situation. Conversely, only one instance of groping or one quid pro quo demand can give rise to an actionable harassment claim.

"When will the employer be held liable for sexual harassment?"

As an employer, you will be automatically liable for any harassment that leads to a significant change in employment status, such as hiring, firing, promotion, or demotion. If the harassment does not lead to a significant change in employment status, you will held responsible unless you can prove that:

* You exercised reasonable care to prevent and promptly correct the harassment.

* The employee unreasonably failed to complain to management or otherwise avoid harm.

"What steps can I take to prevent and correct harassment in order to minimize my risk of liability?"

Most important, you need a written policy prohibiting workplace harassment. While there is no specific form of policy required under the laws, yours should have the following elements:

* A statement that the company will not tolerate harassment, whether sexual or based on religion, race, national origin, age, or disability

* Direct assurance that there will be no retaliation against those reporting harassment

* A clear procedure for reporting complaints and conducting investigations

* A statement that although the organization will protect the confidentiality of all parties to a complaint to the extent possible, it may have to share certain information with those with a need to know

Your complaint procedure should designate more than one individual to whom the employee can report harassment, preferably both male and female, so that complaining employees can select individuals with whom they feel most comfortable. The EEOC has specifically stated that it is not enough that the harassment policy instruct employees to inform their supervisors of harassment; after all, it may be the supervisor who is committing the harassment in the first place! You might consider designating people from a variety of areas in the organization to receive complaints, such as members of the executive staff, legal staff, and human resources staff, and providing a form for employees to fill out to report complaints in writing for those who may not feel comfortable making a face-to-face complaint. A sample complaint form is included in the Tools and Templates section of this book. Some companies successfully use an independent hotline service so employees can report violations to impartial, outside parties.

Some states require employers to conduct mandatory sexual harassment training for managers and supervisors. Inquire whether any harassment education laws exist in your state.

It is essential to conduct a fair and comprehensive investigation of all employee complaints. (See Chapter 8 for more information on effective workplace investigations.) During the investigation, take steps to keep the complaining and the accused parties apart. Reasonable steps may include assigning one or both individuals to different work areas to minimize the opportunity for contact, or placing the accused on paid leave pending the results of the investigation.

If, as a result of the investigation, you determine that harassment has occurred, you must take immediate action to end the harassment and keep it from happening again. The discipline meted out to the harasser should correspond with the seriousness of the offense.

Don't wait until a complaint is filed to work toward eliminating harassment or inappropriate conduct in your organization. Train managers and supervisors to recognize and report harassment and to handle complaints. If you are aware that employees are using the company e-mail system to distribute questionable jokes or that there are sexually graphic pictures hanging in the men's locker room, act now before an incident occurs.

> **Worth Repeating:** *"Not at a company function, you don't!"*
> A young executive was observed propositioning several female employees at an off-premises company-sponsored function. When his boss rightfully admonished him, he claimed his behavior was okay since he was not on company premises. Improper conduct at any company event can be considered harassment, no matter where it takes place.

"If an employee does not complain, can the company still be held liable for harassment?"

Yes, if the failure to complain was reasonable under the circumstances. Generally, an employee is required to take reasonable steps to avoid the harassment and to keep it from becoming worse. Therefore, if an organization has a sound antiharassment policy with clear complaint procedures, the affected employee will normally be expected to use the designated complaint procedure unless there are legitimate reasons for not using it. Legitimate reasons can include fear of retaliation or the knowledge that the company had not acted to investigate and deal with harassment complaints in the past.

It is the employer's responsibility to prove that the failure to complain of harassment was unreasonable. If you create a workplace environment where an employee feels comfortable filing a complaint and knows that you will take the complaint seriously without retaliation, it will be harder for an individual to justify failure to report a problem.

"Can I ever fire a pregnant woman?"

Yes, but not because of her pregnancy. You may properly terminate her employment for performance reasons, layoffs, or any other legitimate circumstances; however, it is important to determine that these conditions are legitimate rather than a pretext for discrimination.

An amendment to Title VII, the Pregnancy Discrimination Act, prohibits discrimination against women because they are pregnant or experience conditions or take leave related to pregnancy. If an employee is temporarily unable to perform her job because of her pregnancy, you are required to make reasonable accommodations, such as modifying her tasks or providing disability leave without pay. When the employee takes a pregnancy-related leave of absence, employers are required to hold her job open for the same period of time as jobs are held open for other sick or disability leaves. Health insurance benefits must cover expenses for pregnancy-related matters to the same extent as coverage is provided for other medical conditions. It is illegal to limit pregnancy benefits to married employees.

"What is this I hear about Title VII reporting requirements?"

If you are a private employer with one hundred or more employees, or a federal contractor with at least fifty workers, you are required to file an EEO-1 employer information report with the EEOC by September 30 of each year. The EEO-1 report provides a breakdown of your workforce by gender, racial/ethnic classification, and job category. You may use employment figures from any pay period from July through September, including both full- and part-time employees.

If you have collected any information from employees after they were hired that identifies their race or ethnicity, you should use this data for your EEO-1 report. If you do not have this data, you are permitted to take a visual survey of your workers and make your best guess as to each worker's race/ethnicity. The EEOC does not recommend that you ask employees directly, but encourages you to provide employees a written form on which they may choose to voluntarily self-identify. A sample of this type of form is included in the Tools and Templates section of this book.

Age Discrimination in Employment Act of 1967 (ADEA)

"Who is covered by ADEA and what types of discrimination does the law prohibit?"

The ADEA applies to all employers with twenty or more employees, including state and local governments. It protects individuals age forty and over from discrimination in employment on the basis of age and from retaliation for making a complaint or participating in an investigation concerning age discrimination.

The restrictions of ADEA are very similar to the prohibitions of Title VII. As with the Title VII laws, employers can be held liable for outwardly neutral policies that have a disproportionate impact on older workers. If you have a policy or practice that tends to have a negative impact on protected employees, make sure you can articulate a valid business reason for maintaining it.

"Is it ever acceptable to make employment distinctions based on age?"

Yes, under very limited circumstances. Age limitations are allowed when age is a bona fide occupational qualification that is reasonably necessary to operate the business. A movie casting agent seeking to cast a role of a young man would not be required to interview or hire older males for the part. Employers may also enforce bona fide seniority systems as long as these systems are not intended to evade the intent of ADEA. In addition, it is allowable to reduce benefits paid based on age if the cost of the reduced benefits for older workers is the same as the cost of providing benefits to younger workers.

"Can our company adopt a mandatory retirement policy?"

No, it is illegal to require an employee to voluntarily retire at a particular age unless age is a bona fide occupational qualification for performing the job.

"Can workers elect to waive their rights under the ADEA?"

Yes, but the waiver must be voluntary and the employee must understand the significance of the document. A valid waiver must be in writing, must specifically refer to ADEA claims, must be in exchange for valuable compensation or other benefits given to the employee, must advise the individual in writing to consult an attorney before signing the waiver, and must provide the individual with at least twenty-one days to consider the agreement and seven days after signing to revoke the waiver. You cannot ask employees to waive future rights or claims. If you are requesting a waiver in connection with an early retirement program or other voluntary termination incentive, there are additional requirements in order for the waiver to be considered proper.

If you are considering requesting an employee to execute an ADEA waiver, consult with an attorney, both to ensure that a waiver is appropriate under the circumstances and that the waiver document complies with the law.

The Americans with Disabilities Act of 1990 (ADA)

"Who is covered by ADA and what types of discrimination does this law prohibit?"

The ADA covers employers with fifteen or more employees. The law prevents employers from making employment decisions that discriminate against qualified individuals with disabilities.

The ADA also prohibits employers from retaliating against individuals asserting their rights under the ADA, and from discriminating against people because of their family or other relationship with a person with a disability. Employers cannot refuse to hire a person with a disabled spouse because of concerns about medical costs or fear that the spouse will cause the employee to miss time from work. In 2008, the Americans with Disabilities Act Amendments Act of 2008 ("ADA Amendments Act") was enacted. The ADA Amendments Act, which applies to discriminatory acts occurring after January 1, 2009, broadened the definition of "disability" under the ADA, emphasizing that the definition of disability should be interpreted broadly and without extensive analysis.

To be protected by ADA, the individual must (1) have a covered disability and (2) be qualified to hold the position in question.

"What is a covered disability under ADA?"

According to the EEOC, a disability is a physical or mental impairment that limits major life activities. This definition covers impairments to hearing, speaking, sight, breathing, performing manual tasks, walking, reading, bending, eating, lifting, communicating, caring for oneself, learning, or working. Impairments to major bodily functions are also considered disabilities under the ADA, including functions of the immune system, normal cell growth, and digestive, bowel, bladder, neurological, brain, respiratory, circulatory, endocrine, and reproductive functions. Temporary or minor impairments do not qualify as disabilities under ADA. If an employee has a broken arm that prevents him from performing his job on the loading dock, this is not a protected disability.

"Who is considered a 'qualified individual' under the law?"

Qualified workers or job applicants must have all the experience and background required by the position. They must have the required degrees, skill, training, and knowledge to perform the essential functions of the job, with or without accommodations. There has been much confusion among employers about what constitutes essential functions and what constitutes minor, noncritical job functions. If you have job descriptions, the major duties listed in these documents are the essential functions. When determining whether specific persons are qualified, it is important to look at whether tasks they cannot perform are really critical functions or ones incidental to the position.

The ADA does not require that you hire a qualified applicant over other applicants or promote a qualified worker over other workers just because that individual has a disability. The law only prohibits discrimination on the basis of the disability. It makes it unlawful to take adverse employment actions based on an individual's disability or need for a reasonable accommodation.

"What reasonable accommodations are employers required to make?"

Employers must make reasonable accommodations for employees with disabilities unless making the accommodation would cause the company undue hardship. A reasonable accommodation is any change in the work environment or the way a job is performed that would allow a person with a physical or mental disability to enjoy equal employment opportunities. An employer must consider a reasonable accommodation upon the written or verbal request of an employee (or the employee's physician). In situations involving obvious disabilities, you may ask the employee whether reasonable accommodation is needed.

The following are examples of types of reasonable accommodations that you might be required to make:

- *Restructuring a position.* This can include shifting minor functions of a position that the employee with a disability cannot perform to other employees who can perform them, or altering when and how the job is performed. You are not required to restructure a position to eliminate a primary job responsibility.

- *Making existing workplace facilities accessible.* Federal and state regulations require employers to adhere to specific standards to make their facilities accessible for persons with disabilities. In addition, an employer may be required to make modifications above and beyond those required by these laws to accommodate the specific needs of its employees.

- *Providing unpaid leave.* If an individual's disability requires unpaid leave, providing this leave may be a form of reasonable accommodation, provided it does not cause your company undue hardship. Persons returning from leave should be reassigned to the same position unless, again, it would cause an undue hardship. You are not required to provide more paid leave to accommodate a person with a disability than you provide for other employees.

- *Providing a modified schedule.* This accommodation may involve adjusting arrival and/or departure times, part-time hours, or periodic breaks, or changing the time of day at which certain tasks are performed.

- *Reassignment.* Unless you can show that it would cause undue hardship to the company, you may be required to reassign an employee who can no longer perform essential job functions because of a disability to a vacant position with responsibilities that the individual can perform. Whenever possible, this new position should be of equal pay and status. You are not required to create a new position, promote the employee, or bump other employees to provide this accommodation. Moreover, the individual must be *qualified* for the new position. You need not provide additional training to enable an unqualified individual to become qualified.

Providing reasonable accommodation can also mean offering employees with disabilities benefits comparable to those offered to other employees. For example, if you provide training to comparable workers, then you must modify the programs, if necessary, to accommodate individuals with disabilities. Examples are providing an interpreter or making training manuals available in braille or on audiotape. Both in-house and outside facilities must be made accessible. Holding your training in a contracted facility or using consultants to conduct the workshops does not excuse you from this responsibility. If your workplace has a cafeteria, lounge, auditorium, or company-provided transportation and counseling services, they must be made accessible to employees with disabilities or you must provide an alternate facility to accommodate them, unless doing so would cause undue hardship.

"What is 'undue hardship'?"

This is the standard by which the EEOC and the courts determine whether a specific accommodation is reasonable. Undue hardship can include significant financial expenditures or measures that would be unduly extensive or disruptive or significantly alter the nature or operation of the business. Each request for a reasonable accommodation should be evaluated individually, taking into consideration the cost of the accommodation, the resources of the employer, the effect on the business, and the impact on other employees. What constitutes undue hardship for one employer will not necessarily constitute it for another. A small start-up business is held to different standards than a multinational corporation. However, a company may never claim undue hardship based on the fears of employees or customers, or their prejudice toward individuals with a specific disability.

"How can I work with my employees to develop appropriate reasonable accommodations?"

The establishment of a reasonable accommodation should result from an interactive process between employer and employee that clarifies the scope of the disability and the specific need for accommodation. You are only obligated to provide reasonable accommodation if you are aware that a disability exists. When disabilities are not obvious, it is up to the individuals to disclose their conditions to you if they feel they need a reasonable accommodation. There is no obligation on the part of the individual to disclose a disability or request an accommodation, but if he later fails to meet the requirements of the job because he did not have the necessary accommodation, this is not the employer's fault. You may not ask applicants or employees about their disabilities during the interview process or after employment (see Chapter 1).

Frequently, an employee will suggest a workable accommodation. Other times, the individual will not know exactly what accommodation is needed and you will need to examine the alternatives together. If there is more than one alternative accommodation that would allow the employee to perform the functions of the job, you may choose the least burdensome and/or least expensive option.

Employers may incur significant legal liability and financial penalties for failing to make reasonable accommodations for an employee with a disability. Therefore, if you are in doubt about whether you are required by law to make a specific accommodation, consult with an attorney before denying the request.

Worth Repeating: *"A very reasonable accommodation."*
A small employer had an employee with a math disability that caused him to make errors transcribing numbers. The company contacted its state department of labor for assistance, which connected the company with a low-cost, state-funded training program to help the employee work with his disability.

The Equal Pay Act of 1963 (EPA)

*"Who does the EPA apply to and
what are its major provisions?"*

The EPA applies to virtually all employers. Under this law, employers must pay equal wages to men and women who perform jobs requiring substantially equal skill, effort, and responsibility under the same working conditions in the same establishment. Here's what these terms mean under the law:

- *Skill.* When comparing the skill sets of two workers, it is important to look at the skills that are necessary for the job, not the total skills possessed by each of the individuals. For example, if a man and a woman are both staff accountants with bachelor's degrees in accounting and ten years' accounting experience, you cannot use the fact that the man has a Ph.D. in English to justify his higher pay rate, because this graduate degree is not related to the job requirements.

- *Effort.* This pertains to the amount of physical or mental exertion it takes to do the job. If you have two individuals in quality inspection positions, but one of them is inspecting small products and the other is examining heavy machinery that he needs to lift, you are permitted to pay the second inspector more than the first.

- *Responsibility.* This refers to the amount of accountability inherent in the position. If only one of two restaurant servers is permitted to handle cash, the increased responsibility justifies payment of a higher wage. If the difference in responsibility is minor—say, for example, that one server is designated to answer the telephone—higher pay is not justifiable.

- *Working conditions.* Working conditions comprise both physical surroundings and hazards. If a hospital employs two nurses' aides, one working in a children's ward and one with violent patients, the increased risk incurred by the second aide could merit a pay differential.

- *Establishment.* An establishment, according to the EEOC, is a "distinct physical place of business." You can generally pay diverse wages to employees doing the same job in different states.

In addition, you may pay employees varying wages if they are based on factors other than sex, such as seniority or merit, but it is your responsibility to prove that you are using valid rather than discriminatory criteria. Audit your salary structure periodically to make sure you are not inadvertently violating the EPA. If you find that your payroll practices need adjustment, you may not reduce the pay of the higher-paid employee but must raise the wages of the lower-paid worker.

The Lily Ledbetter Fair Pay Act of 2009

The Lily Ledbetter Fair Pay Act of 2009 extends the time available to the victim of discriminatory pay practices to file an equal pay lawsuit under federal antidiscrimination laws. This law provides that an act of discrimination occurs with the issuance of each new discriminatory paycheck rather than on the date that compensation was agreed upon by the employer and the employee. Therefore, the statutory 180-day period to file a complaint arises anew on each pay day.

Title II of the Genetic Information Nondiscrimination Act of 2008 (GINA)

Title II of GINA prohibits discrimination against employees due to genetic information, prohibits the use of genetic information in making employment decisions, restricts employer access to genetic information, and limits disclosure of such information. An employer may never use genetic information to make an employment decision, because genetic information does not reveal to the employer anything about the employee's current ability to work. GINA also forbids harassment or retaliation due to genetic information.

"What is 'genetic information' under GINA?"

Genetic information includes information about the potential or current employee's genetic tests and genetic tests of that individual's family members, as well as information about any disease, disorder, condition, or other aspect of the medical history of the individual's family members. Family history is included in the definition of "genetic information" because it is frequently used to determine whether someone has an increased risk of developing a particular disease or condition in the future.

"Can an employer ever acquire genetic information about an employee or his or her family members?"

Yes, but only under limited circumstances. These include genetic information:

- Inadvertently acquired without violating GINA, such as when one employee overhears another discussing a family member's illness.

- Obtained as part of health or genetic services, including wellness programs, offered by the employer on a voluntary basis.

- Acquired as part of the certification process for FMLA leave (see the next section) or leave under similar state or local laws, where an employee is asking for leave to care for a family member with a serious health condition.

- Learned through commercially and publicly available documents like newspapers. However, the employer cannot search these documents with the intent of finding genetic information.

- Acquired through a genetic monitoring program that monitors the biological effects of toxic substances in the workplace, where the monitoring is required by law or strictly voluntary.

- Obtained by employers who engage in DNA testing for law enforcement purposes as a forensic lab or for purposes of human remains identification, but there are significant restrictions on the use of this information.

If you acquire genetic information concerning your employees, you are obligated to keep this information confidential and separate from the individual's employment file, though you may use the same file as you use to keep ADA-related information.

THE FAMILY AND MEDICAL LEAVE ACT

The Family and Medical Leave Act (FMLA) allows covered employees to take up to twelve weeks' unpaid leave of absence per year and requires employers to protect the employee's job and continue health benefits coverage during the periods of leave. The law recognizes that workers may experience health and/or family situations that necessitate a leave of absence. It was designed to help employees achieve a balance between their work lives, their health, and personal considerations.

Many states have laws similar to the FMLA, some providing more generous benefits than the federal laws, which are administered by the U.S. Department of Labor. If you are in a state with leave regulations that differ from those of the FMLA, you are required to give your employees the benefit of whichever law offers the most generous protection.

Employers must post notices informing workers of their FMLA rights in prominent places in work facilities, as well as provide notice either in the employee handbook or upon hire. In 2009, new regulations under the FMLA were enacted that provide additional notice and proof of medical condition requirements in order to help employers combat FMLA abuse. To take advantage of these protections, you must follow the posting requirements and update your policies and forms to comply with the new regulations, and have employees sign a form acknowledging receipt of this information.

"Which employers/employees are covered by the FMLA?"
The Family and Medical Leave Act covers employers with fifty or more full- or part-time employees on the payroll. It covers all public agencies and public or private elementary and secondary schools. To be eligible for FMLA coverage, an employee must:

- Have worked for the organization for at least twelve months

- Have worked for the organization at least 1,250 hours during the previous twelve months

- Work in a location where the company has at least fifty employees working within a seventy-five-mile radius of the location

"When can an eligible employee take FMLA leave?"

Leave is restricted to certain defined conditions:

- *Birth, adoption, or foster care.* Employees becoming parents through birth, adoption, or foster care placement may take a leave of absence within one year after the arrival of the child. In certain situations, the expectant parents can begin the leave before the child arrives. The leave is available to both men and women, but if the husband and wife work for the same employer, their leave may be limited to a combined twelve weeks.

- *Serious health condition of the employee.* The condition must render the employee unable to do his or her job. The law is quite specific and complicated regarding the types of health conditions that qualify for FMLA leave, but generally these conditions include inpatient care, periods of more than three days where the employee is unable to function normally and is under the care of a doctor, pregnancy or prenatal problems, or other material health issues.

- *Serious health condition of a family member.* If a family member has a serious health condition, the employee may take leave to care for this individual. "Family member" under the law is limited to parents, children, or spouses. Other family members and domestic partners are not included.

- *Military status of a family member.* The FMLA was amended in 2008 to extend coverage to employees to care for a family member injured while on active military duty and to take time off in the event of a family member's call to active duty.

"How should employees request FMLA leave?"

Employees should give notice at least thirty days in advance for leave that is foreseeable (such as birth or adoption of a child), or as soon as possible for leave that is unforeseeable (such as emergency personal or family health issues). The notice should specify the reasons for the leave in sufficient detail to allow the employer to determine whether the reasons for the leave qualify under FMLA and the expected duration of the leave.

"Can I request confirmation of a serious health condition?"

When the leave involves a personal or family health concern, you may request that the worker provide medical certification, allowing the employee at least fifteen days to comply. If the worker fails to provide the certification within the time provided or an otherwise reasonable time, you may delay the leave until you receive the information. The Department of Labor has available FMLA request and medical certification forms that you may require the employee to use. If the employee's medical certification is lacking in detail, you must notify the employee in writing about the insufficiency of the information provided and give the employee seven days to provide complete information. While in the past, employers were not allowed to contact the employee's health care provider directly to request details of the health condition, new regulations allow employers to contact the health care provider directly to clarify or authenticate a medical certification after the employee has been given the chance to cure any deficiencies in the information provided. You may not request information beyond what is in the certification form. Most health care providers are required under HIPAA to obtain authorization from the employee to release patient medical information, but if the employee refuses to provide this authorization and otherwise fails to provide satisfactory certification, you may deny the leave.

"What are the circumstances under which employees can request leave due to a family member's military status?"

The FMLA military leave provision generally permits employees to take up to twenty-six weeks of leave to care for a family member who is injured in the line of active military duty, and up to twelve weeks of leave if a "qualified exigency" occurs. A qualified exigency is a permitted reason to take time off in connection with a family member's call to active duty. Qualified exigencies include:

* Short-notice deployments (notice of seven days or fewer)

- Military events (ceremonies, briefings, etc.)

- Financial/legal arrangements related to the call to duty

- Counseling related to the call to duty

- R&R leave (up to five days)

- Postdeployment activities (ceremonies, briefings, etc.)

- Such other activities as the employer may permit

"Do I have to give employees anything in writing when they request an FMLA leave?"

You must provide the worker with a timely written notice specifying employee rights and obligations under the law, preferably within two business days. If you don't provide a notice in a timely manner, you may not be able to deny the leave, even if the employee was not eligible. The notice must specify:

- Whether, and how much of, the time off will count toward the FMLA entitlement.

- Requirements for submitting medical certification and the consequences of failure to do so.

- The employee's right to substitute paid leave, such as vacation time and sick days. As the employer, you may require that available paid leave be used first, provided you notify the individual of this requirement.

- Whether you require a medical certification of fitness to return to duty upon the employee's return from a personal medical leave.

- The employee's right to restoration to his or her position or substantially equivalent position upon return from leave.

- Whether the employee is a "key employee" under the FMLA. Key employees are those salaried employees in the top 10 percent of the company's pay range. The law takes into account that these individuals may be so important to the organization that their extended absence would cause the organization substantial harm. You do not have to guarantee restoration of position to these employees as long as you notify them of their key employee status when they request the leave. You must still give the key employee a reasonable opportunity to return to work from FMLA leave.

- Requirements for making any contribution for health care premiums and consequences for failure to pay on time. You may only require copayments at the same level the employee was required to make prior to the leave.

- Whether workers have the obligation to repay the employer if they do not return to work. This notification applies if your company is paying any portion of employee health care premiums during the leave.

"Can I inquire about employee status during the leave?"

Yes, it is totally acceptable to maintain contact with workers during their leaves, but you cannot contact medical providers or other third parties. You may, with advance notice, require employees to contact you periodically to report on their status, as long as you require all employees on FMLA leave to do so. Requesting that only certain workers report in may be viewed as discriminatory. You may also, with notice, require subsequent medical certifications, but not more frequently than every thirty days.

"Do employees get their jobs back after they return from leave?"

By law, you are required to hold the individual's position open or provide an equivalent position upon her return. An equivalent position is considered one that is virtually identical to the previous one in pay, benefits, working conditions, and status. There are many additional factors that determine whether a job is equivalent, such as duties, location, schedule, fringe benefits, skill, and authority. In some situations it will be easy to offer an equivalent role, especially if an organization has many positions in a particular job category. When a position is highly specialized, it may be harder to prove that a new position is equivalent. Although it may be expensive and inconvenient to hold a job open, if you are not sure that you can provide an alternative position that is truly equivalent, you may have no other choice.

"Can you fire an employee on FMLA leave?"

Yes, under proper circumstances. Although you cannot take any adverse action because an employee is on leave, you are allowed to take any employment actions that you would have otherwise taken if the employee had been on the job. If you conduct a layoff during the leave period and you have valid reasons for eliminating the position, you may do so and you will not be obligated to offer an equivalent job. Your obligations to the employee will end on the date of the layoff—except that you will be required to offer the same termination benefits offered to other laid-off employees. In this situation, be sure to document the legitimate reasons for eliminating this position in the event of future legal challenges.

OCCUPATIONAL SAFETY AND HEALTH ACT OF 1979

As an employer, you are no doubt concerned about keeping your workplace safe for your employees, your vendors, and your customers. The Occupational Safety and Health Act (OSH) was enacted to set certain national standards and guidelines to promote safe and healthful workplaces. The Occupational Safety and Health Administration (OSHA) administers OSH regulations. OSHA has two primary functions: to set workplace safety and health standards and to conduct inspections to ensure that employers are complying with those standards.

Virtually all businesses with employees are required by OSHA to maintain a safe workplace. In addition, OSHA has industry-specific standards that relate to the particular hazards present in that industry. States are allowed to have their own safety plans provided they are at least as protective as the federal regulations. If your business is in a state with its own plan, you must follow state laws. If your state does not have a safety plan, the federal guidelines will apply to you. For more information on applicable state laws, contact your state's labor department.

OSHA standards are divided into four major categories: general industry, construction, maritime, and agriculture. General industry requirements also apply to construction, agriculture, and maritime businesses unless the business category has its own standards on the subject.

Since laws relating to individual industries are broad and complex, we will limit our discussion to general industry requirements. You can obtain detailed information about specific industry standards directly from OSHA.

"What are my basic responsibilities under the OSHA regulations?"

All employers are charged with a general duty to maintain a safe work-place, free of hazards that are likely to cause death or serious physical harm. This means you are responsible for making your workplace safe, even if your business is not subject to industry-specific OSHA regulations. In addition, you must conspicuously post notices informing employees of their workplace safety rights.

Personal Protective Equipment. You must supply employees, at company expense, with personal equipment for protection against certain hazards. Depending on the industry and the hazards involved, this can include helmets to prevent head injury, goggles for eye protection, or respirators for potential airborne hazards.

Hazard Communication. If you manufacture, import, or work with hazardous materials, you are required to conduct an evaluation of these materials and to properly label them if they present sufficient risk under the law. You must include a material safety data sheet (MSDS) in your first shipment to a new customer. Manufacturers and users of hazardous materials must use the MSDS to train their employees to recognize and safely handle them.

Access to Medical and Exposure Records. You are obligated to grant any employee of yours access to any medical records you maintain regarding that employee, including records maintained about the employee's exposure to toxic substances.

Record Keeping and Reporting. All employers with more than ten employees (with the exception of certain low-hazard employers in industries such as retail, finance, insurance, real estate, and certain service businesses) must maintain OSHA-specified records of job-related injuries and illnesses. You can purchase effective software to facilitate your tracking and record-keeping obligations. Employers in all industries are required to report to OSHA, within eight hours of occurrence, any accident that results in a worker's death or in the hospitalization of three or more employees.

"Will OSHA come to inspect my business?"

Unless you are engaged in what OSHA considers a low-risk industry, OSHA may conduct regularly scheduled "programmed inspections" of your facility to determine whether you are compliant. If you have fewer than ten employees, you will be exempt from programmed inspections unless you have had a poor safety record in the past.

Any company may be subject to an OSHA inspection if:

- It has reported an accident involving a worker's death or the hospitalization of three or more employees.

- OSHA receives a complaint from an employee or other party. Under the law, OSHA is permitted to keep the identity of any complaining employee confidential. You are not permitted to retaliate against any employee for filing a complaint or participating in an OSHA investigation.

- OSHA perceives that there is an imminent danger that warrants an inspection.

Generally, OSHA inspectors (or, if your state has a safety plan, the state inspector) will not notify you before their visit to your facility. You have the right to demand that the inspectors obtain an inspection warrant before allowing them to enter your premises. If you don't demand a warrant, then you will be considered to have voluntarily consented to the inspection. You may accompany the inspector on the facility tour, but the inspector is permitted to speak to individual employees privately.

Better Forgotten: *"Is there a traitor in our midst?"*
After an OSHA inspection of a pharmaceutical company plant turned up several safety violations, the plant manager was so busy trying to figure out who reported the violations that triggered the inspection that he did not adequately remedy the violations. Since it is illegal to retaliate against an employee for making an OSHA complaint, this manager would have best spent his time fixing the problems and moving forward.

"What happens if OSHA finds
violations during the inspection?"

If the inspection reveals violations, OSHA will issue a citation to your company that details the violations, notifies you of the proposed penalties, and informs you of your rights to appeal the charges. You may then decide to pay the penalties and correct the violations, enter into settlement negotiations with OSHA to reduce the penalties, or file a "Notice of Contest" indicating your intention to contest the findings before the Occupational Safety and Health Review Commission. This commission is an independent agency unrelated to OSHA or the Department of Labor.

Penalties will vary according to the seriousness of the violation and whether your company has had repeat violations. If your company knew or should have known that it was committing a serious violation, or is aware that a hazardous condition exists that it has taken no steps to remedy, this is considered a "willful violation," which carries a minimum penalty of $5,000 and a maximum of $70,000. If the willful violation resulted in the death of an employee, a court can impose a more substantial fine on the company, as well as imprisonment for those responsible for the violations.

IMMIGRATION REFORM AND CONTROL ACT OF 1986

As discussed earlier in this chapter, Title VII forbids discrimination on the basis of national origin or citizenship. But while businesses in the United States are encouraged to hire a diverse workforce, they must limit their hiring to those who have the right to legally work in the United States. The Immigration Reform and Control Act (IRCA) sets out rules that employers must follow to ensure that they hire people eligible to work here, whether they be U.S. citizens or aliens authorized to work.

"What do I have to do to comply with the IRCA?"

Employers must complete and retain a Form I-9, Employment Eligibility Verification, for all employees hired after November 6, 1986. You can obtain copies of this form from the U.S. Bureau of Citizenship and Immigration Services (USCIS). Make sure you regularly check for the most current form, as regulations, guidelines, and specific requirements change. For each new employee you hire, you will need to take the following steps:

1. Ensure that your employees fill out the information at the top of Form I-9 on the first day of work. If they cannot complete the form themselves or need translation, you may provide them with assistance as long as the preparer or translator fills out the designated certification block on the form. The employer is responsible for making sure that this part of the form is completed in full. An I-9 is required only for workers you actually hire; you should not have all job candidates filling out this information. Since the form contains citizenship and national origin information, you could risk a discrimination lawsuit if you do not hire the applicant.

2. Review documents establishing the employee's *identity* and *eligibility* to work. The employee must present to you original documents from the list of documents considered acceptable by the government. The employee is required to present her documentation within three business days after beginning work. If she is unable to provide the documentation, she must present a receipt for the application for the chosen documentation within the same three-day time frame and the actual document within ninety days after beginning employment.

3. Complete Section 2 of the Form I-9 (pertaining to information about the identity and eligibility documentation presented to you). The IRCA does not mandate that you make a copy of the documentation the employee has presented, and even if you keep copies, you must still complete Section 2 of the I-9. However, copies of the documents can be useful for backup purposes. If you do make copies, attach them to the I-9.

4. Retain the Form I-9 for three years after the date the employee begins work or for one year after the termination date, whichever occurs later.

5. Make the Form I-9 available for inspection by government immigration officials upon at least three days' prior notice. For privacy reasons, do not store the I-9 form in the employee's employment file. Maintain all forms in a central location, such as a three-ring binder, so that you will have them all handy if you are audited. Administration will be easier if you keep I-9s for active employees in alphabetical order in one location, and when employees leave the organization, you move their I-9s to a binder for terminated

employees, kept in alphabetical order by month. This will make it easier for you to identify the I-9s that you can dispose of one year after termination.

The USCIS imposes financial penalties on employers that violate the provisions of the law, with strict penalties for willful violations. Engaging in a pattern or practice of hiring or continuing to employ illegal aliens, or committing fraud in connection with the immigration laws, can result in criminal penalties as well.

Worth Repeating: *"We'll wait for you!"*
A highly qualified foreign technician who did not yet have legal eligibility to work in the United States offered to work as an "unpaid intern" for a prospective employer until her work visa came through. The employer thanked her, but said it would wait instead for her to obtain legal status. It is risky and inadvisable to enter into any questionable arrangements.

"Can I specify which identification and work eligibility documents an employee must present to me?"

No. You must accept the documents given to you as long as they appear to be genuine. You cannot require certain employees to produce more documentation or make government inquiries requesting further information if the documents look valid. If the documents show obvious signs of tampering or forgery, do not accept them or your organization may be charged with knowingly employing an illegal alien. If you suspect that an employee is presenting fraudulent paperwork, you should contact an attorney to discuss a plan of action.

"What is E-Verify and do I have to use it?"

E-Verify is an Internet-based system operated by USCIS that provides an automated link to the Department of Homeland Security and Social Security Administration databases to help employers determine employment eligibility of new hires and validity of their Social Security numbers. Employers may use E-Verify only after a candidate accepts a job offer and completes the Form I-9. Participation is voluntary for most employers, but mandatory for federal contractors and subcontractors with contracts over $3,000. USCIS provides E-Verify training for employers and administers the program after employers sign a Memorandum of Understanding regarding their participation in the program. A number of states also require specified employers to use E-Verify.

"Do I need to maintain a Form I-9 for independent contractors?"

No. If you use contract employees from any source, such as a temporary agency or a food service company, that third-party company is responsible for obtaining the identity and eligibility documentation and maintaining the I-9s. Similarly, if you hire an independent consultant, you need not verify her work authorization. However, you cannot knowingly use contract labor for the purpose of circumventing the laws.

"What do I do about work authorizations that expire during the employment term?"

It is the employer's responsibility to track I-9s and to update them for reverification of employment authorization. It is critical to have some type of a tickler system to track future expiration dates. You should remind employees to renew their work authorizations at least ninety days before the expiration date.

"What should I do if I rehire a person who previously filled out an I-9?"

If you rehire the person within three years of the date of completion of the original document, you may update the I-9 instead of preparing a new one. If the employee's work authorization documented in the original I-9 has expired, you should ask for proof of an extension and then record that information on the form. Don't consider the date of expiration of authorization in making a hiring or employment decision, because this could be considered discriminatory.

8

When Bad Things Happen to Good Employers

How Do I Handle Volatile Workplace Issues?

INAPPROPRIATE OR ILLEGAL EMPLOYEE CONDUCT can create a wealth of problems for any employer. It can result in a decrease in productivity, damage to the organization's business or reputation, injuries to employees and customers, and exposure to costly legal liability. Employee misbehavior can take many different forms—from substance abuse that can create workplace hazards, to workplace violence that threatens individual safety, to improper e-mail and Internet use that can result in exposure to lawsuits and security violations. In this volatile world, all employers should be vigilant about protecting the safety and security of their employees. The potential legal exposure for failing to make reasonable investigations into the background and on-the-job activities of employees is continually on the rise. Employers must understand the warning signs of inappropriate or illegal conduct, the preventive measures to take, and what to do when employees engage in behavior that is likely to put the company or others at risk.

The increasing emphasis on security is, however, combined with mounting concern about individual privacy in all areas of our society. Every day, companies exchange information about our buying habits, track our online activities, and develop and use new surveillance technologies. The outcry from privacy advocates against the increased collection and sharing of personal data has led to heightened public awareness and laws to protect individuals. Employers also need to understand where to draw the line in checking up on the workforce. The employer that goes too far in its quest for knowledge and conducts overly intrusive investigations and monitoring runs the risk of significant legal and human resources problems that may far outweigh the benefits of any information obtained.

How does an employer handle these sensitive issues? How far can and should a business go in the investigation of the conduct of its employees? There are no clear-cut answers to these questions. Employers must carefully balance their proper business needs against the privacy rights and expectations of their employees.

This chapter discusses some of the current hot-button issues related to workforce misconduct and how to deal with them effectively and safely.

First, a rule of thumb . . .

When looking to investigate or monitor any type of employee activity, you should ask yourself these questions:

- Is the scope of the surveillance, monitoring, or investigation *reasonable*?

- Is there proper *business justification* for the surveillance, monitoring, or investigation?

- Are proper steps being taken to *protect* any employee-sensitive information uncovered during the course of the surveillance, monitoring, or investigation from disclosure to parties that do not have a need to know this information?

If you are able to answer yes to all these questions, you are less likely to encounter problems resulting from your actions down the line.

"Does it matter whether my company is a public or private employer?"

Different standards apply to public and private employers. Public employees (i.e., employees of state and local governments and their agencies, school districts, and special districts, etc.) are expressly protected by Fourth Amendment rights to privacy in the workplace, whereas private employees are not. As a general rule, public employers must always either inform workers of surveillance or monitoring or position all surveillance equipment in visible locations.

ELECTRONIC MAIL, INTERNET, AND COMPUTER USE

Computers are indispensable to today's workforce, and most of us cannot imagine life without e-mail, the Internet, and smart phones. To complicate matters, Facebook and other social networking sites play a major part in many companies' business strategies, but are also used by individual employees, often blurring the line between personal and business communications.

"Is inappropriate employee e-mail, Internet, and computer use really a serious problem?"

Potentially, it can be. Misuse of these electronic tools can create a host of legal problems for an employer. E-mail transmissions are considered "documents" and can be used against an employer in a lawsuit in the same way as any written letter or memorandum. Today, employee e-mail messages play a role in a majority of corporate lawsuits and have been presented as evidence in claims of discrimination, sexual harassment, and other illegal activities. Even when the user deletes messages, they do not just "go away": They remain in the company's electronic archives. Deleted messages can be recalled, and an improper message can come back to haunt an employer months or years after the message was first transmitted.

Similar issues arise with general computer use. Employees commonly create and store personal documents on employer-supplied hardware. Furthermore, excessive non-business-related Web surfing can impede business productivity, and improper browsing—for example, viewing pornographic material in the workplace—can lead to charges of sexual harassment or discrimination from employees who are involuntarily exposed to this material.

"What steps can I take to reduce improper e-mail, Internet, and computer use?"

You must develop and communicate a policy regarding online issues, which should apply to all employees with access to these tools. Depending on the specific business concerns and risks faced by your individual business, you may additionally consider using some form of electronic monitoring.

"Do employees have the right to privacy in their e-mail, Internet, and computer use?"

Generally, an employee sending personal e-mails in the workplace and using company-supplied Internet access does *not* have the right to privacy, nor does a right to privacy exist related to Internet use or personal files stored on a company desktop or laptop computer, or sent on a company-owned BlackBerry or other smart phone device. The electronic mail systems and computers at work are the employer's property. As an employer, you have the right to expect that employees will use these tools for proper business purposes, and you have the right to monitor employee activity for potential violations of this expectation. In addition, because e-mail messages and computer files can be used against a company as evidence in a court of law, you have the right to take steps to minimize the risk that an employee may create documentation that is discriminatory, harassing, or otherwise illegal or improper.

However, there is a limited exception to the general rule that employees have no expectation of privacy in the workplace. Under the laws of some states, if an employer is found to have created for its employees a "reasonable expectation of privacy," employees may be able to legitimately claim that employer screening violates their individual privacy rights.

"How can I protect myself from claims that I violated an employee's reasonable expectation of privacy?"

The best way to protect yourself is to directly let employees know, both verbally and in writing, that they have no right to expect privacy in any of their activities related to company e-mail, Internet, and computer use. Make it clear that all these systems are company property. Even if you do not currently conduct electronic monitoring, do not promise employees that you will not do so in the future.

"Is it advisable to monitor employee e-mail, Internet, and computer use?"

There is no single answer to this question; the decision is entirely up to the employer. There are a number of sound business reasons for monitoring. Not only are employers concerned with preventing legal exposure, but they also want to ensure that employees are working productively on company time. In addition, the issue of security is paramount.

> **Better Forgotten:** *"I received that e-mail too!"*
> During discussions about a separation agreement from a manufacturing company, an executive requested details of a benefits package via e-mail. The human resources staff member responding to the request sent out a summary of the issues that had led to the separation. The wrong document was also mistakenly sent to a wide distribution list within the company. The departing executive negotiated a significantly larger severance package because of the damage to his reputation.

Organizations wish to protect the safety of their employees and customers, and they have a strong interest in ensuring that their confidential and proprietary information is not being sent out of the company without authorization.

On the other hand, there may be some good reasons *not* to monitor employee e-mails and other computer activity, or at least to use some discretion in the scope of the monitoring undertaken. Excessive surveillance can be damaging to employee morale. Monitoring without notifying employees that they are being monitored may lead to a lack of trust in the integrity of the organization. If the organization decides to monitor employees, it is best to limit the scope of the monitoring to concentrate on proper business concerns and to notify employees of this practice on a regular basis.

In deciding whether to conduct electronic monitoring of employees, a company should first clearly establish what *purposes* it has for doing so, as well as the *extent* of the screening to be conducted.

Purpose of Screening. Not all the reasons mentioned previously will apply to every company. Make a list of the ones that apply to your organization. If you clearly understand the specific business interests that you wish to address, you will be better able to determine the scope of monitoring activities and credibly communicate to employees the reasons for the screening.

Extent of Screening. If you decide to monitor e-mail, Internet, and computer use, carefully consider the extent of the screening you plan to conduct. Electronic screening can vary widely in scope, but generally falls into the following categories:

- Random spot checks of messages

- Restriction of monitoring to use with individuals suspected of some form of wrongdoing

- Use of software that scans employee e-mails for certain keywords that are likely to signal a harassing or discriminatory message, or the transmittal of proprietary information

- Continuous surveillance of all employee computer-related activities

Limit the scope of screening to that which is necessary to achieve your legitimate business purposes. The more intrusive the monitoring, the more likely it will be to have a negative impact on employee morale and perception of the company—especially if you are unable to present a credible explanation of why the company is taking these steps. These problems could potentially outweigh the benefits of any information uncovered by the screening.

Availability of Other Protective Measures. There are various software filter packages that can help employers limit access to pornography or other sites that are inappropriate or can drain productivity. Using these filters can help employers prevent problematic Internet browsing in a less intrusive way than full-scale monitoring.

"What problems are presented by Facebook, Twitter, and other social media, and how can I prevent them?"

If you think employees are too busy at work to use Facebook, you are mistaken. A recent study found that Facebook is used significantly more often than Google. Social networking can be more than a productivity drain, however. In some instances, employees have used these tools to divulge company secrets or malign the organization. Unless the employee's job involves recruiting, marketing, public relations, or other interaction with potential clients, it is unlikely that the individual's job requires access to social networking sites. Again, it is an individual choice whether to ban social networking at work altogether or to develop a policy that advocates judicious, sensible use of these tools and that sets forth guidelines regarding an acceptable middle ground.

"How can I adopt and communicate standards regarding proper e-mail, Internet, and computer use?"

Whether or not you decide to monitor employee online activities, it is critical to develop and communicate a sound policy regarding proper use of the company electronic systems. Most employees who misuse these tools do not do so intentionally. In situations involving e-mail use, employees often do not understand that these transmissions, by their nature, are *not* private documents and that inappropriate use of the system opens both the company and the individual to potential legal exposure and personal embarrassment. Similarly, employees using Facebook and other social networking sites do not understand the public nature of their posts or the damage that a business can suffer as a result of ill-considered disclosures. You may choose to block employee access to these sites, as well as access to Web-based e-mail accounts such as Google or Yahoo. If you do not choose to do so, a well-drafted, well-communicated company policy will instill in employees the instinct to think twice before clicking the "send" button or posting inappropriate messages on Internet sites.

"What should the policy say?"

A sound e-mail, Internet, and computer use policy should contain the following elements:

- A statement that the employer's e-mail system is company property, to be used for the purposes of furthering company business.

- A statement as to whether personal e-mails and Internet use are permitted, defining any limitations on personal use of the system. This definition should be as specific as possible; for example, using a phrase such as "personal computer use should be reasonable in duration" leaves much more to interpretation than "personal computer use should be limited to twenty minutes per day."

- An explanation of the rules governing the use of the e-mail, Internet, and computer system. For example, employees should be informed that use should comply with all applicable laws and regulations and that the system should not be used to:

  1. Transmit or receive confidential or sensitive information, or information about the business

2. Transmit or receive discriminatory, harassing, sexually oriented, offensive, or other illegal or improper messages

3. Download unauthorized software onto the employer system

- A statement explaining the business reasons for conducting electronic monitoring (if you intend to do so), as well as the circumstances under which monitoring will take place.

- A statement that the employee has no expectation to privacy regarding *any* e-mails, any computer documents sent, received, or stored at the workplace, or any activities related to the Internet.

Worth Repeating: *"But I sent that message from my laptop!"*
A small medical products manufacturer had communicated a well-crafted policy indicating that the e-mail system and its contents were company property. A salesperson who resigned felt that she did not receive proper incentive payouts and subsequently raised an issue of sexual harassment, with e-mails as proof, by another employee. The company reviewed all the messages between these two employees and found that there was clearly a personal involvement between the two, with inappropriate messages written by both. These salespeople thought that since they were in the field, using their laptop computers, the correspondence could not be traced! They did not realize that all electronic communication traveled through the same company server.

"How should I communicate the policy?"

Distribute the policy regularly to all employees. Require all employees to sign an acknowledgment that they received, read, understood, and agree to abide by the rules. If you are adopting this type of policy for the first time, hold employee meetings to explain the rules and answer individual questions.

VIOLENCE IN THE WORKPLACE

No employer wants to think that there is potential for violence in its workplace, but workplace violence is a disturbing fact of life. A recent report by the Bureau of Labor Statistics indicated that workplace homicides account for 10 percent of all fatal work injuries—the second highest cause of workplace deaths. When workplace violence does strike, the results can be devastating and can include not only harm to employees and/or customers, but also negative publicity, workers compensation costs, OSHA charges, and lawsuits.

Obviously, not all incidents of employee violence can be predicted or prevented, but companies today are expected to take reasonable measures to keep informed of potential threats to the health and safety of employees and customers. Employer liability is most likely to arise when the company has failed to take the appropriate measures to:

- Screen potential employees for incidents of violence related to their past employment

- Recognize the warning signs in present employee behavior that may foreshadow potential violence and act appropriately to analyze these signs

- Take reasonable steps to prevent violent behavior from occurring

The measures taken by the employer must be balanced against employees' privacy rights. This means that companies must take care both to avoid undue intrusion into a worker's private affairs and to limit disclosure of employee confidential information to those individuals within and outside the organization with a need to know.

"What are my rights and obligations as an employer regarding preemployment screening for a history of workplace violence?"
In Chapter 1, we gave guidelines for doing a preemployment background check and discussed ways to avoid liability for negligent hiring resulting from failure to make proper inquiries into a candidate's background. These guidelines are especially applicable to situations involving workplace violence.

"Do I have any obligations if I discover during
preemployment screening that an employee
has a history of workplace violence?"

In the course of a proper background or reference check on a potential employee, you may discover a history of workplace violence and decide not to hire this individual. Once you have made this decision, refrain from any further discussion of the details of the applicant's history, either internally or externally. Since your company has not personally experienced any incidents of violent conduct, you do not have the duty or the right to further disclose any information you may have gleaned from background or reference checks. Improperly disclosing this information can lead to defamation or other legal charges. The results of the background or reference checks should simply be retained in the event that the individual reapplies for employment.

"What are the warning signs of workplace violence?"

While there is no comprehensive list of predictors that an employee or group of employees is about to turn violent, some common indicators can include:

- Explicit threats and verbal abuse

- Inappropriate displays of anger, such as screaming and slamming doors

- Continually disgruntled attitude

- Paranoid behavior

- Exhibition of wide mood swings, unexplained attendance problems, or other erratic behavior

Except in situations involving specific threats, you cannot always tell whether an employee who exhibits one or a few of these characteristics is likely to become violent. After all, everyone becomes angry sometimes, disagrees with decisions, or breaks the rules, and an occasional display of this conduct does not mean that an individual is dangerous. The more often and intensely an employee displays these behaviors and carries out these patterns, the more closely you should watch this individual.

"What do I do when an employee exhibits these warning signs?"

As uncomfortable as management may feel in confronting an employee who exhibits the warning signs, you cannot afford to ignore the problem. While there is a chance that the conduct will "go away by itself," the risk is much greater that the problem will escalate into a more dangerous situation. In situations involving ambiguous behavior (i.e., behaviors other than direct threats, which should be dealt with immediately, under company policy), observe the following guidelines:

- *Have a discussion with the employee.* The manager and/or the HR representative should sit down with the employee and discuss the company's concerns about the behavior. Keep the conversation focused on objective, observable aspects of specific behavior rather than subjective or speculative thoughts. If the employee has been having attendance problems or nodding off to sleep at the job, discuss these behaviors rather than asking, "Are you on drugs?" If the worker has been screaming and throwing objects, say, "You were screaming and throwing objects," rather than, "Are you having personal problems?" Let the employee know that this is not acceptable behavior in the workplace. Document the meeting in writing. Not only will a written record help you in the event that you have to eventually terminate this employee, but if this behavior escalates to violence at some point, it will enable you to prove that, as an employer, you recognized and attempted to deal with the problem.

- *Do not become involved in "managing" the problem.* During the course of the discussion, the employee may reveal specific problems that he or she may have that are contributing to the behavior. Rather than becoming involved in hearing the details of these problems, be prepared to refer the individual to outside help, through a formal employee assistance plan (EAP) or other outside counseling source (see Chapter 6 on benefits). If you do not have an EAP, you can find an outside counselor through your benefits or workers compensation insurance provider. Employers are not trained to diagnose and deal with the multitude of complex problems that employees may face, nor are they qualified to determine whether an individual has the potential to become dangerous. Often, employees who exhibit high-risk behavior will not admit they have a problem or even that they are doing anything wrong.

*   *Keep results of investigations confidential.* As you investigate and deal with an employee's high-risk behaviors, keep all information learned from any source completely confidential, and do not share any details with anyone who does not have a *need to know*. This will usually be limited to the EAP, a member of the human resources department, company attorneys, the employee's manager, and/or any outside counselor who is involved. Do not encourage, or take actions that encourage, gossip or speculation about the employee. When investigating an employee's behavior, limit your inquiries of coworkers to *specific facts* about the behavior rather than asking other employees their opinions on what might be causing the conduct. For example, instead of asking, "Do you think Mary is cracking under the stress here?" you might ask, "Have you observed Mary having problems with her supervisor?"

"Can I force an employee to undergo psychological testing and/or counseling as a condition of employment?"

It will be easier for you to do so if your organization has developed and communicated a clear written policy against workplace violence and included in the policy a provision mandating referral for employees who have displayed behavior that the employer has reason to believe may lead to violence.

"Can I prevent employees from bringing guns to work?"

Not always. Several states have enacted laws that prohibit employers from banning employees from bringing guns to work and leaving them in their cars. This creates serious problems for businesses and increases concerns of potential violence, especially from disgruntled employees. If you do business in a "guns at work" state, check whether your state statute has an exemption that includes your business or provides extra protections such as allowing employers to set up a secured parking area for vehicles carrying guns, or prohibiting guns in company-owned or company-leased vehicles. Create and implement a policy that makes clear that while guns may be permitted in vehicles, they are not permitted outside vehicles or inside company buildings. These policies should include the express consequences for violation, up to and including termination.

*"How can I prepare my company for the occurrence
of an incident of workplace violence?"*

No matter how vigilant you are in spotting and dealing with potential trouble situations, there is no way to eliminate all workplace violence. With the help of attorneys, trauma and security experts, and human resources professionals, develop a comprehensive safety plan for dealing with incidents of workplace violence. This plan should identify the following:

- Emergency crisis procedures that outline a chain of command for emergency response

- Counseling resources for employees, victims, and families of employees and victims

- Steps to reestablish a secure workplace and to determine when the workplace is sufficiently safe for employees to return to work

- A public relations team that will handle internal and external communications

The way you, as an organization, respond in the face of an emergency will be critical in reestablishing a sense of safety among employees and generating goodwill from the community as a whole.

SUBSTANCE ABUSE IN THE WORKPLACE

As with workplace violence, the issue of substance abuse in the workplace is an unpleasant one to face. Some employers will deny that the problem exists at their organizations; others might feel certain that they would be able to recognize the problem in employees when and if it occurred. The costs of substance abuse at work, however, are staggering and can be quite a revelation for those employers in denial about the problem.

According to the U.S. Department of Labor, almost 75 percent of illicit drug users are employed full or part time. Furthermore, the DOL estimates that between 10 and 20 percent of workers who die on the job are using alcohol or other drugs. These sobering statistics show that all employers must understand the consequences of drug and alcohol use at the workplace and take appropriate steps to prevent and eliminate the problem.

> **Worth Repeating: Meeting the Face Behind the Program**
> An employer in a service industry had a representative from the EAP
> come in to speak briefly to employees during their benefits orientation.
> During this introduction, human resources representatives left the
> room. An EAP counselor also spoke at least twice a year to a supervi-
> sors meeting, providing information on spotting and handling these
> issues. These introductions put a face and familiarity behind the pro-
> gram and made it user-friendly—not merely a policy on paper.

"How can I reduce substance abuse in the workplace?"

The rights and obligations of employers in this area are covered by individual state laws and, if applicable, the Drug Free Workplace Act of 1988
(DFWA). As a preliminary step, determine whether your business is covered by this legislation. The DFWA applies to some federal contractors
and all federal grantees. Employers who do not have or do not intend
to apply for federal contracts or grants are not subject to these drug-free
workplace requirements. In addition, even if the act applies, it does not
apply to the entire company; only employees working on the covered
grant or contract must comply.

"What are the requirements of the
Drug-Free Workplace Act of 1988?"

The law requires that covered companies take the following actions:

✓ Publish and give a policy statement to all covered employees
  informing them that the unlawful manufacture, distribution, dispen-
  sation, possession, or use of a controlled substance is prohibited in
  the workplace and specifying the actions that will be taken if an
  employee violates this policy.

✓ Establish a drug-free awareness program to make employees aware of
  (a) the dangers of drug abuse in the workplace; (b) the policy of maintaining a drug-free workplace; (c) any available drug counseling, rehabilitation, and employee assistance programs; and (d) the penalties that
  may be imposed on employees for drug abuse violations.

✓ Notify employees that as a condition of employment on a federal contract or grant, they must (a) abide by the terms of the policy statement and (b) notify the employer, within five calendar days, if they are convicted of a criminal drug violation in the workplace.

✓ Notify the contracting agency within ten days after receiving a notice that a covered employee has been convicted of a criminal drug violation in the workplace.

✓ Impose a penalty on—or require satisfactory participation in a drug abuse assistance or rehabilitation program by—any employee who is convicted of a reportable workplace drug conviction.

✓ Make an ongoing, good-faith effort to maintain a drug-free workplace by meeting the requirements of the DFWA.

Worth Repeating: *"Where do I go for the test?"*
In implementing a drug testing program, make certain the provider meets your needs. If you are a multiple-location employer you do not have to find labs in many locations. Testing companies will coordinate multiple locations for you. Verify that the locations are accessible for your candidates and employees and that the environment and service reflect your standards. You can also look for a company that will set up testing and provide results via the Internet.

"What substances are covered under the DFWA?"

The DFWA applies only to defined controlled substances. It does not cover abuse of prescription drugs or alcohol.

"What happens to employers that fail to comply with the provisions of this legislation?"

Employers that are covered under the DFWA that do not comply with its requirements are subject to certain penalties, which can range from cancellation of the grant or contract to being barred from participation in federal contracts and grant or award proceedings for up to five years.

"What steps should employers that are not governed by this law take to reduce substance abuse in the workplace?"

Employers not required to comply with the DFWA have more flexibility in handling employee substance abuse issues, but it is still advisable for all employers to take proactive steps to maintain a drug- and alcohol-free working environment. These actions can include:

✓ Writing and communicating a clear and comprehensive policy prohibiting the use of drugs and alcohol at the workplace. The document should state why the policy is being implemented, describe the behaviors that are prohibited, and explain the consequences for violating the policy.

✓ Training supervisors in the organization's drug-free workplace policy, the supervisor's specific responsibilities in implementing the policy, and ways to recognize and deal with employees who have job performance problems that may be related to alcohol or drug abuse.

✓ Educating employees about the details of the company policy and the dangers inherent in drug and alcohol abuse, as well as the types of help available for employees with substance-related problems.

✓ Providing assistance for employees with substance abuse issues, either through company-sponsored EAPs or by providing an accessible way (such as help lines) for employees to get information about treatment programs.

✓ Establishing a drug testing program. This action involves determining whether drug testing is appropriate for an individual employer and, if so, implementing a sound, legally compliant program.

"Should I conduct employee drug testing?"

Drug testing is required by law for certain positions. For example, the Department of Transportation mandates these tests for individuals who operate motorized vehicles as part of their jobs.

However, most drug testing is optional. Drug tests have traditionally been—and still are—controversial. Some employers believe that the risk of employee death and disability, and the cost to business of drug and alcohol abuse, are more important than the personal freedoms of employees. Other organizations believe that such testing is an undue intrusion on personal liberties and that the tests are not infallible. Each business must carefully weigh the pros and cons of drug testing in light of its individual circumstances and the results it wants to achieve through drug testing.

"What factors should I consider in developing a drug testing program?"

Before implementing a drug testing program, carefully evaluate your specific purposes for conducting the program. You can then develop policies and procedures that will accomplish your objectives without risking damage to employee morale from excessive intrusions on privacy. Among the factors you should consider are:

✓ *Who will be tested?* Will all employees be subject to the tests, or just employees in safety or security-sensitive positions?

✓ *When will tests be conducted?* Will the tests be limited to preemployment screening, or will they be conducted during the course of employment as well? If post-employment tests are conducted, will they be random or periodic? Will they be based on reasonable suspicion or for cause? Will they be done after an accident or after rehabilitation?

✓ *Which drugs will be tested for?* Will testing be limited to the substances for which many federal government agencies require testing (i.e., marijuana, opiates, amphetamines, cocaine, and PCP), or will testing be broader, covering alcohol and prescription substances as well?

✓ *How will tests be conducted?* A number of tests are available, including urinalysis, saliva tests, hair tests, breath alcohol tests, sweat patches, and blood tests. The laws in individual states vary as to types of testing that may or may not be performed. All federal drug testing programs must conduct tests in accordance with the Guidelines for Federal Workplace Drug Testing Programs published by the U.S. Department of Health and Human Services.

✓ *What state and federal laws apply?* Employers should completely familiarize themselves with the federal laws and all relevant state laws regarding drug testing. Before implementing any program, contact an attorney to ensure compliance with these regulations.

MONITORING OTHER WORKPLACE DISHONESTY

There may come a time when your company experiences other acts of employee dishonesty, such as theft of company property or the property of other employees, or fraud. Depending on the nature of your business, you may run a high risk of exposure to these violations of trust. How far can you go in using other techniques—such as the search of employee property or employees themselves, video surveillance, and telephone monitoring—to root out the wrongdoer or prevent these incidents from occurring in the first place? You should again take into account whether the actions you want to take are reasonable and necessary for proper business purposes and balance this consideration against the privacy expectations of your employees.

"Do I have the right to conduct searches of employees or their property?"

Generally, employers do have this right, provided they have not created a reasonable expectation of privacy for employees. The best way to ensure that employees do not have a reasonable expectation of privacy is to create policies that state that the company has the right to search their belongings or persons. The policy should also spell out the types of items or places that the employer may search, such as persons and belongings, automobiles parked on company premises, work areas, and lockers. If the company intends to conduct random searches, the policy should also state this.

"Is it advisable to conduct random searches of employees?"

In businesses where there is a high incidence of employee theft, such as retail or manufacturing industries, random searches are common. For other types of businesses, random searches may create more problems than they solve, especially in the areas of employee morale and productivity. For this reason, it is best for the companies in lower risk businesses to limit searches to situations where there is probable cause or reason to believe that they will find what they are searching for.

"What should I consider when conducting a probable-cause search?"

First, consider what factors give you reason to believe that a certain object will be found on a particular employee. Your decision should focus on factors that you have seen or heard about, or on which you have a legitimate basis to suspect an employee or group of employees. Never rely on any preconceived notions you may have about a person's race, gender, economic background, or other illegal or inappropriate criteria, or you may face charges of discrimination or harassment.

You will also need to consider where you will search. This search should focus on where you reasonably expect to find the item in question. Do not use a search to go on a "fishing expedition" to find instances of wrongdoing that you have no reason to legitimately suspect. If a television manufacturer suspects an employee of stealing from its inventory, the company may search her car, or perhaps her locker if it is large enough to hold a TV product, but it should not search her person to determine whether she is also carrying illegal drugs.

Better Forgotten: *"You found what in my locker?"*
A hotel in a mid-size city adopted a policy of random locker searches followed by termination of employees with company property in their lockers. The random search policy was developed and conducted by the human resources department. Even though the policy was communicated clearly, the resulting mistrust of HR led to serious morale problems. HR quickly developed a reputation as the place you went only if you were being fired!

"Suppose the employee objects to the search?"

When confronted with a search of their personal belongings, employees may object on the grounds that the area the employer wants to search also contains confidential items that the employer has no right to see. For example, an employer may want to search an individual's briefcase for a handgun, but the owner of the briefcase may state that it contains confidential paperwork. One way around this problem would be to give the employee the option of having the briefcase searched by an independent third party. This third party would only tell the company whether there was a handgun in the briefcase, supplying no further details of its other contents.

If the employee refuses to consent to any search, you will generally have grounds for discharging the individual. In these situations, carefully document the circumstances of the attempted search and the employee's conduct and responses. Do not attempt to physically restrain the employee or to detain the individual against his or her will. This may result in assault, harassment, or false imprisonment charges. If you believe that the employee is trying to remove something from the premises that will cause great damage to the company if removed—for example, a very expensive piece of equipment or confidential company information—it may be appropriate to detain the individual for a short period of time until law enforcement arrives. Scrupulously document your reasoning and the actions taken.

"Can I monitor regular mail addressed to the employee at the workplace?"

Even though federal law prevents the obstruction of mail delivery, according to the U.S. Postal Service, mail is "delivered" when it arrives at the premises of the employer. Therefore, employers are entitled under federal law to read personal employee mail sent to the workplace. Under the laws of some states, however, this type of activity can constitute invasion of privacy.

It is not advisable to read employee mail unless you have a sound and legitimate basis for doing so. Companies that believe they have a proper business purpose in monitoring personal mail should inform employees of their intent to monitor and should state that they have the right to review all mail, even that which is marked "personal" or "confidential." If, when reviewing an item of employee mail, you discover that it is truly personal and unrelated to anything for which you are screening, stop reading. Never disclose any personal information that you learn from monitoring personal letters.

"Can I listen in on employee telephone conversations?"

In certain situations, an employer is permitted to monitor employee telephone conversations. While telephone monitoring is generally restricted under federal and state wiretap laws, there is an exception to these laws for secret monitoring "in the ordinary course of business."

There is no clear-cut definition of what constitutes the "ordinary course of business" for monitoring purposes, and different states have different standards for determining how far an employer can go. The ordinary course of business can encompass what is reasonable for a particular job or customary in an industry. It is common and acceptable, for instance, for employers to monitor customer service providers and telemarketers to assess their performance. When courts look at whether an individual instance of monitoring is legal, they will examine the extent of the monitoring and whether it was reasonable to achieve a proper business purpose. Proper business purposes have included allowing businesses to listen in on conversations when they believed employees were disclosing confidential company information to outside parties, and permitting the monitoring of calls after an employee was heard denigrating his supervisors.

Under some state laws, it is also legal to monitor even those employee telephone conversations that do not fall under the "ordinary course of business" standard, provided the employer obtains consent. The standards concerning what constitutes "consent" vary by state. Some states deem consent to exist if only one party to the conversation agrees to the monitoring. Other states require the consent of both parties. Before you undertake any telephone monitoring, it is best to consult counsel as to the laws of the specific state in which your work site is located *and* the state of the party that the employee is calling.

Even if the monitoring you are conducting is permissible by law, this does not entitle you to listen in on all employee telephone calls. Under federal law you *must* stop monitoring a call when you determine that the nature of the call is personal. To avoid invasion of privacy claims, you must also keep confidential any personal information you discover from the call.

If you plan to conduct telephone monitoring, have a clearly stated policy informing employees that you reserve the right to listen in on telephone calls.

"Can I conduct video surveillance
of employee workplace activities?"

Yes, but you should have a legitimate reason for the surveillance, and you should limit the video monitoring to places where the activity you want to prevent or gather evidence on is likely to take place. Avoid areas where the employee can reasonably expect privacy. If you are concerned with preventing employee theft, you might use video surveillance in the warehouse or display area. For security reasons, you may want to place video cameras at exits and entryways and other high-risk areas.

Do not place cameras in break areas, bathrooms, and employee changing rooms. Some states specifically prohibit monitoring in these "private" areas, but even in states without these specific laws, this type of intrusive surveillance can lead to invasion of privacy claims and be devastating to employee morale. In addition, use video equipment that does not have sound-recording capability, or else you will be subject to the same restrictions as apply to telephone monitoring. Before investing in and installing any type of surveillance equipment, it is advisable to consult with an attorney.

"Can I give my employees a polygraph test?"

As a general rule, private employers cannot require or request that an employee take a lie detector test, and they cannot fire an individual who refuses to take a test. Use of polygraphs is covered under the Employee Polygraph Protection Act (EPPA), which limits the polygraph testing to specific circumstances. The EPPA does not apply to government employees or to private individuals hired by the federal government to engage in certain national security activities. Employers covered by the EPPA must prominently post a notice explaining employee rights under the law. Some employers desire to use preemployment polygraph tests to verify the details provided by the applicant. Under the regulations, employers cannot do preemployment polygraph testing, with the exception of security services firms or pharmaceutical manufacturers and distributors.

If you want to test employees you suspect are stealing from the company, you may test only those employees with access to the stolen property, and even then only with their consent. The EPPA also sets out guidelines and standards concerning the length of the test and the conduct of the test. Some states have passed additional laws related to employer polygraph testing. If you believe your company falls under the limited exemptions of the EPPA and you desire to test any of your employees for any reason, contact legal counsel to discuss your responsibilities under federal and applicable state laws.

CONDUCTING EMPLOYEE INVESTIGATIONS

To obtain further details about any form of employee misconduct, employers will usually need to conduct an investigation. It is critical that companies understand how to conduct effective investigations, since improper investigations expose the company to claims of discrimination, invasion of privacy, false imprisonment, and other charges. Although the details and extent of investigations will vary with the circumstances, there are certain basic rules that apply to all these actions.

"When do I need to conduct an investigation?"
In situations involving fraud or theft, the employer may need to investigate to uncover the identity of the wrongdoer or, if the identity is already known or suspected, further evidence of the illegal conduct. In other circumstances, such as allegations of harassment, discrimination, drug use, or potentially violent behavior, the investigation may stem from a complaint by another employee. Some problems can be resolved quickly and without a formal investigation. In deciding whether to conduct an investigation, consider factors such as:

- The complexity of the issues involved

- The number of employees involved in the complaint

- The level of seriousness of the reported conduct

- Whether more fact finding must be done before the company takes action

"Who should conduct the investigation?"
Again, the answer depends on the nature of the offense and the expertise of company employees. Some companies have employees in the legal, security, or human resources departments who are familiar with the proper method of conducting an investigation. If you do not have

this in-house expertise, it is advisable to hire an attorney or other independent investigator to perform the investigation or, at a minimum, consult with an attorney before proceeding.

When using an outside investigator, you may be subject to the provisions of the Fair Credit Reporting Act, which could trigger an obligation to get permission from the accused individual for the third party to conduct the investigation. Professional outside investigators can generally provide the required consent forms.

Better Forgotten: *"Did you talk to everyone?"*

A customer service representative was brought in to the human resources department and told she was being fired for making personal phone calls using a manager's telephone access code. HR had the records showing that the calls were made to the employee's home from her desk, during her shift, using the code. After the employee composed herself, she stated she had a sick relative at home and had expressed her concern to a manager, who had given her a code with permission to make the calls during work.

"How do I conduct a proper investigation?"

If the employees in question are covered by a union collective bargaining agreement, the agreement may contain specifics about how to conduct employee investigations, and it is important that employers adhere to these procedures. In general, there are three steps to any investigation:

1. Planning

2. Fact finding

3. Analysis and conclusions

"How should I plan for the investigation?"

Your goal should be to develop an objective and fair plan that is designed to gather the necessary information without violating the rights of the accused or suspected individuals. First, you will need to determine who, within or outside the company, should conduct the investigation. Assemble all relevant documentation, such as the employment files of the employees under investigation; written documents such as letters, memorandums, e-mails, expense records, or time sheets, and any company policies that pertain to the conduct involved. Speak to legal counsel and understand the relevant laws that apply to both the alleged misconduct and the investigation of the misconduct, and determine whether it is necessary or advisable to suspend the accused employee with or without pay until the investigation is resolved. Determine what other resources may be necessary, such as translators for non-English-speaking employees who will be interviewed, law enforcement for situations involving illegal activities, and public relations assistance, if the situation is likely to cause the employer negative publicity.

"Should I send the accused employee home, with pay, pending the investigation?"

If the accusation centers on a violent act or other activity that could threaten the safety of employees or customers or significantly damage the morale or effectiveness of coworkers, it is advisable to keep the accused away from the premises until the matter is resolved. It is significantly less costly to suspend an employee with pay than suffer potential threats to safety or productivity. In other circumstances, there is usually no reason the accused cannot continue to report to work until a final determination is made.

"During fact finding, who should be interviewed?"

The answer to this question will vary with the situation, but generally your investigators will interview:

- The person(s) making the complaint (if applicable)

- The person(s) accused of the misconduct

- Witnesses to incidents relevant to the misconduct

- Supervisors of the person(s) making the complaint and those accused

- Individuals the complaining party or the accused have requested be interviewed

To avoid claims of invasion of privacy, interview only those people who are involved in or may have direct knowledge of the conduct being investigated.

"How should the interviews be conducted?"

All interviews should be conducted in a private setting to ensure confidentiality and avoid embarrassment. It may be more comfortable and afford more privacy to conduct employee interviews off-premises. Inform all parties interviewed about the purpose of the investigation, the reason you are interviewing them, the seriousness of the investigation, and the importance of their full cooperation. In addition, assure them there will be no retaliation against any participant in the investigation. Often, participants in an investigation are concerned about the confidentiality of the information they provide. While you cannot assure these individuals that you will not share any information, you should inform them that all information will be kept as confidential as possible and will be disclosed only to those with a need to know.

Treat all persons interviewed in a dignified and professional way. Avoid jokes or threats, and do not provide personal opinions about the information discussed. Do not physically restrain employees or tell them that if they don't cooperate, they cannot leave the workplace. These restrictions can lead to charges of false imprisonment. It is proper, however, to make cooperation a condition of an individual's continued employment.

Ask questions that are relevant to the substance of the investigation. Do not allow the interview to deteriorate into a general discussion about problems at the company or personality issues with any of the parties involved. Focus questions on the specific behaviors and conduct that are central to the investigation, and ask open-ended rather than leading questions. For example, if investigating a sexual harassment complaint, you may want to ask, "Have you observed any tension in the department between Mr. X and Ms. Y?" rather than saying, "Do people in the department talk about Mr. X touching Ms. Y?"

Distinguish facts from speculation and focus on the facts. Limit your conversations with witnesses to what they personally know or have seen rather than what they heard through the grapevine. Conclude the interview by thanking each participant for cooperating and confirming the company's policies concerning confidentiality and nonretaliation.

Encourage witnesses and complaining parties to report any relevant information that may later occur to them, and to come forward if they witness or experience any future incidents of the conduct being investigated.

Most important, document all interviews. Take careful notes and prepare written statements summarizing each interview. These statements should include the substance of the information obtained from employees, as well as any special instructions given to them during the course of the interview. Ask participants to sign and date the summaries of their individual interviews. If the interviewed individual refuses to sign this statement, at a minimum have the interviewer sign and date it.

"What should I do after I gather the facts?"

You must analyze the facts, reach a conclusion, and take action. Often it is difficult to reach a conclusion after an investigation because the information gathered will conflict. Many investigations come down to assessing the credibility of the participants, examining the facts, and determining the motivations of the individuals. However, it is appropriate to evaluate all these factors and reach an informed conclusion to avoid employee perception that the company does nothing about complaints.

In certain situations, you may decide that the evidence presented does not allow you to reach a firm conclusion about what took place. Even so, it is important to warn the accused to avoid similar conduct in the future and to encourage the complaining party to report any further incidents.

When the investigation yields a more conclusive result, you must determine the action to be taken. This will depend on a number of factors, including whether any policies or procedures were violated, how similar situations had been handled in the past, any legal requirements for handling the situation, and whether there are special circumstances that warrant handling the matter more leniently or strictly than it might otherwise be handled. An employer's actions can encompass a wide range of options, including:

- Verbal warnings

- Written warnings

- Probation or suspension

- Demotion

- Transfer

- Termination of employment

Once you have analyzed the facts, reached a conclusion, and determined what actions to take, you should inform both the accused and the complaining party of the results of the investigation. It is neither necessary nor advisable to inform witnesses of the results and conclusion. If witnesses ask about the outcome of the investigation, tell them that the matter is confidential and thank them for their cooperation.

"Should I maintain documentation of the interview?"
The investigators should prepare a report of the investigation, summarizing the issues involved, the steps taken in the investigation, the substance of each witness interview, and the findings and actions taken. This report should also include any signed statements of participants in the process.

It is important to recognize that every document prepared that relates to the investigation may one day be admitted as evidence in a lawsuit. For this reason, all documentation should be factual and objective. In preparing your documentation, remember that your goal is to show a jury or other third party that you took the complaint seriously, responded appropriately, and did your best to reach an informed and responsible conclusion and take the necessary actions. This report will also be useful for reference if the same, or similar, misconduct occurs again in your workplace.

Termination and Discharge

How Do I Fire an Employee Legally and Humanely?

WHENEVER YOU HIRE AN EMPLOYEE, you have high hopes that you have made a good decision and that the employment relationship will be a long and mutually beneficial one. Sometimes, however, the arrangement does not work out as anticipated and you may want to end the employment relationship and hire someone more suitable for the position.

Firing an employee is never easy. Since it is difficult to tell people that they are going to lose their jobs, some employers will ignore a situation until it gets out of hand—and then suddenly and swiftly discharge the problem employee. This type of rash action can have painful consequences. Wrongful termination lawsuits are common, expensive, and time-consuming. In addition, you must consider that every time you terminate a worker, your remaining employees will be watching your actions very carefully. If you are perceived to be arbitrary, heartless, or unfair, employee morale will suffer, along with your reputation in the community as a desirable employer.

While firing in haste can create legal liability, taking the opposite approach and being afraid to terminate employees who are not working out can be just as hazardous for a business. As organizations face the challenge of developing a leaner workforce to remain competitive, it is more critical than ever to retain the flexibility to replace problem employees with those who will make positive contributions.

Do not let fear of legal action paralyze your decision making. There is no way to completely insulate your business from lawsuits; some individuals will sue whether or not they have a legitimate case. The practical goal is to minimize the risk of liability and negative employee perceptions—which you can do by developing, implementing, and consistently adhering to a system based on sound policies, guidelines, and procedures to support your terminations. This chapter will guide you in making the right termination decisions and carrying them out in a way that will decrease your potential exposure.

THE TERMINATION PROCESS

Every termination process must include the following four elements:

1. Determining whether the employee can be properly terminated

2. Ensuring that the proposed termination is adequately documented

3. Conducting the termination responsibly

4. Promptly handling follow-up matters

Never act rashly. Discipline your organization to follow these four steps *every time* you consider terminating an employee.

"Can't an employer fire and rehire people as it wishes?"
Not really. The laws concerning what constitutes wrongful discharge vary by state, but there are certain instances where termination will always be considered illegal. In addition, there are other variables that will have a bearing on whether a particular termination is appropriate, such as whether there is a written employment contract, the wording of any employment handbook or policy manual, and the prior actions and practices of the company.

"What about 'employment at will'?"
Some state laws support an "employment at will" doctrine, which maintains that both employer and employee are free to terminate the employment relationship at any time and for any reason (as long as that reason is not illegal). However, the concept of employment at will con-

tinues to be eroded in the courts, and even companies located in so-called "at will" states have incurred liability when the circumstances of the termination suggested that the fired employee was wronged in some way. It is therefore essential to adopt sound termination practices no matter where your business is located.

"What do I need to consider in determining whether I can terminate an employee?"

First, you need to determine whether your reasons for conducting the termination are proper and legal. There are many legitimate reasons why you might consider firing an employee. He may not be performing the job satisfactorily. She may have behavior or attitude problems, such as excessive absences or lateness or lack of cooperation with coworkers, which are affecting productivity and morale. The individual may have engaged in illegal or unacceptable activities such as drug use on the job or threats of violence. Or your business may simply be moving in a direction that requires that you replace an existing worker with some-one with a different skill set.

On the other hand, there are some reasons that will always be considered inappropriate and illegal. As discussed in Chapter 7, firing an employee for reasons involving discrimination related to age, sex, religion, ethnicity, or other protected-class status is against the law. It is also improper to discharge a worker in retaliation for that person's reporting a violation of an antidiscrimination, harassment, or safety law, for serving on jury duty, or to deny retirement benefits. Individual states have additional laws regarding employment terminations. You will need to be aware of the applicable laws of both the state where your company headquarters is located and the state in which the employee works.

Once you have determined that your reasons for firing are appropriate, you must consider whether there are additional factors that will complicate the termination process. Each time you conduct a termination, ask yourself the following questions:

* Can this termination reasonably be interpreted as being *discriminatory* or *retaliatory*? In other words, you may want to fire an individual for poor performance, but if this same individual recently complained of an instance of sexual harassment in her department, it is likely that she will claim that she was terminated because of her complaint.

- Did you make *verbal promises* to the employee about her employment status or term of employment? It is never advisable to make representations such as, "You will have a job here as long as we are profitable" or "You will only be fired for good reasons."

- Is there an *employment agreement* between the company and the employee? If so, you will need to carefully review the agreement to ensure that the termination does not violate the company's contractual obligations. Many employment agreements spell out the term of employment, as well as reasons and procedures for discharge, and provide for severance payments or other penalties if the contract is terminated.

If you answer yes to any of the questions above, it is still possible to terminate an individual for a legitimate cause, but you will have to take further steps to set the right legal groundwork to support your actions. Consult an attorney to help you with this process.

If your reasons for the firing are proper and you have answered no to all the previous questions, you still have more work ahead of you before you can discharge the employee. There are very few instances in which you can safely terminate an employee on the spot. These include extreme situations involving violence or threats to harm others; fraud, significant dishonesty, or other criminal activity; possession or use of alcohol or drugs in the workplace; and unauthorized disclosure of trade secrets. In other circumstances that do not involve immediate threats to the company, its employees, or its customers, you will need to take the time to ensure that you set the stage for the termination through adequate documentation and communication.

"How do I ensure that the proposed termination is satisfactorily documented?"

In Chapter 3, we discussed the progressive disciplinary system and how to document performance and behavioral problems. It is critical that before conducting a termination, you make sure there is adequate documentation of the reasons for termination and of the fact that the performance issues have been communicated to the employee. Because you never know who will file a suit for wrongful termination, it is prudent to look at every employee termination as a potential lawsuit and have the data available for each discharge to defend yourself and demonstrate that you acted responsibly and within the law.

When you are considering a termination, review the individual's employment file to ascertain whether the following documentation is in place:

- Records that clearly note and explain incidents of unacceptable performance or conduct and that show that the employee was notified of these deficiencies

- Documentation reflecting that the employee was notified that his or her employment may be terminated if improvements did not occur

- Documentation that the employee was offered a reasonable opportunity within a reasonable time frame to make the necessary improvements, and that the improvements did not occur

If any of these elements are missing from the file, it is better to hold off on the termination until the actions can be documented properly. While the prospect of postponing a termination can be inconvenient, the costs of acting too hastily are potentially far more serious.

"How do I prepare for and conduct the actual termination?"

As a guiding principle, keep in mind that no matter what the specific circumstances, it is important to treat the departing employee in a dignified manner at all times during and after the discharge. Employees who feel humiliated during the process are more likely to spread damaging comments to others or take legal action than those who believe they were respected. The way you conduct a termination sends a message to all employees—let that message be that you are a responsible and concerned employer.

- *Scheduling the termination meeting.* Schedule the meeting when the employee will be at work and not on leave or vacation. Friday afternoon is the worst time to fire. Sending the employee home for the weekend fresh from the shock of losing a job is heartless, and it does not give the company time to assess and control the situation if there is negative fallout among other employees. Conducting the termination earlier in the week, at the end of the day, gives the employee time to emotionally prepare for the weekend ahead and allows the individual to leave the office without having to give embarrassing explanations to colleagues.

Plan to have the meeting in a quiet and private place, such as a supervisor's or human resources representative's office. If no private office is available, use a conference room. Have two people present for the termination discussion, usually the individual's manager and either a human resources professional or another manager who has had contact with the employee. This way you will have a witness if the employee later disputes what was said or done at the meeting.

Limit information concerning the discharge to those employees with a need to know, such as discharged employees' managers, functional area heads, and the appropriate legal and human resources representatives. Make sure these individuals understand the need to keep the matter totally confidential. If the affected employee feels he was the last to know about his termination, this will only elevate resentment.

Better Forgotten: *"Just this one last business trip . . ."*
A national consulting firm routinely flew managers from remote locations to corporate headquarters asking them to "attend a meeting," only to deliver news of their termination upon their arrival. Don't have employees take a long trip home alone after being let go. Travel to the employee's location when you need to deliver bad news.

- *Conducting the termination interview.* How you open the meeting will set the tone for everything that follows. Although you may be anxious about the unpleasant task before you, you must be clear, courteous, and direct. Do not engage in extraneous conversation, but state the fact that you are terminating the individual's employment and offer the reasons for your decision.

  It is common that even when you state the purpose of the meeting directly, employees may not fully understand that they are being fired. Give them a chance for the message to sink in, and be sure they comprehend the action you are taking. You will want to give people the chance to ask questions, but do not let the session become argumentative or allow an employee to revisit the details that led to the termination. Gently explain that the decision you have made is final, and move on to the rest of your agenda.

Different people react to bad news in different ways. Some may cry; others may get angry or defensive; some may say nothing or show no emotion. Allow emotional workers to regain their composure before moving on. Do not respond to anger by getting angry yourself. It is your role to stay in control of the meeting.

You will then want to explain about COBRA and other benefits (see the next section on post-termination) that are available to assist the employee in transition to new employment. Give the employee a written description of these benefits or say that details will be mailed in the near future. Provide the name of the proper person to contact if there are questions about transition benefits. Collect any company property, such as security ID cards, laptops, cell phones and smart phones, company credit cards, and file cabinet or office keys. Finally, document the termination meeting, including the date, time, attendees at the meeting, and major points discussed, and place a copy of the documentation in the individual's employment file.

- *Collecting personal belongings and leaving the premises.* After the meeting, allow the employee to return to his work space to gather personal belongings and any additional company property to be returned. Again, permitting the individual to retain his dignity is key. While it is usually advisable for terminated employees to leave company premises as soon as possible, this is not necessary in all situations. If there is no valid security concern, do not add insult to injury by sending them back to their desks accompanied by uniformed security guards or escorting them off the premises. Use alternative methods of addressing security issues, if available, such as deleting employee access codes to the company's computer systems, remotely, while the termination meeting is taking place.

Worth Repeating: Let the Boss Know

A mid-size company made it common practice to let the president know in advance of termination actions at all levels. This way, when and if the terminated employee contacted the president, he was not blindsided and could respond based on the facts.

"What if the employee requests to resign instead of being fired?"
Occasionally, an employee may feel that it is less of an ego blow to resign than to have the employment file reflect a termination. There is no reason not to agree to this request. When you agree to a resignation in lieu of a termination, do not attempt to challenge the individual's collecting unemployment benefits. The unemployment agency will view this type of resignation as a discharge and almost always allow the worker to collect.

POST-TERMINATION COMPENSATION AND BENEFITS

When you terminate an individual's employment, there are certain compensation and benefits that you must offer and others that are optional. Before the actual discharge meeting, make a list of the required and optional items you will provide and review them with the employee during the termination meeting.

*"What post-termination compensation and benefits
am I required to offer to discharged employees?"*

- *Final paycheck.* No matter what the circumstances of the termination, you are obligated to pay the employee for time worked through the date of discharge. State law varies as to when the final check must be delivered; understand your obligations before acting. You are not permitted to "offset" amounts that the employee owes you against wage or vacation time payment. For instance, if the final paycheck amount is $500, but you claim that the employee owes you $100 for failing to return a company-provided cell phone, you cannot deduct $100 from the paycheck or withhold pay until the phone is returned. All such matters must be settled separate and apart from the payment of wages.

- *Vacation pay.* Most state laws do not require that you compensate employees for earned but unused vacation time upon termination of employment, but many states mandate that if an employer takes or omits to take certain defined actions, it will be required to pay unused vacation time. In addition, if you have a policy or practice of making these payments, you will be required to do so on a consistent basis. Any vacation pay due the terminated employee should be included in the final paycheck.

- *Stock option, 401(k), pension, and non–health insurance benefits.* If the employee has vested stock options, 401(k) or other retirement savings, or pension benefits, provide instructions for continued participation in the plan (if allowed under the plan) or for distribution of funds. If the company's life insurance or other non–health-related insurance plans offer participants the option to convert to individual coverage, inform the individual of this feature.

- *Continuation of health insurance coverage (COBRA).* The Consolidated Omnibus Budget Reconciliation Act (COBRA) requires employers with twenty or more employees (with the exception of plans provided by the federal government and certain church-related organizations) to provide the opportunity for continued health insurance coverage for employees who lose their coverage due to a "qualifying event" such as termination of employment. Generally, you must provide the same level of benefit to any employee, spouse, or dependent who was covered on the date of termination. The period of coverage continuation is usually eighteen months, but it may be extended up to thirty-six months in certain disability situations. Employees elect to continue the coverage at their own expense, at a rate no greater than 102 percent of the cost of the premium.

    COBRA provides certain specified notification and action requirements, as follows:

Key Event	Time Frame
Company must notify plan administrator of a "qualifying event"	Within 30 days of termination or other "qualifying event"
Plan administrator must notify individual of rights under COBRA and period for electing to participate	Within 14 days after notification to plan administrator (described above)
Individual must notify company of his or her election to participation under COBRA	Within 60 days after receiving notice from plan administrator (described above)
Participating individual must pay initial premium	Within 45 days of electing coverage

If you have questions about COBRA requirements, your company's health plan administrator is a good place to start. The Department of Labor also makes available comprehensive employer compliance information. In addition to COBRA, many states have insurance continuation laws that provide additional or extended rights or benefits to terminated employees, or so called "mini-COBRA" laws, that extend benefits to terminated employees of companies too small to be covered under federal law.

Better Forgotten: *"We'll only fire some thieves!"*
A small products manufacturer had a policy stating that all employees caught taking company property would be automatically terminated. Yet when it conducted random locker inspections and found stolen property, it fired only those workers that the plant manager disliked. One of the terminated workers filed a discrimination complaint against the company. Apply your discipline and termination policies consistently.

"What types of optional post-termination compensation and benefits might I consider offering?"

* *Severance pay.* Severance pay is an amount of compensation, in addition to money owed for time worked, that is paid to the terminated employee. Severance serves both as a gesture of goodwill and to help tide workers over until they obtain new employment. An employer generally has no legal obligation to pay severance, and the amount you pay will usually be totally within the discretion of the organization. Some companies have structured severance policies that clearly spell out the conditions under which discharged employees are entitled to severance and the amounts they will get. Most businesses prefer to handle severance on a case-by-case basis without locking themselves into a formula that they might not always want to apply. Severance payments will either be "mitigated" or "unmitigated." Mitigated severance cuts off if the employee finds a new job within the severance period; unmitigated severance is payable whether or not the employee becomes employed while severance is being paid.

- *Outplacement.* Several types of outplacement arrangements are available to help the fired worker accept the loss of a job, acquire job search skills, and move on to new employment. These services can range from half-day workshops on resume preparation and interview techniques, to expensive senior executive programs providing private offices and administrative support. Providing outplacement not only eases an employer's guilt over a discharge, but can also demonstrate to employees that the company cares. Good outplacement counseling can help to diffuse employee anger and redirect energies toward planning for the future. The quality and cost of outplacement services vary widely. Before retaining the services of an outplacement professional, ask for details on the program and check references.

  You cannot force anyone to participate in an outplacement program. Often workers will say they don't need any outplacement assistance, requesting instead that you pay them directly the money you otherwise would have spent on the program as part of their severance package. It is best not to agree to this request, because direct payment will not serve the purpose of diffusing anger or focusing attention on new employment. Explain gently but firmly that the outplacement is being offered not as compensation, but as a benefit to encourage success in the job search process.

- *Other compensation and benefits.* You can create other features of a severance package tailored to a specific situation. You may offer an executive with a company car the opportunity to continue using the vehicle for a designated period of time until she purchases a new one. Or you might forgive an employee loan or allow a manager to keep his laptop computer or other equipment. If you can accommodate a person within reason, you can go far toward easing a difficult situation.

"Am I free to pick and choose what optional benefits I will offer individual terminated employees?"

Yes, as a general rule you are—provided you do not create a situation where employees can claim they are entitled to certain separation benefits that would normally be considered optional. If your handbook has a written severance policy that states, for example, that employees will be paid severance of two weeks for every year worked, you will be obligated to abide by the policy for all terminated employees. Similarly, if you have a signed employment contract with a stated severance provision, you are bound to the terms of the agreement. Even if you have no employment contracts or written severance policies or procedures, you may be obligated to provide certain severance benefits and payments if the company has a history of providing severance to employees who were discharged under similar circumstances.

When you are deciding what optional severance benefits to offer in a given situation, be fair and rational in your determinations, and do not discriminate among certain classes of employees. For example, a practice of offering larger severance payments to men than to women will likely get you into trouble.

"Are all terminated workers entitled to unemployment benefits?"

No, they are not. Although the decision whether to award unemployment insurance to a given employee is up to the state and not the company, most states do not allow employees fired for serious cause or misconduct to collect benefits. The conduct that would disqualify a person from receiving unemployment benefits generally needs to be intentional and seriously injurious to the employer, its employees, or its customers. Sexual harassment, on-the-job drug use, and theft are, as a rule, offenses serious enough to prevent a worker from collecting unemployment. Merely having a difficult personality, being a sloppy worker, or not being skilled enough to perform a job are not sufficient justifications to deny someone unemployment benefits.

Even an employee who quits voluntarily may be entitled to unemployment benefits if he had good cause for resigning. "Good cause" means that the worker would have suffered some compelling harm or injury if he continued on the job. Quitting a job because of serious company safety violations or because the organization asked the employee to do something illegal are examples of good cause. Workers who quit in lieu of being fired usually will not be denied unemployment compensation.

"Should I contest a terminated employee's application for unemployment insurance?"

If the employee was not terminated for misconduct sufficient to justify the withholding of unemployment benefits, you should not contest the claim. You have no grounds to do so, and your baseless opposition to the claim will reflect poorly on you. Even if you terminated the employee for serious misconduct and you have grounds to contest the claim, you may want to think twice before doing so. Although each unemployment claim you pay may have an impact on your company's insurance rates, it costs money and manager time to oppose a claim, and you will be sure to engender the animosity of the terminated worker. Sometimes, this animosity is great enough to lead the worker to file a wrongful termination lawsuit when he had not previously planned to do so. Before you decide to oppose any claim, carefully analyze your reasoning, the risks involved, and your anticipated benefits.

If you decide to contest a claim, you have the burden of proving that the employee is not entitled to unemployment benefits. The state unemployment office will request certain information in writing, and it is important that you adhere to any deadlines established by the agency. You may be asked to appear at an administrative hearing to discuss the case.

Better Forgotten: *"Are you talking about me?"*
A senior HR executive and a division vice president were exchanging e-mails about the termination process for the vice president's assistant, forgetting that the assistant was able to view her boss's inbox. Not only is it inadvisable to discuss confidential matters via e-mail, but you should also be mindful of individuals who might have access to these communications.

What is a "waiver" or "release," and should I get discharged employees to sign one?

A waiver or release is a legal document in which the employee agrees not to sue the company over matters taking place during the course of employment. While you need not obtain a release from every terminated worker, it is helpful to request one in situations where you believe the employee is likely to file a wrongful discharge claim. A valid release in an individual's employment file can save you many headaches down the road.

For a release to be valid, it must conform to specific criteria. As the document has significant legal ramifications, ask an attorney to prepare it. In general, all waivers must:

1. *Provide an additional benefit to the employee.* The employee signing the waiver must receive in exchange a benefit to which she would not ordinarily be entitled. This could be additional severance, outplacement, or other optional payments or benefits. It is not sufficient to offer benefits detailed in the company's standard severance policy, nor can you withhold vacation pay, 401(k) plan funds, or any other items already due to the employee in order to obtain a release.

2. *Be voluntary on the part of the employee.* You cannot threaten, force, or coerce an individual to sign a release of claims. Give the employee a reasonable amount of time to review (or have an attorney review) and sign the release document. Do not make the waiver language unduly complicated or you risk employees arguing later that the release was not voluntary because they did not understand it.

3. *Afford legally required protection to older workers.* The Older Workers Benefit Protection Act (OWBPA) places certain additional requirements on employers when they obtain releases from workers age forty or older. Under this law, the release document provided to the employee must contain language that specifically:
    *   References the Age Discrimination in Employment Act and gives the employee up to twenty-one days to review and consider the document (forty-five days in situations involving a group termination).
    *   Advises the employee to consult with an attorney regarding the document.
    *   Allows the employee to revoke the release within seven days after signing.
    In situations involving workers covered by the OWBPA, it is appropriate to withhold the payment of additional benefits until the revocation period has expired. However, do not hold up benefits or payments that are required to be paid beforehand.

4. *Preserve the right of the employee to file a charge with the EEOC.* Release documents that specify that the employee is waiving his rights to file a charge, testify, assist, or cooperate with the EEOC are unenforce-

able. The release can state, however, that if the employee files a charge with the EEOC or other administrative action, he agrees to forgo the right to collect monetary damages.

5. *Not require that the employee waive future damages.* The release covers claims arising up to the date of signature. You cannot ask the employee to waive damages that arise after the agreement is signed.

OTHER POST-TERMINATION MATTERS

"What do I tell remaining employees about a coworker's termination?"

After terminating a worker, it is good practice to call together the employees in the affected employee's workgroup or department and make a simple announcement, such as, "As of this afternoon, John is no longer employed by the company. His duties will be split between Mary and Jim until we find a replacement." To avoid liability for defamation, avoid going into details about the reasons for termination or any of the circumstances surrounding the discharge.

Sometimes employees will seem especially upset or distracted after a coworker is fired. Understand that they are probably wondering whether they will be the next to go. You can help the situation by taking care to acknowledge good performance, especially in the wake of the termination. Let employees know that their work is valued.

"Are there steps I should take to protect company confidential information when an employee leaves?"

If your employees signed a confidentiality agreement at the commencement of their employment, you will want to remind them upon termination that their obligation not to disclose or improperly use trade secrets or other proprietary company information extends beyond the term of employment. In addition to the other termination paperwork provided to workers, you should also include, and ask employees to sign, a document that states that they understand their obligations under the confidentiality agreement and that they agree not to violate the contract. If the employee refuses to sign this document, send a letter explaining that the individual is bound to maintain confidentiality and that the company will prosecute violations.

"Is it appropriate to provide references for terminated employees?"

This decision is entirely up to you. Often a discharged employee will request that the employer provide references to potential new employers. Deciding whether to give a reference is confusing to many organizations, mostly because of the fear of defamation lawsuits. As a result, many organizations adopt policies that confine reference information to the position held and dates of employment—so-called neutral or "name, rank, and serial number" references.

It's true that when you give a negative reference, you run the risk of exposure to defamation, invasion of privacy, or discrimination lawsuits by former employees. However, there are often good reasons to provide more comprehensive references. If an employee is discharged for reasons other than poor performance or unacceptable conduct— such as lack of work or the company's need for a different skill set— failure to pass along positive information may unfairly penalize good workers. In addition, just as your company wants to learn as much as possible about a prospective worker before extending an offer, other employers want to gain knowledge as well.

Increasingly, courts are recognizing that employers have a legitimate need to exchange performance-related information and are protecting companies that opt to provide more detailed employment references, as long as employers provide information that is *job-related, based on reasonable evidence*, and *without malice*. If you do decide to give more detailed references, follow these guidelines:

- *Obtain a release form.* Provide a reference release form for employees to sign upon leaving the organization, releasing you from any liability for responding truthfully to any questions asked during the course of giving references. Tell departing employees that without a signed release, the organization will provide "neutral" references only.

- *Establish a point of contact.* Assign a point of contact within the organization responsible for handling all reference inquiries. Instruct employees not to provide any information, but to direct all reference calls or letters to this individual. Make sure the individual designated as the point of contact is properly trained as to the organization's reference policy, as well as the do's and don'ts of providing reference information.

- *Provide only accurate and verifiable information.* An employee cannot win a defamation suit unless the reference provides intentionally false information. Provide only honest opinions, and express opinions as opinions rather than statements of fact. Do not respond with malice. Limit the information given to the employee's job-related performance. Do not divulge gossip or information that might invade the former employee's privacy, such as information about an individual's medical condition, political beliefs, or religious practices. Do not provide unsolicited information; address only the specific questions asked.

- *Give references to proper parties only.* Verify the identity of the person requesting the reference. Make sure that the person is an appropriate individual to be receiving the information and that the former employee knows that her references are being checked. If in doubt about the identity of the person requesting the reference, ask for the request in writing. Do not give out any information to parties unless they have a legitimate need to know (e.g., an employee or agent of a prospective employer, a job placement firm, etc.).

"Do I have any obligation to pass on negative information in a reference?"

In general, you are not required to do so. If you fire a worker for poor performance or unacceptable conduct, the employee will probably not request that you provide references or sign a reference release, and you are well within your rights to give a simple neutral reference. However, if the reasons for termination involved fraud, theft, violence, or some other form of illegal or egregious behavior, you could be held liable for failure to disclose this information to a future employer when called for a reference—even if your company policy does not allow detailed references. In these situations, consult with an attorney before providing an employment reference.

"Can I now expect terminations to go more smoothly in the future?"

Terminations are not pleasant, but they are a necessary part of operating a successful organization. As long as you remember that they are business decisions, not personal decisions, and if you follow consistent guidelines, then the termination process will be less painful for everyone involved.

10

Workforce Reorganizations

How Do I Manage Workforce Size in a Changing Business Climate?

IN TODAY'S EVER-CHANGING BUSINESS ENVIRONMENT, companies need more than ever to be able to remain nimble to satisfy the demands of the marketplace. New market trends require some organizations to add products or services to existing offerings, or even completely change the nature or scope of their businesses. Other companies choose to grow by acquisition and are faced with the challenges of integrating two or more companies in a short period of time. And unfortunately, there are companies that experience a downturn in their fortunes and need to find ways to cut expenses in order to survive.

Though these situations may be quite different in nature, all have a common thread: These corporate changes will usually cause a business to rethink the organization and structure of its current workforce. Companies undergoing these changes will ask themselves questions such as, "Do I have too few or too many workers?" or "Do we have the right people with the right skill sets to get where we want to go, or do we need to make changes?" Companies involved in recent mergers and acquisitions are traditionally faced with too many people for available positions in the new organization. And those with fiscal woes or urgent pressures to increase profits will often look to reducing head count as a solution.

Layoffs. Downsizing. Restructuring. Reductions in force. Reorganization. Terminations. No matter what the term used or the reason behind the action, layoffs are, by their nature, unpleasant for all involved. It is therefore tempting to move through the process as quickly as possible in an attempt to get the bad news over with and proceed with business. However, many organizations learn too late that an inadvisable or hastily conducted reduction in force results in costs that far outweigh the benefits obtained—including a sharp drop-off in productivity, risk-averse decision making, increased legal liability, low employee trust and commitment, bad publicity, and a negative reputation in the community. Before implementing a major reduction in force or reorganization that will result in terminations, instead of giving into reflexive, short-term-only decision making, it is far wiser to adopt a strategic approach that will best position the organization to meet its objectives, minimize legal liability, and increase the chances that, going forward, the company will continue to be perceived as a responsible employer.

ACQUISITIONS AND MERGERS

"How should I make staffing decisions in an acquisition or merger situation?"

An acquisition or merger tends to be an exciting event for the surviving organization. Overnight, the enterprise has increased in size and is poised to become a more formidable competitor in its existing business or to enter an entirely new area of the market. For individual employees, however, the outlook is more uncertain. What are the plans for the new company? Is there a place for me? If I am terminated, will I get any severance or other assistance? The anxiety is generally heightened for the employees of the acquired or merged organization, who may believe (often justifiably) that if there are cuts to be made, they are more likely than their counterparts at the acquiring company to be designated for termination.

Companies almost always make acquisitions thinking they can create strategic efficiencies, which will usually include streamlining the workforce of the new, combined entity. Even in the best-case scenarios, there are likely to be redundancies—or situations where there is a person from each company presently in a particular job function, but room for only one person in that job function in the merged business. How the company handles these redundancies will chart the shape of the business and create an early impression concerning the corporate character of the new entity.

The acquiring company should begin planning the shape of the post-acquisition workforce long before the transaction is consummated. Develop a blueprint of the combined organizational structure, identifying both duplications and gaps in talent. Identify key employees or positions in both entities that will be essential to ongoing success, as well as those that are needed for a shorter transitional period. Devise a retention incentive program to discourage defection, which usually involves offering cash incentives, or "stay bonuses," to appropriate individuals. Where duplications or excess personnel are identified, create a plan and timetable for making the terminations, and identify the severance, benefits, and other assistance you will make available to affected workers.

Deciding which employees will stay and which will go is one of the most strategically and emotionally challenging parts of the merger/acquisition process. Too often, when redundancies exist, the acquiring company automatically chooses its own employee over the one from the acquired entity. After all, it is human nature to see the merger situation as "us" vs. "them" and to opt for the known over the unknown. Don't make this mistake. Instead, think of the situation as the chance to upgrade your workforce and to choose the best employee for each available position. Moreover, if your process is perceived as fair by both sides, you will better establish the trust and commitment necessary to build a successful culture for the new, combined enterprise.

For each position where you are choosing between two or more people, treat the decision the same way as if you were choosing among the candidates to fill a new position:

- Review the personnel files of each employee to determine experience, performance, and other relevant factors.

- Speak with each employee's manager and peers to gain perspective on the individual's strengths, weaknesses, and potential for growth.

- Interview the employee, also paying attention to the individual's willingness and ability to participate in the desired corporate culture.

- If possible, retain the services of a third-party consultant who can provide an unbiased assessment using consistent criteria.

ECONOMIC CHALLENGES

Downsizing offers an immediate reduction in payroll costs and thus the opportunity to quickly impact the bottom line and appease investors. Reducing head count is not the only alternative for reducing costs, nor is it the best response in every situation. Before planning and implementing a layoff, it is important to assess the options to determine whether a layoff is right for your business.

"How do I determine whether a layoff is the right solution for my company?"

You will need both to look at your options to see whether another solution may be preferable to downsizing and to conduct an honest appraisal of whether your business can in fact absorb a reduction in force without serious adverse consequences.

Assessing Your Options. Many innovative companies lose their creativity when it comes to considering their options. Management often assumes that a reduction in head count is the only workable solution, when in fact a detailed examination of corporate spending across the company may reveal other viable ways to cut costs. These solutions may include:

- Decreased spending in other areas of the business, such as freezes on purchases of new equipment, limitations on the use of outside contractors, or restrictions on business travel expenses. Often employees can be the best sources of identifying corporate waste and suggesting ways to save money. Give employees the assignment or challenge to come up with cost savings and revenue-enhancement concepts

- Streamlined work processes, which can save a business time and money and ultimately increase productivity.

- Available federal, state, or local programs or funding to assist struggling employers.

- Early retirement or voluntary separation programs, which offer incentives to certain employees to leave the organization voluntarily.

- Other personnel-related measures, such as reduction of hours, temporary shutdowns, offsite work or flexible hours, restrictions on overtime, leave without pay, transferring and retraining employees, hiring freezes.

Can You Really Afford to Downsize? As we mentioned above, a layoff can cost a company significantly more than it saves. In addition to the indirect costs, such as decreased morale and employee security and the increased risk of litigation, there will be additional direct costs. Make sure your cost analysis accounts for potential increases in your organization's unemployment tax rate, expenses connected with retraining, and severance and outplacement costs.

Take a realistic look at whether your business can adequately absorb the planned cutbacks without causing a significant drop-off in productivity. Will there be enough people remaining to adequately perform the tasks at hand? Will these workers have the skills and training to absorb the responsibilities of departing employees? Staff reductions without a significant productivity increase from remaining employees are likely to lead to a decline in customer service and quality that not only may inhibit future growth, but also may damage the reputation of the organization.

"How do I go about conducting the downsizing?"

Whether your need to conduct layoffs arises from a merger or acquisition, challenging economic times, or any other circumstances, it is critical that you carefully plan and implement your layoff to comply with applicable federal and state laws, minimize adverse employee reactions, and reinforce company strategy going forward. There are three stages to effective downsizing:

1. Planning

2. Implementation

3. Support of remaining employees

Handle all steps with care and forethought to achieve maximum results.

PLANNING THE LAYOFF

"What do I need to consider when planning a reduction in force?"

First and foremost, put the layoff in its proper perspective. If you have done the necessary analysis in deciding that you need a reduction in force to begin with, you should be looking at the reduction and everything that flows from it as an essential, long-term strategy rather than a crisis-management situation. Instead of creating "head count targets," develop a forward-looking vision of your company and a restructuring plan that will further this vision. Are there certain areas of your business that are booming and others that are dying? Are you looking to move into new areas of growth? Cutting staff across the board will do nothing to speed your progress and will probably hinder you in reaching your goals, but a focused approach to determining exactly who you can spare and who you must keep can help your company emerge a stronger business force.

- *Create the action plan.* Develop a written plan that includes the business rationale and objectives for the downsizing. This plan will serve as a reference point in determining the nature and scope of the staff reduction. It will also help protect the company in the event of future legal challenge by demonstrating that your actions were reasonable and fair. The plan does not have to be elaborate, but can be a brief document, outline, or summary of meeting notes. Identify those people who will be making the decisions about the layoffs. In most situations it is helpful to involve a cross-functional team, which may include representatives from affected business areas, human resources, and the legal department. Because layoffs have so many potential legal ramifications, involve an outside attorney or other experienced professional if you lack the in-house knowledge.

- *Look for any contractual restrictions.* Some employee handbooks contain layoff policies that detail the procedures under which layoffs will take place, as well as severance benefits payable to laid-off workers. Or you may have employment contracts or collective bargaining agreements that will mandate certain actions. If your company has written layoff policies and procedures or employment or union contracts, you will have to follow them carefully when conducting your downsizing. Even if you do not have written policies, if you have offered workers severance compensation in the past when they were fired for financial or other reasons not related to their performance, you will risk litigation if you do not offer downsized workers similar compensation. If you are cutting jobs in a merger situation, be sure to do a thorough search regarding severance contracts the acquired company may have with its employees. As the acquiring company, you will be bound by contracts entered into by the business you purchased. Absent severance agreements, you will likely still be bound by the acquired company's severance policy when you release its employees.

- *Decide which jobs and functions will be reduced.* Sometimes layoffs will occur only at specific sites or in specific job categories or functional areas. Other times you may choose to reduce head count across the business as a whole. Either way, your plan should focus on positions, not the individuals in the jobs. Detail the areas that will be affected by the action, as well as who in each area will make and review termination decisions. If your plan involves eliminating certain departments or positions, you will not have to decide which individuals to terminate, as all employees holding the positions to be eliminated will be terminated. If, on the other hand, you are not going to eliminate positions entirely, but want to reduce the number of people in these positions and consolidate the work, you will have to develop criteria to determine which employees in similar job categories will be fired.

Better Forgotten: *"What happened to that budget line?"*
An international sales company thought it was doing an excellent job of keeping secret its plans to eliminate its Latin American marketing group. But when it distributed its budget reports to help managers with the coming year's budgeting process, line items showing salaries and expenses for these employees had been eliminated! This is no way to inform employees about your plans. Check all paperwork and reports you distribute in times of change to make sure you are not inadvertently leaking information.

- *Establish criteria for determining employees to be downsized.* Make your criteria as clear and objective as possible. Examples of objective criteria are factors such as skills, performance, and seniority. Try not to use subjective factors such as motivation or commitment to the company. Objective criteria are more easily measured and less ambiguous, and thus easier to apply uniformly and defend in a future lawsuit. Once you have established the criteria, use them consistently in your termination decisions. Do not make exceptions for sentimental or arbitrary reasons. Document the criteria you used and how the results you achieved reflect your criteria.

- *Analyze the proposed reductions.* Once you have a list of proposed staff reductions, analyze it to ensure that the group does not include a disproportionate number of members of any protected class (minorities, females, older workers, etc.). You must conduct this review *after* you determine the initial group of employees under your set criteria. You will risk discrimination lawsuits if managers and others in the decision process use employee demographic data during the selection.

  The demographic balance of laid-off workers should reflect the general demographic population of the organization as a whole. If before the reduction in force, women made up 50 percent of your managers but the restructuring would reduce that number to 30 percent, the resulting imbalance could lead to future discrimination claims that you may have difficulty defending. If you find that your affected population is skewed in any way, you may wish to make adjustments to your criteria to achieve a more equitable result. Make sure in this situation that you are adjusting your measurable criteria, *not* making exceptions for individuals based upon their membership in a particular class. In circumstances where it is inappropriate to adjust your criteria and there exists an unbalanced result, reexamine your decision process to be certain there are legitimate, nondiscriminatory reasons for your selections and that the documentation reflects these reasons. You should be prepared to defend the layoff decision for *every* affected employee. Having an attorney review your proposed plan will help to head off any potential problems.

  Your termination list may include individuals you believe are likely to sue for discrimination or retaliation, particularly workers who have filed a claim or grievance in the past, are on medical or maternity leave, are close to vesting in a retirement or benefit plan, or have litigious personalities to begin with. Again, do not make exceptions, as this will undercut the integrity of the process—if your criteria are reasonable, nondiscriminatory, and well-documented and you follow them consistently, you will be more likely to succeed in a future lawsuit.

Analyze the proposed layoffs to determine whether there are enough remaining employees, and whether they possess the required skills, to get the work done. Many organizations do not learn that they have an inadequately staffed workforce until after the downsizing, and they end up having to hire new employees, rehire terminated employees, or use contract workers. Not only does this approach negate any financial benefits achieved by the reduction, but it also damages morale and will cause your workforce to question management decision making.

● Decide what severance benefits you will offer downsized employees. There are certain compensation and benefit items you will be legally required to offer, such as payment of accrued wages and vacation time, COBRA continuation, the opportunity to exercise vested stock options, and 401(k) and/or pension benefits (see Chapter 9 on termination). You may also decide to offer severance payments, outplacement, or other optional benefits. The amounts and types of post-termination benefits you offer are totally up to you, unless you have specific policies or employment contracts covering severance concerns or you have set past precedents regarding severance during layoff situations.

In the long run, it pays to be as generous as you can be under the circumstances. Employers that send hordes of workers out on the streets with "nothing" tend to get bad press and suffer in the eyes of the community. Former employees who believe that they received an unfair severance package will be more likely to air their grievances in court. Strongly consider offering outplacement or other transition counseling to assist individuals in dealing with their anger and fears and moving on with a new job or career. Even if you cannot afford an extensive outplacement program, providing just one or two group sessions can assist workers in preparing their resumes and understanding basic job search methods.

If you decide to pay severance compensation or offer other optional severance benefits, above all be consistent! While you can vary amounts based upon such factors as years worked for the company or job category, apply these standards evenly and without exception to all employees in a given classification. Unequal treatment may give rise to discrimination claims.

● *Keep the details of the changed organization confidential.* Emphasize to everyone involved in the decision-making process the importance of keeping the planning and decisions confidential. Store layoff documentation and lists of affected employees in a safe, secure place. Do not conduct communications about the downsizing over the company e-mail system. The e-mail system is not private, and it is easy to inadvertently send a message to the wrong party.

Better Forgotten: *"Hmmm, I wonder what this box is for?"*
A technology company gave its maintenance chief a list of employees that would be terminated in a downsizing the following day, but did not give any further instructions. The next morning, the employees to be laid off arrived at their offices to find empty boxes at their doors to help them pack—before they had been told about the layoff! Be careful to whom you give the news, and provide detailed instructions.

"What is the Worker Adjustment and Retraining Notification Act and will it apply to our layoff?"

If you are a private employer with (a) one hundred or more employees (not counting those who have worked less than six months or who work less than 2 hours per week) or (b) one hundred or more employees, including part-time workers, who in the aggregate work at least 4,000 hours per week, excluding overtime, the Worker Adjustment and Retraining Notification (WARN) Act will apply if you plan to:

- Completely close a facility or discontinue an operating unit for a period of six months or more, resulting in the loss of employment of fifty or more full-time employees; or

- Conduct a "mass layoff" affecting more than five hundred full-time employees at a single site of employment during a thirty-day period, or at least fifty workers if they constitute at least 33 percent of the workforce at the single site of employment.

There is a limited exemption from this law for companies that close temporary facilities or conduct a closing or mass layoff as a result of the completion of a project. To qualify for this exemption, you must have informed workers at the time of hire that their employment would be limited in duration.

The WARN Act mandates certain detailed timing and notification requirements and imposes substantial penalties for violations, including back pay and benefits for affected employees. The major procedural requirements are as follows:

✓ You must give affected employees at least sixty days' advance notice.

✓ If you have a series of small terminations during any ninety-day period, you must add them together to determine whether the total number of affected workers meets the WARN standards. For example, if you lay off 250 employees on May 1 and an additional 300 on July 15, these two actions will be considered one mass layoff, requiring you to follow WARN procedures.

✓ Notices must be in writing and in clear language that employees can easily understand. It is sufficient to send the notice to employees' last known addresses, or to include the warning with pay stubs.

✓ When your layoff will affect union employees, you must deliver written notice to the chief elected officer or the employees' exclusive representative or bargaining agent and to the local union officials representing the workers, in addition to any notice requirements in your collective bargaining agreement.

✓ You must also send notices to the state dislocated worker unit and to the chief elected official of the local government where the site is located. Your state department of labor can tell you how to contact the dislocated worker unit.

Under the WARN Act, there are certain limited circumstances where a sixty-day notice may not be required. These include:

• *Faltering company.* When a company can prove that during the time the sixty-day notice would have been required, it was actively seeking capital financing or business in order to avoid a plant closing and that the required notice would have caused the company to lose the financing or business. This exemption applies only to plant closings and not mass layoffs.

• *Unforeseeable business circumstances.* When a shutdown or mass layoff is necessitated by significant circumstances outside of the employer's control and not reasonably foreseeable at the time the sixty-day notice would have been required.

- *Natural disasters.* Circumstances falling under this exemption include floods, earthquakes, storms, etc. that directly led to the plant closing or layoff.

It is the employer's responsibility to prove the existence of circumstances sufficient to qualify for an exemption to the notice provisions of WARN. In addition, several states have their own notice requirements for plant closings that may impose additional obligations on employers. Consult with an attorney before acting to ensure that you comply with federal and state mandates.

IMPLEMENTING THE LAYOFF

"How do I implement my downsizing plan?"
The way you handle your reduction in force not only impacts affected workers, but will also influence the attitude and productivity of those remaining, and the perception of your business in the eyes of customers and the community as a whole.

"Should I give employees advance notice of the layoffs?"
Unless you are covered by the provisions of the WARN Act, whether you give advance notice is up to you. In most cases, though, it is advisable to notify workers of the impending actions. Layoffs are rarely a complete surprise to employees. Your workforce knows that some cuts will be made after an acquisition and it senses when business is bad, and the closed-door meetings and stressed demeanor of management that usually accompany a downsizing will encourage rumors and heighten anxiety. Honesty and openness with employees is almost always the best approach. Don't wait for office gossip to get out of hand or, worse yet, let employees first read of impending layoffs in the local newspaper. Even if you believe you can keep word of the reductions from spreading, springing surprise layoffs on your workers can damage trust in management.

Top management should deliver the news in person. Never delegate the task of messenger to nonexecutive personnel or resort to e-mail, newsletters, or written memoranda to spread the word (although you can and should use these written communication methods to follow up on or reinforce what has been communicated verbally). Call a meeting or series of meetings and explain that there will be job cuts. Be forthright. Communicate the reasons for the downsizing, the strategies to be pursued, and the time frames involved. Reinforce that this is a business decision to strengthen the company or weather a storm, not a personal action intended to clean house. Explain the company's plans for a more efficient and profitable future and how the restructuring will help the organization attain its goals. Be positive and optimistic about the future rather than going into panic mode. Listen and respond carefully to employee concerns. This is a difficult time for everyone concerned, but all eyes will be on management, looking for a reasoned game plan and to see whether the company is treating employees with sensitivity and fairness.

"Should I lay off employees in groups?"

Under most circumstances, it is best to conduct your layoffs personally. When you are terminating a very large group it may be impractical to have one-on-one meetings, and personal conversations may be unnecessary for short-term, temporary layoffs. Yet as a general practice, group layoffs are insensitive and demeaning. Just because you are firing several employees rather than a single individual, there is no reason to sacrifice their dignity or treat them with any less consideration than you would in any other termination situation (see Chapter 9). While you may decide to hold subsequent group meetings regarding explanation of benefits continuation or outplacement assistance, a group setting is an inappropriate place to break the news of a job loss.

"Who should conduct the actual layoffs?"

As with individual terminations, it is best to have two people in the termination interview, one to conduct the meeting and the other to serve as a corroborating witness. Usually, the two persons will be the affected worker's manager and a member of the human resources department or someone who has worked closely with that individual, but there are no hard and fast rules. You will need to decide what works best in each situation, especially when the downsizing affects entire departments or units and the managers and supervisors are losing their jobs as well.

Even if top management is not involved in terminating individual employees, it is important that they maintain visibility during the process. Executives who disappear during difficult moments such as layoffs do not demonstrate the leadership that is necessary during challenging times and will lose the respect of the staff.

"How should I break the news to terminated employees?"

In Chapter 9, we discussed the general guidelines applicable to termination interviews. These guidelines are equally applicable to downsizing situations. However, be especially sensitive to the fact that layoffs resulting from mergers and tough economic times are unlike traditional terminations, in that you may be firing individuals who are good workers. Do not make employees feel like they have done anything wrong to lose their jobs, but explain why the layoffs were necessary and the process used to make decisions. While you need not—and should not—go into intricate detail about the reasons an individual was selected for the reduction, prepare a simple statement like, "After our recent acquisition of the XYZ Company, we have decided to consolidate the two sales forces," or "In reducing the number of financial analysts, we decided to release those analysts with the least seniority." Even though you may have a number of terminations to conduct in one day, do not rush through the process and make the individual feel unimportant.

If the layoff will be of limited duration, or if the worker will be eligible for potential recall, explain this during the meeting. Provide clear, written information about benefit continuation options, collect or arrange to collect any company property in the employee's possession, have someone on hand to answer any immediate questions, and let workers know whom to contact with future concerns. Take notes of the meeting and place them in the worker's employment file.

"Should I obtain a waiver and release from employees terminated in a layoff?"

It is often a good idea to get downsized employees to sign a waiver and release, as long as you are offering them some form of benefit in addition to those they are entitled to by law, policy, or custom (see Chapter 9 for criteria governing valid releases). However, unlike situations involving individual discharges, where it is acceptable and common to negotiate release provisions, providing differing release documents, amounts, and terms and conditions in layoff situations can be considered discriminatory. Therefore, it is best to stick with the predetermined severance formula and not allow separate negotiation of release documents.

Also remember that workers over forty years of age who are terminated in a group termination situation are entitled to an extended period of forty-five days in which to review and consider the waiver and release document. In addition, the employer must provide information about the ages (not the names) and job titles of those employees selected and those not selected in the "decisional unit." A decisional unit consists of the group of employees who were considered for layoff, such as a specific department.

"Is it best to stagger the layoffs?"

Conducting layoffs in stages is rarely advisable, as it will prolong the distraction and uncertainty, and delay the process of recovery and return to business. If possible, conduct all necessary downsizing at one time.

Worth Repeating: *"Keeping downsized employees in mind."*
Soon after a layoff in her department, a manager heard about a position opening in another functional area that was perfect for one of her former direct reports. The manager recommended this employee, and he was able to return to work within two weeks. The company bridged his service so he didn't lose any seniority or other benefits.

"Are downsized employees entitled to collect unemployment insurance?"

Yes. You will not have grounds to contest unemployment compensation for individuals who were laid off.

CONSIDERATIONS FOR REMAINING WORKERS

Employers are often so preoccupied dealing with the terminations that they neglect the employees who are left behind. It is a huge mistake to assume that layoff survivors will be happy merely to have retained their jobs. In reality, they will be beset by a variety of questions and emotions. They will be fearful about their own job security. They will be saddened by the loss of their coworkers and overwhelmed by their increased responsibilities. They will be concerned about the future of the company and wondering whether they should be exploring other employment opportunities. Just as important as treating departing employees fairly is keeping remaining employees loyal and motivated. Your success as a business will depend on your current workforce.

"What should I tell surviving employees after the downsizing?"

Senior management should communicate with remaining employees immediately after the layoffs. Do not rely on memoranda or e-mails to do the job for you. Like all important layoff communications, the situation calls for personal contact from the top. Your communication has several purposes: to inform employees about what happened, to acknowledge and deal with the thoughts and emotions that workers are having during this difficult period, and to motivate them to move forward and help the organization prosper.

✓ Candidly inform survivors about the downsizing actions that you took, explaining the business motivation and the rationale for decisions. By being open with workers, you will help to quell rumors and show that the layoff determinations were reasoned rather than random.

✓ If the layoff resulted from a downturn in business, never blame the terminated workers for the company's woes. Explain that it was the *positions* that were no longer needed by the company, not the individuals.

✓ Do not ignore the fact that survivors will have deep feelings about the layoffs. Some may feel angry with the company or guilty that they survived and others did not. Do not try to keep people from discussing what happened; rather, acknowledge to employees that this is a difficult time and allow them to air their emotions and concerns.

✓ Detail any changes in management or organizational structure resulting from the actions.

✓ Discuss how work will be redistributed and how to handle telephone calls for and reference requests regarding terminated employees.

✓ Reassure workers that they are important to the organization and will be a critical part of the company's plans going forward.

✓ Never promise that there will be no further reductions. Such statements will erode trust if further downsizing does become necessary.

Better Forgotten: *"Who has the straight story?"*
A major local employer that had just conducted a large reduction in force was upset to find out that two executives who had been interviewed by different newspapers about the layoffs had contradicted each other! Appoint one senior manager as the company press spokesperson and have all other employees direct interview requests to this person.

"How do I keep employees motivated and focused?"

There are several steps you can take, both in the immediate aftermath of the layoffs and on a continuing basis going forward.

- *Provide necessary training.* Survivors will be worried about their workload as well as whether they will be able to succeed in any new roles and support the company's new direction. If they need additional training, provide training in-house or though outside sources. Don't expect people to learn all the necessary skills on the job. You may also want to consider providing training or coaching on dealing with change, especially for those employees who are experiencing particular difficulty coping with the events.

- *Provide reassurance.* Meet with individuals to let them know that their contributions are valued. This message should come from the company's top executives as well as individual managers. Discuss strategies for career development within the organization. Recognize and reward good performance—this may be a good time

to beef up your reward and incentive programs. Give excellent performers the message that you are really committed to keeping them,
but never make statements such as, "Your job is secure" or "We want
you to stay." These comments, though well-meant, can lead to
implied contract claims if you terminate the employee in the future.

* *Be sensitive to conspicuous spending.* No matter what the financial condition of the organization, the post-layoff period is not the time for
  management to purchase a new company jet or to buy fancy new
  furniture for the offices of senior executives. Employees are already
  questioning whether the staff reductions were actually necessary—
  don't give them a reason to believe that management sacrificed
  employees senselessly.

* *Communicate on a continuing basis.* The communication should not
  stop in the immediate aftermath of the downsizing. No matter what
  the reasons for the layoffs and how effectively they were conducted,
  it will take time to rebuild lost trust. Generate a practice of ongoing communication to rebuild security and confidence, and diffuse
  the damaging perception that employees will be expected to always
  do more with less. Focus on plans going forward, project momen-
  tum and purpose, and involve employees in actively helping the
  organization succeed and prosper.

Tools and Templates

THROUGHOUT THIS BOOK, we suggest that in creating human resources documents, you refrain from merely copying materials gathered from other companies and instead take the time to develop forms and materials that reflect the unique culture and goals of your organization. The tools and templates presented in this section are not intended to be the last word on the subject, but they are designed to help you put some of your thoughts in focus. You can revise each of these forms as you see fit.

1. Ten Questions to Ask by Phone Before Scheduling a Candidate for an Interview
2. Applicant Flow Log
3. Preemployment Telephone Reference Check
4. Sample Health Plan Comparison
5. Sample Acknowledgment of Receipt of Employee Handbook
6. Sample Goals Form for Performance Management
7. Management Focus Group Preparation for Updating a Performance-Management System
8. Self-Evaluation
9. Telecommuting Checklist
10. Discrimination/Sexual Harassment Formal Complaint Form
11. EEO-1 Voluntary Self-Identification Form
12. Termination Checklist
13. Exit Interview Questionnaire
14. Employment Reference Request

TEN QUESTIONS TO ASK BY PHONE BEFORE SCHEDULING A CANDIDATE FOR AN INTERVIEW

1. What is the correct spelling and pronunciation of your name?
   Constant misspelling and mispronunciation make people feel unwelcome.

2. What position(s) are you applying for?
   You may give a very brief description of the job. Job titles can be misinterpreted.

3. Where are you currently employed?
   The resume you have may indicate that the candidate is employed, but his or her status may have changed to unemployed or another position.

4. Why did you leave your last job?

5. When are you available to start a new position?

6. What hours/shifts/days can you work?

7. What are your salary requirements for a new position?
   Candidates may not want to be specific about an answer here; ask for a range or tell them a range for the job. You do not want to take the time to bring in a candidate seeking a $100,000 a year position to interview for a job paying $60,000.

8. _____
   Identify any special skill, knowledge, or licensing/certification needed for the position, such as software knowledge or a driver's license. You should know if the candidate possesses these basic requirements before you bring her or him in.

9. Why are you interested in this position?

10. When are you available to come in for an interview?
    If you have interview availability and you want to bring the person in you should say, "Can you come in on Wednesday at 10:00 a.m.?"

Name of Telephone Screener: _____ Date: _____

If the answer to any question indicates that a candidate should not be invited in for the interview or needs further discussion prior to an invitation, thank the candidate for his or her time and say you will review the matter and call if an interview is appropriate. If you are not interested, send the candidate a brief letter as you would any candidate you interview in person and do not pursue. If it is clear to both the interviewer and the candidate that this is not an appropriate position, acknowledge this at the time of the telephone conversation, say thank you, and conclude the conversation. If it is possible that the individual would be considered for another position at any time, mention this.

APPLICANT FLOW LOG

Candidate Name	Date Resume Received	Source of Resume	Date of 1st Interview or Call	Interviewer	Date of 2nd Interview	Interviewer	Position	Status	Reason
Carl Brown	9/1/11	Local College	9/7/11	Holly Morgan	9/14/11	Molly Burton	Sales Manager	Not a Good Candidate	Lacks high-volume sales experience

If spreadsheet software is used to develop an applicant flow, it can be sorted by candidate name, date of application, or even position, which will facilitate locating candidates in the employment process. Change column headings to suit your needs. You may also create abbreviations and explain their meaning on the bottom of the log.

PREEMPLOYMENT TELEPHONE REFERENCE CHECK

Name of Candidate: _____

Position: _____

Name of Person Contacted: _____ Telephone: _____

Title/Company: _____

1. Please verify dates of employment: _____

2. Please verify position(s) held: _____

3. How would you describe this candidate's quality of work? _____
    _____

4. Please give me a specific example. _____
    _____

5. Please describe this candidate's relationships with other employees.
    _____
    _____

6. How did this candidate interact with his or her immediate supervisor?
    _____
    _____

7. What was this candidate's greatest accomplishment while he or she
    worked for you (your company)? _____
    _____

8. If you would work with this employee again what would you like
    to see him or her change or improve? _____ _____
    _____

9. Is there anything else you would like to add that would help us to
    make our decision? _____
    _____

Name of Person Obtaining Reference: _____

Signature: _____

Date of Reference: _____

SAMPLE HEALTH PLAN COMPARISON

ABC Health Plan Comparison			
	ABC HMO	**ABC PPO**	
Covered Service		In Network	Out of Network
Primary Care Office Visit Copay	$15	$15	Deductible & Coinsurance
Specialist Office Visit Copay	$40	$40	Deductible & Coinsurance
Routine Adult Preventative	$0	$0	$0
Well Child Care (up to age 19)	$0	$0	$0
DXL/Lab Fees	$0 at Participating Lab	$0 at Participating Lab	Deductible & Coinsurance
Annual Deduct., Indiv.	$0	$500	$1,000
Annual Deduct., Family	$0	$1,000	$2,000
Coinsurance	$0	90%	70%
Hospital Stays Pre-approved or contact ABC Health within 48 hrs for emergency	$150 Copay per Incident	Deductible & Coinsurance	Deductible & Coinsurance
Emergency Room	$100 Copay	$100 Copay	$100 Copay
Outpatient Mental Health	50% Copay, 30 visits per calendar yr.	50% Copay, 30 visits per calendar yr.	50% Copay, $25 max, 30 visits per calendar yr.
Chiropractic Care	$30 Copay	$30 Copay	Deductible & Coinsurance
Employee Contrib.	**ABC HMO**	**ABC PPO**	
Employee Only	$46.59 per pay period	$65.77 per pay period	
Employee plus spouse	$272.11 per pay period	$289.22 per pay period	

SAMPLE ACKNOWLEDGMENT OF
RECEIPT OF EMPLOYEE HANDBOOK

I, _____, acknowledge that I have received a copy of the XYZ Company (the "Company") Employee Handbook (the "Handbook") and that I have read the policies and procedures contained in the Handbook, understand them, and agree to abide by them. I understand that during the course of my employment with the Company, questions may arise that are not explicitly addressed in the Handbook, and I agree to consult with my supervisor or other member of the Company management regarding these matters.

I understand that the Handbook is intended to serve as general information about policies and procedures of the Company, but in no way constitutes, creates, or forms a part of an express or implied employment contract with the Company, nor does it guarantee employment for any definite or indefinite period of time. I recognize that my employment is employment "at will," and that either the Company or I can terminate my employment at any time, with or without cause or notice.

The Handbook supersedes any and all prior written or unwritten policies, procedures, or practices of the Company pertaining to or inconsistent with the subjects detailed herein. The Company reserves the right to clarify, change, or supplement any information contained in the Handbook, and the Company will notify me if and when such changes occur. No changes to this Handbook may be made without the approval of the President of the Company, and any such changes will not be deemed to affect my "at will" employment status.

Signature of Employee: _____

Print Name: _____

Date: _____

SAMPLE GOALS FORM FOR PERFORMANCE MANAGEMENT

Priority	Goal	Steps required to achieve goal	Expected completion date
The priority can be taken from the overall action that needs to be taken, or the mission or vision of the organization.	The goal is the specific measurable target.	List the steps that need to be taken to achieve the goal.	This can be a specific date, the end of a time period such as a calendar quarter, or ongoing.

(Here we provide an example of the types of questions you might prepare before convening an employee focus group.)

MANAGEMENT FOCUS GROUP PREPARATION FOR UPDATING A PERFORMANCE-MANAGEMENT SYSTEM

We are looking forward to a successful focus group session to gather information for updating the Performance-Management System. Your involvement in this process will ensure that the final product will meet your needs as a manager, the needs of your employees, and company goals.

Our session will last no more than two hours. In order to make the most out of this time and to gather the best information, please complete the following questions that we will discuss during the focus group.

1. Why is performance measurement important?

2. What happens when a company does a good job of measuring performance?

3. What happens when a company does a poor job of measuring performance?

4. Think about any best practices in the area of performance management that you have seen at other companies.

5. Identify the best practices in performance management at our company

6. Describe the mission/goals of our company.

7. What are some organizational obstacles you face in setting and achieving goals and expectations at this company?

8. What are some personal obstacles you face in setting and achieving goals and expectations at this company?

9. List five results expected at our company for a successful employee.

10. List and describe five words or phrases frequently used here to describe or measure performance or results.

11. In your opinion when is the best time to review performance?

12. What training do you need to measure performance effectively?

SELF-EVALUATION

Name: _____   Position: _____

Reviewing Manager: _____

Date in Position: _____   Original Hire Date: _____

Evaluation Period: From _____   To _____

A. Describe your major accomplishments that have been achieved during the period covered by this review.

_____

_____

_____

_____

B. Would you prefer to remain in your present position, or if you were to be considered for a new position in the near future (6–12 months) what position(s) do you feel you would be most qualified to assume?

_____

_____

_____

_____

C. In what areas do you see the greatest need for development and what training or experiences would meet these development needs?

_____

_____

_____

_____

D. What are your long-range career goals and how does your employment at this company help you to reach these goals?

_____

_____

_____

_____

TELECOMMUTING CHECKLIST

Employee Name: _____

Department: _____

Primary Business Location: _____

Telecommuting Location: _____

Supervisor Name: _____

Number of days/week telecommuting requested: _____

Requirements of Job	YES	NO
Measurable and definable work outputs	_____	_____
Concentration required	_____	_____
Extensive coworker interaction	_____	_____
In-office reference material needed	_____	_____
Work is autonomous	_____	_____
Permits e-mail, fax, phone interaction	_____	_____

Personal Characteristics		
Self-motivated	_____	_____
Able to work without supervision	_____	_____
Computer literate	_____	_____

Equipment Requirements (check all items relevant and specify whether they will be provided by the Company ("C") or the employee ("E")).

	C	E
Desktop or laptop computer	_____	_____
Printer	_____	_____
Software (specify)_____ _____	_____	_____
Modem	_____	_____
Additional telephone line	_____	_____
BlackBerry or smart phone	_____	_____
High-speed Internet connection	_____	_____
Copy machine	_____	_____
Voice mail	_____	_____
Office furniture	_____	_____
Other (specify)	_____	_____

	YES	NO
Individual approved for telecommuting?	_____	_____

Manager Signature: _____   Date: _____

DISCRIMINATION/SEXUAL HARASSMENT
FORMAL COMPLAINT FORM

Instructions:

The Company is committed to providing a working environment that is free from discrimination and harassment. It is not a requirement that you use this form to file a complaint. If you do choose to use this form, please include all the information requested below in your complaint. By being as specific as possible when discussing incidents of harassment, discrimination, or retaliation, you will assist the investigators in the fact-gathering process. Be sure to include the date(s) the incident(s) occurred, the name(s) of the person(s) involved, and the name(s) of those who may have witnessed the incident. Your complaint is not limited to the space provided. You are encouraged to use additional paper as needed and to attach additional materials that may assist in the investigation process. Please note that information provided on this or any other form is not considered an official complaint unless it is signed by you and dated.

Upon receipt of your complaint, the members of the Company's Anti-Discrimination and Harassment Committee (the "Committee") will review and investigate it. You will be informed of the outcome of the investigation.

To investigate your complaint, it will be necessary to interview you, the alleged offender(s), and any witnesses with knowledge of the allegations or defenses. The Company will notify all persons involved in the investigation that it is confidential and that unauthorized disclosures of information concerning the investigation could result in disciplinary action.

It is the expectation of the Company that those who file a complaint will remain active and cooperative in the investigation process, and will keep the complaint and investigation process confidential except to the extent necessary to participate in the investigation process. The Company will not condone or permit any retaliation as a result of the filing of any complaint or participation in the resulting investigation.

Submit this completed and signed form by mail or in person to any member of the Company's Human Resources Department or the Committee. The names of members of the Committee can be found on the Company intranet site and are posted on bulletin boards in your facility.

Name: _____
      First   *Middle*   *Last*

Location: _____ Department: _____

I wish to complain against: _____

(Identify the person(s) directly responsible for the alleged violation.)

Date of incident of alleged discrimination: _____

Place of incident of alleged discrimination: _____

Nature of alleged discrimination: _____

_____

(Sexual harassment; discrimination on the basis of your race, sex, sexual orientation, national origin, age, disability, color or religion; retaliation because you filed a complaint.)

Describe in detail the specific incident that is the basis of the alleged discrimination:

_____

_____

(Describe each incident of harassment, discrimination, or retaliation separately. Please be as detailed as possible, giving names, dates, and place. Use additional paper if needed.)

Did the person you are complaining against state a reason for the action prompting your complaint? If yes, please describe:

_____

_____

Describe why you believe the incident you described was related to your race, sex, or whatever basis you indicated above, or why you believe you were retaliated against:

_____

_____

List and describe all documents, e-mails, records, materials, and other evidence pertaining to your complaint:

_____

_____

_____

Name

List and identify all witnesses to the incident(s) or persons who have personal knowledge of information pertaining to your complaint:

_____

_____

Have you previously reported or otherwise complained about this or related acts of harassment, discrimination, or retaliation to the Company? If so, please identify the individual to whom you made the report, the date you made the report, and the resolution:

_____

_____

Please submit any additional information pertaining to the alleged discrimination/harassment:

_____

_____

Describe the injury or harm you suffered because of the alleged discrimination/harassment:

_____

_____

Complaint Acknowledgment:
I certify that to the best of my knowledge the information I have provided is accurate and the events and circumstances are as I have described them.

Signature: _____   Date: _____

EEO-1 VOLUNTARY SELF-IDENTIFICATION FORM

The Equal Employment Opportunity Commission (EEOC) requires organizations with one hundred or more employees to complete an EEO-1 report each year that collects workforce data about gender and race/ethnicity by type of job groupings. The information is used for reporting purposes only and is kept confidential by the EEOC.

Completion of this data is voluntary and will not affect your opportunity for employment or terms or conditions of employment. This form will be used for EEO-1 reporting purposes only and will be kept separate from all other personnel records accessed only by the Human Resources Department. Please return completed forms to the Human Resources Department.

Name: _____ Job Title: _____

Gender: *(Please check one of the options)* _____ Male _____ Female

Race/Ethnicity:
(Please check one of the descriptions below corresponding to the ethnic group with which you identify.)

____ *Hispanic or Latino* A person of Cuban, Mexican, Puerto Rican, South or Central American, or other Spanish culture or origin regardless of race.

____ *White (Not Hispanic or Latino)* A person having origins in any of the original peoples of Europe, the Middle East or North Africa.

____ *Black or African American (Not Hispanic or Latino)* A person having origins in any of the black racial groups of Africa.

____ *Native Hawaiian or Other Pacific Islander (Not Hispanic or Latino)* A person having origins in any of the peoples of Hawaii, Guam, Samoa, or other Pacific Islands.

____ *Asian (Not Hispanic or Latino)* A person having origins in any of the original peoples of the Far East, Southeast Asia, or the Indian Subcontinent, including, for example, Cambodia, China, India, Japan, Korea, Malaysia, Pakistan, the Philippine Islands, Thailand, and Vietnam.

___ *American Indian or Alaska Native (Not Hispanic or Latino)* A person having origins in any of the original peoples of North and South America (including Central America) and who maintain tribal affiliation or community attachment.

___ *Two or More Races (Not Hispanic or Latino)* All persons who identify with more than one of the above six races.

Date completed: _____
Please return form to the Human Resources Department.

Thank you for your participation.

TERMINATION CHECKLIST

Employee Name: _____ Date of Termination: _____

Termination is: Voluntary _____ Involuntary _____

Before employee's last day of employment

Human Resources

_____ 1. Prepare COBRA letter or contact COBRA administrator

_____ 2. Schedule exit interview

_____ 3. Notify insurance carriers

_____ 4. Compile all benefits conversion information and forms

_____ 5. Request final paycheck

Accounting/Finance

_____ 1. Prepare final paycheck including any benefit days due

_____ 2. Cancel any company credit cards

_____ 3. Ensure final expense reports are submitted or provide a
         timetable for submission

_____ 4. Pay outstanding expenses

IT/Telecommunications

_____ 1. Cancel voice mail access on appropriate date

_____ 2. Cancel network access on appropriate date

Last day of employment

_____ 1. Nondisclosure agreement   date received: _____

_____ 2. Reference release   date received: _____

_____ 3. Last paycheck   date received: _____

_____ 4. Collect keys

_____ 5. Collect ID/access cards

_____ 6. Collect cell phone, BlackBerry

_____ 7. Verify address

_____ 8. Provide benefit conversion information (this can be done
         before last day)

After the employee's last day

_____ 1. Check if any additional amounts owed (commissions, expense reports, etc.)

_____ 2. Mail final pay stub to former employee if necessary

_____ 3. Check to ensure that COBRA notification was sent

Reason for leaving: _____

Employee Signature:_____ Date: _____

Company Signature:_____ Date: _____

EXIT INTERVIEW QUESTIONNAIRE

We would appreciate your taking a few minutes to answer the following questions about your decision to terminate your employment with our organization. This information will assist us in analyzing our employee turnover and in making this organization a better place to work. Please answer these questions honestly. Your responses will be treated as confidential and will *not* be placed in your employment file.

Name: _____

Position: _____

Department: _____

Supervisor: _____

Dates of Employment: _____

What factors contributed to your accepting a job with this organization? _____

_____

_____

_____

Did you understand the job expectations of the position when you were hired? _____

_____

_____

Did you receive the support of the organization in meeting these expectations? _____

_____

_____

Please rate the following on a scale of 1 to 5, 5 being the most positive:

Enjoyment of your work: 1 2 3 4 5

Fairness of workload: 1 2 3 4 5

Salary: 1 2 3 4 5

Opportunity for growth: 1 2 3 4 5

Organizational effectiveness: 1 2 3 4 5

Group insurance benefits: 1 2 3 4 5

Other benefits (vacation, paid
holidays, etc.):   1 2 3 4 5

Treatment by management: 1 2 3 4 5

Work environment
(stress, frustrations, etc.)   1 2 3 4 5

Physical working conditions: 1 2 3 4 5
Quality of supervision: 1 2 3 4 5
Quality of training: 1 2 3 4 5
Recognition of achievements: 1 2 3 4 5
Opportunity to express grievances: 1 2 3 4 5

What did you most enjoy about working for this organization? _____
_____
_____
_____

What did you like least about working for this organization? _____
_____
_____
_____

What is your reason for leaving the organization? _____
_____
_____
_____

Could this organization have done something to prevent your leaving?
_____
_____
_____

If asked, would you recommend employment at this organization to a
prospective employee? _____
_____
_____
_____

Please comment on any other areas you believe would improve the
workplace quality of this organization. _____
_____
_____
_____

Employee Signature: _____   Date: _____

EMPLOYMENT REFERENCE REQUEST

I, _____ [print name], acknowledge that I have been informed by the XYZ Company (the "Company") that it is the policy of the Company to disclose only limited information in response to the request of a prospective employer for reference information about a current or former employee, including dates of employment, title of job performed, and confirmation of salary.

By executing this document, I am requesting that the Company depart from its general reference policy and provide to any and all prospectors that may contact the Company to request employment-related information about me, any information about my employment that the Company considers appropriate, including but not limited to opinions and assessments about my performance and conduct as an employee; job duties; evaluations; reasons for separation; and eligibility for rehire.

In exchange for the Company's agreeing to my request to provide additional employment-related information to prospective employers, I hereby release and discharge the Company, and its employees, officers, directors, and successors and assigns from all claims, liabilities, or actions arising in connection with this Employment Reference Request and any related exchange of records or other communication related to my employment with the Company.

_____   _____
Employee Signature   *Date*

_____
Witness Signature

Index